The New Zealand

CYCLE TRAILS

NGA HAERENGA

RANDOM HOUSE

UK | USA | Canada | Ireland | Australia
India | New Zealand | South Africa | China

Random House is an imprint of the Penguin Random House group of
companies, whose addresses can be found at global.
penguinrandomhouse.com.

Penguin
Random House
New Zealand

This revised edition published by
Penguin Random House New Zealand, 2017

10 9 8 7 6 5 4 3 2 1

Text © Jonathan Kennett, 2013 and 2017

All photographs by Jonathan Kennett unless credited otherwise
Maps and elevation profiles by Geographx
Cover photograph by Colin Monteath/Hedgehoghouse.com/Adventure
South (Alps 2 Ocean Cycle Trail, beside Lake Pukaki, with Aoraki/Mount
Cook in the background)
Back cover photographs by Jonathan Kennett (top and bottom) and
Hamish Seaton (middle)

Original design by Anna Seabrook
Updated design by Rachel Clark © Penguin Random House New Zealand
Prepress by Image Centre Group
Printed and bound in China by RR Donnelley Asia Printing Solutions Ltd

A catalogue record for this book is available from the National Library of
New Zealand.

ISBN 978-0-14-377131-9

penguin.co.nz

A Guide to New Zealand's 22 Great Rides
and Introducing Tour Aotearoa

The New Zealand
CYCLE TRAILS
NGA HAERENGA

Jonathan Kennett

RANDOM HOUSE
NEW ZEALAND

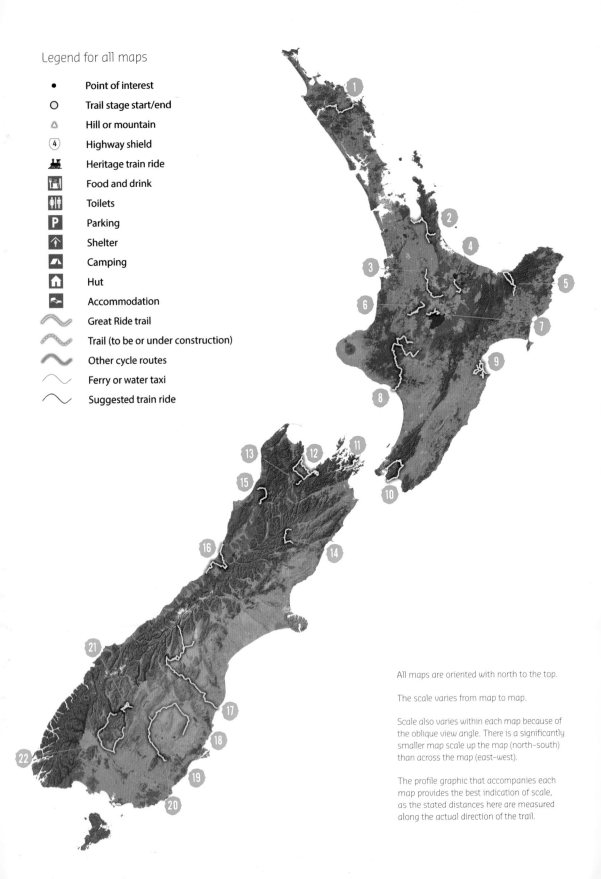

Legend for all maps

- **•** Point of interest
- **○** Trail stage start/end
- **△** Hill or mountain
- **④** Highway shield
- **🚂** Heritage train ride
- **🍴** Food and drink
- **🚻** Toilets
- **P** Parking
- **↑** Shelter
- **⛺** Camping
- **🏠** Hut
- **🛏** Accommodation
- **〰** Great Ride trail
- **〰** Trail (to be or under construction)
- **〰** Other cycle routes
- **⌒** Ferry or water taxi
- **⌒** Suggested train ride

All maps are oriented with north to the top.

The scale varies from map to map.

Scale also varies within each map because of the oblique view angle. There is a significantly smaller map scale up the map (north–south) than across the map (east–west).

The profile graphic that accompanies each map provides the best indication of scale, as the stated distances here are measured along the actual direction of the trail.

CONTENTS

INTRODUCTION

BACKGROUND AND HISTORY OF NGA HAERENGA

The simple pleasure of cycling is a joy that can be experienced by everyone, from the youngest child mastering movement and gaining independence on two wheels to the 'renaissance rider' shedding years as they jump on a bike for the first time in decades. Thankfully, it is a pleasure that is becoming increasingly accessible as most countries in the world are creating more cycle paths than ever before. New Zealand is no exception.

In the last seven years, over 1000 km of cycling routes have been built as part of Nga Haerenga the New Zealand Cycle Trail, which has a long-term vision of developing a network of cycle routes covering the entire country. Nga Haerenga means 'the journeys' in both a physical and spiritual sense. These trails, and others built before them, provide an ideal way of connecting with New Zealand's diverse culture and celebrated natural environment. All of the trails are open to walkers as well as cyclists, and some of the trails provide great tramping experiences.

The idea of going on a holiday by bicycle harks back to the first bicycle boom in the 1890s. Of course, there were no motor vehicles back then, so no cycle trails were needed. Cycle touring boomed three times throughout the twentieth century, with the last really big one coinciding with the invention of the ten-speed and oil shortages in the 1970s. This was followed by the mountain-bike mania of the 1990s and beyond, which saw fit people head for the hills, and the numbers cycling on roads drop right off. By the turn of the century, many New Zealanders felt our roads were unsafe for cycling. For an easy, safe biking holiday, we had the Otago Central Rail Trail, and that was about it. Until now!

CONCEPTION

Many of the best ideas come from a combination of the most unlikely factors. In February 2009, in response to the global economic meltdown, the New Zealand Government initiated a job summit to brainstorm how to limit the damage and save jobs.

Meanwhile, a luxury real estate agent, Aucklander Graham Wall, bumped into a couple of English cyclists at the beach. They were having a great old time, and told Graham about cycle paths developing across the UK. Now, Graham was an ideas man. He hadn't been on a bike for 40 years, and knew nothing about cycling, but he thought, 'What if you could go cycling without cars around? Imagine doing it from the top of the North Island to the bottom of the South?' His mind was racing, and he fell more and more in love with the idea.

Graham wrote a few ideas for a national cycleway down on a bit of paper and passed it on to then Prime Minister John Key. Along with a lot of other ideas at the job summit, the PM threw the idea of a cycleway on the table.

As the summit progressed, the ideas were assessed, separating the wheat from the chaff, and the cycleway rose to the top. It was purely a business proposition — if a 150-km rail trail in Otago had managed to generate over 200 jobs, imagine what 2000 km of cycle trail could do.

The idea of a cycle path the length of the country soon changed into a vision for a network of iconic rides, like the Otago Central Rail Trail, connected by quiet country roads. Just a few months after the job summit, the Prime Minister articulated the vision to the *New Zealand Herald*, saying:

> 'I see the national cycleway developing from a series of "Great Rides" through some of New Zealand's most beautiful scenery. Our long-term goal is to create a network that links these "Great Rides" into a uniquely New Zealand set of cycling experiences that connects and passes through our cities.'

The pressure was really on to create jobs and a cycle trail! Political advisers were worried that the cycleway could become a source of ridicule. In New Zealand, some people still stereotyped cycling as an activity for kids, or the poor. Yet the new cycling boom was instigated mostly by healthy, wealthy people, many of whom, like Graham Wall, hadn't been cycling for decades.

This didn't stop old-school cyclists wanting a slice of the action. Graham Wall has pointed out, 'Lots of people had this idea, I just got the credit for it.' One of the keenest old-school cyclists who'd had the same idea was Green Party MP Kevin Hague. It was one of the few projects, along with home insulation, where the Greens and National could see eye to eye, and so they partnered up. Kevin Hague had a lot of cycling expertise, and John Key could unlock the money. In May 2009, Cabinet approved funding for Nga Haerenga the New Zealand Cycle Trail. An investment of $50 million was put towards its design and construction.

DEVELOPMENT

There was so much political pressure to begin constructing trails that the Ministry of Tourism started looking for instant opportunities. They approached the Department of Conservation (DOC) and mayors from around the country, as well as consulting with key cyclists. The result was seven 'Quick Start' trail-building projects.

DOC had already been considering three projects: the St James Cycle Trail, the Timber Trail and Mountains to Sea. So these were all brought on board.

Four other Quick Starts were announced in July 2009: the Twin Coast Cycle Trail in Northland, the Hauraki Rail Trail on the Coromandel, the Waikato River Trails south of Hamilton and Southland's Around the Mountains.

Success has been mixed. Five of the Quick Starts were open by mid-2013, and three of them were hugely successful (the Timber Trail, Mountains to Sea and Hauraki Rail Trail). The Twin Coast Cycle Trail was fully opened in early 2017 and Around the Mountains Trail is close to complete.

Almost exactly one year after announcing the Quick Starts, a further 12 cycle trails were announced. These had been selected from 54 proposals received from around the country. The interest was huge, and $50 million was not enough to satisfy everyone. However, most of the trails were backed by other organisations, mostly DOC and local councils. Officially, other organisations have supplemented The New Zealand Cycle Trail by $30 million, but in reality the figure is closer to a dollar-for-dollar match of the Ministry of Tourism's $50 million.

Kiwi cyclists were literally right behind the construction of the cycle trails.

In hindsight, selecting the trails was the easy part. Ahead lay three hurdles that varied in difficulty from trail to trail: land access, resource consents and actually building the trail to a decent standard.

The first and most important was land access. Without access, there could be no trail. Most trails had challenges they never expected. The Clutha Gold Trail had to negotiate access across 121 land parcels. The chance of 100 per cent approval was slim, but after moving the trail around a bit, they managed to get there. In the case of the Roxburgh Gorge Trail and the Great Lake Trail in Taupo, the solution has been to provide a boat service, bypassing land where permission wasn't granted. Some trails were all on public land, so access wasn't such a problem.

The second hurdle was resource consents. While most councils were supportive of the project, some organisations opposed the consents because the trails would open to the masses areas that had previously been enjoyed by a select few. Sometimes it was fishermen or hunters who wanted an area to themselves. In one case, opposition by Fish & Game New Zealand put the trail's development four years behind schedule.

And the third hurdle was designing and building the trails. With so much trail building on the go, New Zealand suddenly had a shortage of experienced track designers and builders. Some trails got the best track builders in the country; others had track builders who were learning on the job. The results were mixed, and left one of the New Zealand Cycle Trail project managers to comment that there was still a lot of work to be done even after the trails had been opened.

The first trail to open was the 64-km St James Cycle Trail in November 2010. No one who rode it on the opening day honestly thought that it was finished. Many felt that they had had a great time, but it wasn't a 'Great Ride'. Over the following two years, significant improvements were made, including a magnificent upgrade of the last 10 km. Riding it reminded me of my first ride along the Otago Central Rail Trail — how terribly rough that had been and how far it has come since 1996. Just like that venerable trail in Otago, every New Zealand Cycle Trail that has opened has had significant improvements made over the following months and years. All of them seem to get better year by year.

At the easy end of the scale, Hawke's Bay soon followed with the first of several openings. The Hawke's Bay trail developers already knew how to build cycle trails since the local Rotary groups had been knocking them out since 2002. Now the local councils put in a huge amount of co-funding and created a 200-km network of smooth, mostly flat, off-road paths that not only attracted tourists but also caused a local cycling boom. What had previously been a fringe activity became an everyday one. Bike shops and cafes reaped the financial benefits, while everyone on their bikes enjoyed the health benefits.

After construction got under way on the new cycle trails, other existing Great Rides were added to the network. Not surprisingly, the first to be added was the Otago Central Rail Trail.

It was officially opened in 2000, and had become the model to which most other cycle trails aspired; adding it was a no-brainer. Then the Queen Charlotte Track was added. Both were the fine work of DOC in partnership with local landowners and communities. Despite their early success, 10 years passed before other parts of the country recognised the benefits of creating local cycle trails. Plenty of groups had been quietly working away at planning and building trails, but they lacked adequate resources until the New Zealand Cycle Trail project was born. Suddenly, with the funding behind them, they really got off the ground. Incredible progress has been made within seven years and it's not over yet. The government is now investing a further $6 million per year into major enhancements and extensions, which will result in significant changes from 2020 onwards.

FUTURE

In mid-2017, three trails were still under construction.

Great Taste Trail Over the next five years, another major section will be added to the trail between Wakefield, Kohatu, Tapawera and Woodstock.

Alps 2 Ocean Cycle Trail is actually a great ride already, but there are plans to move some of the on-road sections off-road during 2017 and 2018.

Around the Mountains started construction in June 2013 and completed Stage 1, the section from Kingston to Mossburn, in 2015. Stage 2 involves building an off-road trail from Mossburn towards Mavora Lakes and then following existing gravel roads to Lake Wakatipu.

Also, there are significant extensions planned for several other trails.

Hauraki Rail Trail has just extended from Thames to Miranda and now plans to extend the trail from Te Aroha down to Matamata. Impressive!

Queen Charlotte Track has plans to extend from Anakiwa to Picton in 2017–2018.

St James Cycle Trail plans to extend north to Lake Tennyson and south to Hanmer Springs, as well as build a new hut in the middle of the trail.

The Queenstown Trail plans to extend down the Kawarau to Cromwell and eventually connect to the Otago Central Rail Trail at Clyde.

The Roxburgh Gorge Trail still hopes to close the 12-km gap they have in the middle.

Clutha Gold Trail hopes to extend from Lawrence to Milton and Lake Waihola.

It is an exciting time for cycling in New Zealand, whether for a holiday or as a local day trip. In 2010 there were only two multi-day trails available — Otago Central Rail Trail and Queen Charlotte Track. Seven years later, there are 22 Great Rides and a 3000-km length of New Zealand cycling route called Tour Aotearoa. No wonder cycling is booming.

PAUL KENNETT

The opening of the Wineries Ride, Hawke's Bay.

THE CYCLE TRAIL NETWORK

As well as the Great Rides that are described in this book, the New Zealand Cycle Trail network consists of many other cycling routes. Some are just short country roads that connect Great Rides with the nearest town or city, and others are long cycle-touring routes through heartland New Zealand. The network in its entirety represents the safest and most enjoyable way to explore New Zealand by bike.

In 2011 the first cycle-touring route was added to Nga Haerenga — the 180-km Forgotten World Highway. From Taumarunui it follows one of the country's least-used highways, then old stock roads and finally a stunning concrete path weaving along the Taranaki coast to the centre of New Plymouth. It has proved very popular.

The Forgotten World Highway has been followed by several others, including the wonderful Manawatu Cycleway from Mangaweka to Palmerston North, the classic Rainbow Trail along the Rainbow Valley to Hanmer Springs and, most recently, a trio of rides from Cape Reinga to downtown Auckland.

These rides are predominantly on-road and suit experienced adult cyclists. All of them are Grade 3 (Intermediate) and above. They require good road sense, and sometimes enough fitness to cover 70 or 80 km in a single day.

The New Zealand Cycle Trail network is similar in concept to networks overseas, such as Sustrans in the United Kingdom, EuroVelo in Europe and the Adventure Cycling Association network in the United States. It is likely to continue developing for many years. As roads are improved and cycle lanes and paths are built, more routes will be added to Nga Haerenga. The long-term goal is to develop a network the length and breadth of the country that connects with all the Great Rides. The maps over the page show what this network is shaping up to look like.

For a comprehensive look at the cycle-touring routes of the New Zealand Cycle Trail network, check out my other book, *Classic New Zealand Cycle Trails*.

Te Rewa Rewa Bridge, New Plymouth.

Hokianga Harbour, on the Kauri Coast, Northland.

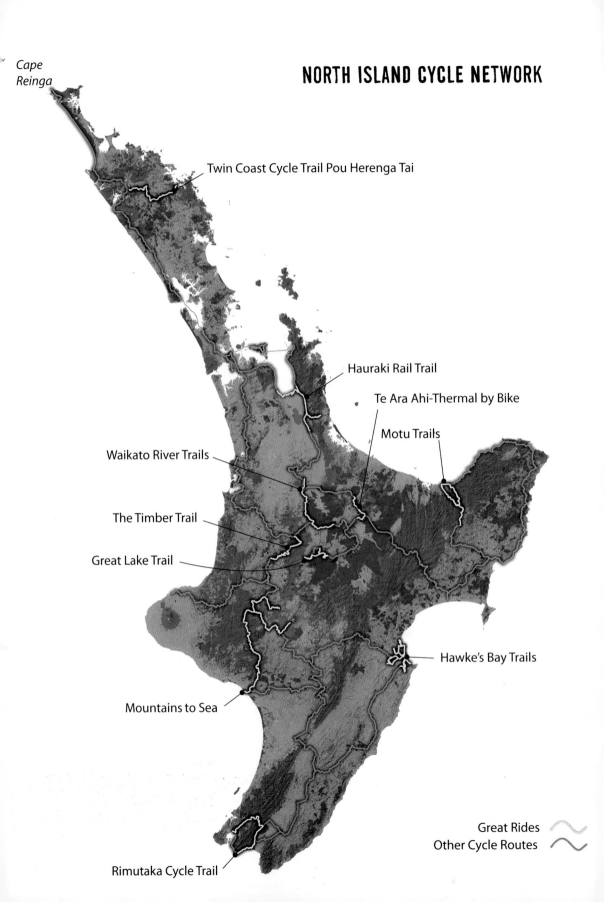

Cape
Reinga

NORTH ISLAND CYCLE NETWORK

Twin Coast Cycle Trail Pou Herenga Tai

Hauraki Rail Trail

Te Ara Ahi-Thermal by Bike

Motu Trails

Waikato River Trails

The Timber Trail

Great Lake Trail

Hawke's Bay Trails

Mountains to Sea

Rimutaka Cycle Trail

Great Rides
Other Cycle Routes

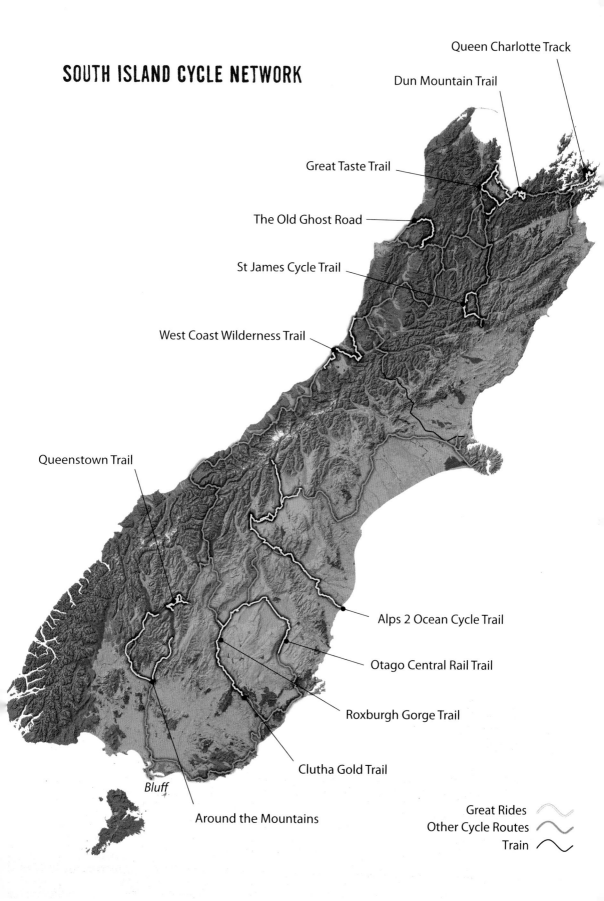

SOUTH ISLAND CYCLE NETWORK

Queen Charlotte Track

Dun Mountain Trail

Great Taste Trail

The Old Ghost Road

St James Cycle Trail

West Coast Wilderness Trail

Queenstown Trail

Alps 2 Ocean Cycle Trail

Otago Central Rail Trail

Roxburgh Gorge Trail

Clutha Gold Trail

Bluff

Around the Mountains

Great Rides
Other Cycle Routes
Train

ABOUT THIS BOOK

This book provides a summary of each trail, along with the vital information you need before starting your ride. The following topics are covered in the summaries.

Start and end points Start points and end points are given for those who want to ride the full trail. They are not compulsory. All of the trails are made up of sections, allowing you to dive in and out of the ride. It is easy to select the best bits of a trail if you only have time for a short ride.

Distance This is the full riding distance, which is often longer than the trail distance listed on most websites. This is because you usually have to veer off the trail for a variety of reasons — for instance, to visit a cafe or stay at a motel.

Likely time The times shown are based on riders averaging 5–10 kph on gravel roads or tracks, and up to 10–15 kph on sealed roads. Allow extra time for stopping for picnics, cafes, hot pools, a walk, or simply to take a breather.

Grading The trails vary hugely, from smooth, flat concrete paths, right through to steep rocky tracks in the middle of wilderness. To have a good time, it's important to choose

Family fun on the West Coast Wilderness Trail.

a trail that suits your riding skill and fitness.

Trails such as The Old Ghost Road and the St James Cycle Trail are much, much harder than the Otago Central Rail Trail or the Hawke's Bay Trails.

Each trail is given an overall grade from Grade 1 (Very easy) to Grade 5 (Expert) depending on the following three elements:

- The fitness level required (how steep and long the hills are)
- The skill level required (how narrow and rough the track is)
- The traffic sense required (how much traffic there is, the speed limit and how much space there is on the road)

Combining all of these into one grade can create some confusion. To drill down on the details, check out the table on pages 296–297.

Bikes bound for Waihi.

Surface All of the trails are unique, and the riding surfaces vary from volcanic ash to limesand, asphalt and concrete. Make sure your bike tyres are suited to the surfaces of the trail.

Maps Where a trail has produced its own paper map, this is listed. Otherwise the next best map available is listed. Some of these maps can be bought from bookstores and i-SITEs, whereas a few are only available from specialist map shops or outdoor stores.

Websites For trails that do not have their own website, the official New Zealand Cycle Trail website (www.nzcycletrail.com) is listed.

Bike type The two most common types of bikes ridden on these trails are mountain bikes and hybrid/comfort bikes.

Mountain bikes are incredibly versatile and can be ridden on every type of trail in this book, from rough Grade 4 tracks to smooth Grade 1 rail trails.

Hybrid/comfort bikes are great for smooth Grade 1 and 2 tracks. They are generally less expensive, more comfortable to ride and easy to attach carriers to.

Road racing bikes are fast but not comfortable and handle poorly on gravel tracks.

Touring or cyclo-cross bikes are like road bikes but with fatter tyres, stronger brakes and a wider range of gears.

BMX bikes and kids' bikes are only suitable for flat Grade 1 and 2 tracks.

Bike hire Businesses that hire bikes on the trails are listed. Taking your bike on a plane can be expensive and it takes time to pack and unpack, so you may prefer to hire one at the trail. Most bike-hire businesses can also arrange trail transport (shuttles around the trail) and offer advice on where to stay and eat.

Getting there The most common way of travelling to the trail, which is usually driving, is
provided for each ride. If you wish to cycle between these Great Rides, refer to *Classic New Zealand Cycle Trails* for details on the full network.

Trail tales This section summarises the natural and cultural history of the trails,
providing a fascinating insight into how the region developed. It also includes some of the stories that have made the local culture what it is today.

Food and accommodation Remaining flexible, if you can, is one of the beauties of cycling
— stop and start where you like, and eat when you're hungry. However, be mindful that flexibility may not be possible during popular holidays, such as Christmas, Easter, school holidays and long weekends. You will find in each trail chapter a list of the towns you will pass, with information on businesses and services. If there is not much accommodation, then contact details for that accommodation are given. If there is abundant accommodation, I have indicated the best general website that lists all of the local options.

Shortcuts and detours If you are short on time, or are looking for more options, refer to
this section for a summary of the best shortcuts, other trails and activities. These are sometimes the most memorable parts of a cycling holiday.

GRADES

Grade 1: Very easy

Flat, smooth and wide trails suitable for absolutely everyone. The surface will be asphalt, concrete or smooth gravel. Any on-road sections will have little to no traffic, travelling at 50 kph or slower.

Grade 1 trails include: Hawke's Bay Trails, Hauraki Rail Trail, Otago Central Rail Trail.

Bike type Any bike with moderately wide tyres is suitable, even single speeds.

Grade 2: Easy

Some gentle climbs and narrow sections but still mostly wide enough to ride side by side. The surface is generally smooth gravel, and any on-road sections will have very little traffic.

Grade 2 trails include: Clutha Gold Trail, Roxburgh Gorge Trail, most of West Coast Wilderness Trail.

Bike type A multi-geared bike with medium or wide tyres is recommended; for example, a hybrid/comfort bike or mountain bike.

Grade 3: Intermediate

These trails include off-road sections that may be rough and narrow, and some good-sized hills. On-road sections of trail will mostly be on quiet country roads, with fewer than 1000 vehicles a day on average. Young riders should be accompanied by an adult.

Grade 3 trails include: the Timber Trail, Te Ara Ahi-Thermal by Bike, Motu Road (Motu Trails).

Bike type A mountain bike is recommended for off-road Grade 3 trails.

Grade 4: Advanced

Off-road Advanced trails have steep climbs with lots of obstacles and possibly a few short walking sections. On-road Advanced trails will probably include long hills and possibly gravel sections. The roads will be open to 100 kph traffic, with up to 1000 vehicles per day, possibly more, but only if there is a good road shoulder.

Grade 4 trails include: Mountains to Sea, The Old Ghost Road and St James Cycle Trail.

Bike type A mountain bike with suspension is highly recommended for off-road Grade 4 trails, and it should have less than 10 kg of gear loaded on it.

Grade 5: Expert

Hardly anything in this book is Grade 5. These trails require either excellent mountain-biking skills or a sensible willingness to get off and walk. You must be fit and very experienced to ride Grade 5 safely.

Grade 5 trails include: short sections of The Old Ghost Road, St James Cycle Tail and Queen Charlotte Track.

Bike type A quality mountain bike with full suspension is ideal for off-road Expert trails.

PRACTICAL ADVICE

CHOOSING A BIKE

If you want to do only Grade 1 and Grade 2 trails then a hybrid/comfort bike is perfect and a mountain bike is also fine. But if you are considering doing harder trails (Grade 3 and Grade 4), then you will need a mountain bike.

The best type of mountain bike for these trails is a hard-tail, 29er mountain bike. Such a bike only has suspension on the front forks, and its wheels are 29 inches in diameter. Between $1000 and $4000 will get you a good durable bike.

Hybrid bikes are similar to mountain bikes but have narrower tyres, more upright handlebars and special 'braze-ons' that make it easy to attach a carrier to the bike. They are generally less expensive.

Comfort bikes have more comfortable seats, sometimes with a suspension seat post and higher handlebars, making the riding position more comfortable.

Some specialist 'bikepacker' bikes have features that make them well suited for the easier cycle trails, but they can also be more expensive. One of the better-known specialist bikes is the Salsa Fargo, which is a practical combination of a mountain bike and a road bike.

Size matters. The most important aspect when choosing a bike, no matter what type, is the size. A bike shop or bike-hire business can help you find the right-sized bike.

As a rough guide, your leg should be almost fully extended as you pedal. If the bike is too big, then you won't be able to reach the pedals comfortably, and if the bike is too small, then your knees will be too bent.

GEAR

Helmets New Zealand law states that you have to wear a helmet while cycling in any public place. This law is often enforced on public roads, but I have never heard of it being enforced on trails.

Locks The best bike insurance is a solid D-lock. However, D-locks are also the heaviest. A thin cable lock is a good lightweight compromise.

Bags Load your bike up, not your back. A heavy backpack is uncomfortable on long trips.

On Grade 1 and Grade 2 trails, traditional bike panniers are a much better option. However, on bumpier trails it is harder to handle fully loaded bikes, so then you really need to split your gear between a backpack and panniers, or bikepacking bags. Bikepacking bags have become widely used since 2014 and they don't require a carrier.

Carriers There are three common types of carrier in New Zealand: conventional carriers that bolt to the front or back of the frame; carriers that clamp to the seat post; and Freeload carriers that clamp onto the front or rear of almost any style of bike.

Conventional carriers are cheap and light but can only be attached to bikes with no rear suspension, such as hybrid bikes and touring bikes.

Seat post carriers are also cheap, and convenient, but only carry up to 9 kg of gear.

Freeload carriers are the most expensive, but they can be attached to most bikes with both front and rear suspension. Hint: This carrier can jiggle loose, so make sure you take the small tool that comes with it.

Tools As a general rule, the longer and more remote the ride, the more tools you should carry. At the very least, take a spare tube, a tyre lever, a pump and a small multi-tool. All four of these together will cost less than $100 and be worth their weight in gold if you need them in the middle of nowhere.

Additional tools, in order of priority, are: puncture repair kit; small bottle of oil; spare brake blocks/pads; chain breaker and a spare chain link; spoke tool; spare pannier bolts; and a crank tool.

A group of cyclists may also feel it is worth throwing in a pedal spanner, some brake and derailleur cables, a freewheel tool and a spare tyre, just in case.

MURRAY DRAKE

Loaded up on the Timber Trail.

Bike seats Bicycles these days often come fitted with horribly uncomfortable saddles, so you may want to simply buy a larger one with more padding, or even springs! It will make a world of difference. Gel seat covers also make a difference and are easy to put on, but their extra width can introduce chafing problems.

Special cycling clothes Lycra cycle shorts with padding are very comfortable. Even if you hate the look, there is no denying the comfort. If you're really not keen on tight Lycra, you can buy casual-looking baggy cycle shorts with padding (check out www.groundeffect.co.nz).

Lycra cycle tops aren't so important. They have pockets at the back which are handy, but otherwise aren't really a big advantage.

High-visibility tops make it much easier for people to see you and are recommended when riding on roads at night or in low light conditions.

Cycling gloves are recommended for Grade 3 and Grade 4 trails. They are comfortable, help prevent sunburn and offer some extra protection should you fall off your bike.

Lights Don't forget to use good lights if riding road sections at night or during poor visibility. Also remember to replace or charge up the batteries regularly.

IN EMERGENCIES

Always have a contact person if you are riding alone. Leave the details of where you are going with a reliable friend and make it clear when they are to contact the police if they have not heard from you.

Take a first-aid kit and know how to use it. Also consider taking some form of communication with the outside world. On some of these trails there is little or no cellphone coverage. If you are in a remote area, the only way to contact emergency services would be to have an emergency personal locator beacon (PLB) or a Spot™ tracker. PLBs can be hired from outdoor stores and some businesses near the more remote trails. A Spot™ tracker has the advantage of showing your location on a website for family and friends to see.

Twin Coast Cycle Trail Pou Herenga Tai Good cellphone coverage on this trail.

Hauraki Rail Trail 100% cellphone coverage.

Waikato River Trails Approximately half the trail has cellphone coverage.

Te Ara Ahi-Thermal by Bike The majority of the trail has cellphone coverage.

Motu Trails Cellphone coverage around Opotiki and at Matawai. Most of the trail has no coverage — consider carrying a PLB.

The Timber Trail There is very little cellphone coverage on this trail. There is coverage between the 14-km and 16-km marker posts.

Great Lake Trail There is cellphone coverage along 90% of the trail.

Mountains to Sea Only 15% has cellphone coverage. A PLB is recommended.

Hawke's Bay Trails 100% cellphone coverage.

Rimutaka Cycle Trail Very patchy coverage from Te Marua to Cross Creek, and around the south coast.

Queen Charlotte Track Cellphone coverage is available along most of the trail, but not all.

Dun Mountain Trail Up to 50% of the trail has cellphone coverage.

Great Taste Trail There is coverage on almost all of the trail.

St James Cycle Trail There is no cellphone coverage on this trail. A PLB is recommended.

The Old Ghost Road There is very little coverage on this difficult and remote trail. Only at the Big Slips, just before Mt Montgomery, at Heavens Door and Ghost Lake Hut. A PLB is recommended.

West Coast Wilderness Trail Patchy cellphone coverage in the middle half of this trail, but it is improving every year.

Alps 2 Ocean Cycle Trail 95% of this trail has cellphone coverage.

Otago Central Rail Trail Generally good coverage, although there are a few black spots.

Roxburgh Gorge Trail There is little cellphone coverage in the gorge, but this section of the trail is not long.

Clutha Gold Trail There is 70% Spark coverage and 30% Vodafone coverage on this trail.

Queenstown Trail Good coverage on this trail.

Around the Mountains There is little cellphone coverage on half of this trail.

Tour Aotearoa Cape Reinga to Bluff. Mixed coverage. Consider taking a Spot™ tracker.

TRAINING AND PREPARATION

If you are planning on doing your first bike ride in months, years or even decades, then you will benefit from doing some pedalling in preparation for your cycling holiday, especially if you want to enjoy riding for more than one day in a row.

I recommend you do three one-hour rides a week, starting a few weeks out from your trip, building gradually up to one ride that is 80 per cent of the longest day you have planned. The more you ride, the easier you will find it.

Bike checklist

Before any big ride, or after storing your bike for a long time, check the following parts:

Tyres On a mountain bike or comfort bike, pump both tyres up to between 35 and 55 psi. 35 psi is relatively low and will be comfortable but sluggish, especially for heavy riders. 55 psi is quite a hard tyre, providing a fast ride but one that feels bumpy. After pumping your tyres up, inspect them to check there are no bulges, cuts or cracks.

Brakes Check both the front and rear brakes work properly. The cables might be undone or the brake blocks/pads worn out.

Oil the chain Apply a thin layer of oil to the whole chain.

Now load up the bike, checking that the panniers fit securely, and ride it around the block, making sure the gears don't skip and there are no other problems. If there are, take it to a bike shop for a check-up.

TRANSPORTING YOUR BIKE – CAR, BUS, TRAIN, PLANE

There are a few train networks that connect with towns and cities near to the trails and these provide good, relaxing travel, if a bit slow. The few long-distance train services that remain are very scenic, and some are highly recommended as a way of starting a trip — the train from Dunedin to the start of the Otago Central Rail Trail is the best.

Buses service more of the country, but taking your bike on a bus in New Zealand can be a hassle. You can't book your bike, and the drivers reserve the right to refuse to carry a bike if they don't have enough space. In actuality, I've never been refused, but every now and again you hear stories of others who have.

Ferries are much better set up to take bikes, and are never a hassle. In fact, it is often a joy to relax on a ferry, and recharge your batteries.

In all major cities you can get shuttle vans with trailers that can take bikes. These are not cheap, but they are convenient, as you can leave when you want and from where you want.

If you're on a tight budget or want to do a through trip, public transport might be your best option. Here are the websites for nationwide transport:

KiwiRail (train) www.kiwirail.co.nz
Interislander (ferry) www.interislander.co.nz
Bluebridge Cook Strait Ferry www.bluebridge.co.nz
Air New Zealand www.airnewzealand.co.nz
InterCity Coachlines (bus) www.intercity.co.nz

Smaller operators are mentioned in the relevant ride notes.

Fees for carrying bikes

Some ferries and trains, and most buses, charge $10–15 for an unbagged bike.

The Interislander ferry charges $15 for a bike. Bluebridge Cook Strait Ferry charges $10 for a bike. You'll be required to walk your bike on and off these ferries.

Air New Zealand does not charge for bikes but does charge for your second bag or item ($15 for a bag up to 25 kg). They expect you to pack your bike in a bike box or bike bag (most bike shops give away bike boxes).

Qantas charges $20 per bike and sells bike boxes for $25. If your bike weighs more than 15 kg, there may also be an excess luggage charge.

Budget airlines will charge an arm and a leg!

WEATHER

New Zealand is famous for its variable weather. It is not unusual for storms or fine weather to occur at any time of the year. Weather forecasts are reasonably accurate a few days out, but they are sometimes overly pessimistic. Three excellent weather forecast websites are: www.metservice.com; www.metvuw.com and www.weather.com

Seasonal patterns enable us to predict the best times of year to ride the trails.

Twin Coast Cycle Trail Pou Herenga Tai The winterless North is seldom too cold to go riding, but it can be stinking hot over summer. Take plenty of water.

Hauraki Rail Trail Moderate climate for most of the year but can be frosty in winter.

Waikato River Trails Generally moderate climate but cold during winter mornings.

Te Ara Ahi-Thermal by Bike Mostly good riding weather all year round with frosty mornings in winter.

Motu Trails Moderate climate for most of the year but can be frosty inland.

The Timber Trail Mostly good riding weather, but it can be very cold in winter, and the mountain section gets boggy after long periods of rain.

Great Lake Trail Mostly good riding weather all year round with frosty mornings in winter.

Mountains to Sea Expect a range of weather as this trail starts in the alpine zone at 1600 metres and finishes at sea level. Some of the off-road sections become unrideable after a couple of days' steady rain.

Hawke's Bay Trails Excellent cycling conditions, except for cold winter mornings and sometimes sweltering summer days.

Rimutaka Cycle Trail Moderate climate all year round, however the south coast is very exposed to southerly storms.

Queen Charlotte Track Moderate climate but the track is slippery after rain.

Dun Mountain Trail Moderate climate. However, the trail's highest point of 900 metres can experience extreme storms.

Great Taste Trail Moderate climate all year round, but expect some frosty winter mornings.

St James Cycle Trail Good weather in summer and autumn but often closed by snow over winter. Some side streams can flood, blocking the track.

The Old Ghost Road It is important to choose your weather on this trail. The region is famous for rain, which can flood side streams, closing northern parts of the track. Autumn brings long dry spells. Sections of the track can be closed in winter due to snowstorms.

West Coast Wilderness Trail Moderate weather, although the region receives plenty of rain. Take a good waterproof coat.

Alps 2 Ocean Cycle Trail Snow can close the higher-altitude parts of this track during winter. Otherwise, mostly great weather.

Otago Central Rail Trail Famous for its low rainfall, hot summers and freezing winters.

Roxburgh Gorge Trail This is a desert. It can be extremely hot in midsummer and completely frozen in winter.

Clutha Gold Trail Expect a moderate climate, with cold weather during southerlies.

Queenstown Trail Winter is Queenstown's ski season, so it gets very cold. Generally good weather for the rest of the year, but summer can get very hot.

Around the Mountains This trail can be bitterly cold in winter, with regular snow. Save this ride for summer or early autumn.

Tour Aotearoa Prepare for four seasons on this journey that takes you the length of New Zealand.

TOUR GUIDES

There are roughly three ways you can organise your cycling holiday.

Independent Self-organised from go to whoa. You arrange transport, food and accommodation. This is the cheapest and most flexible option.

Supported This is the hassle-free option, where you pay a business to organise your trip. They arrange shuttles, book accommodation, possibly organise meals and maybe even supply a bike.

Guided A guiding company will arrange everything and join you on the ride so that you don't have to worry about losing your way, your bike breaking down, or going hungry.

ENVIRONMENTAL CARE CODE

Protect plants and animals Treat New Zealand's plant life and birds with care and respect. They are unique and often rare.

Remove rubbish It irritates landowners to have rubbish left behind, it's not pleasant for other users and it's harmful to wildlife. Take all your rubbish with you.

Toilets Plan your day to use the public toilets marked on the maps. If you get caught short, make sure you do your business well out of sight and away from waterways.

Keep streams and lakes clean When cleaning and washing, do so well away from streams and lakes. Soaps and detergents are pollutants.

Take care with stoves and fires Fires can destroy forests and huts. Never leave a fire unattended, and make sure you put it out when you are finished with it.

Share with care The trails in this book are open to the public, including walkers. Share them with care. Slow down and sing out before overtaking other cyclists or walkers.

Respect our cultural heritage Many places in New Zealand have a spiritual and historical significance. Treat these places with consideration and respect.

The Mokihinui Gorge on The Old Ghost Road.

MURRAY DRAKE

Crossing from the Bay of Islands to the Hokianga Harbour, the Twin Coast Cycle Trail Pou Herenga Tai is the country's northernmost cycle trail, and the only one that runs from coast to coast. The trail starts in Opua, a small harbour on the east coast. It's a slice of paradise where sheltered waters and tantalising scenery attract boaties and tourists by the droves. From the car park behind Opua marina, the trail skirts around the coast and heads inland past Taumarere Station and across farmland to the main street of Kawakawa, a vibrant small town inviting exploration.

After a coffee at Kawakawa, you're back on your bike, heading west past Moerewa and several historical sites en route to Kaikohe, the hub of Northland, the largest town on the trail and a convenient overnight stopping point. The old railway line leads you north, to Okaihau, which was the end of the line for decades. From there, it is mostly downhill through farmland and beside a meandering stream to the oldest tavern in New Zealand, perched right on the edge of the Hokianga Harbour.

The popular tourist town of Paihia is only 6 km from the start of the trail and is a base for all sorts of activities, including fishing, sailing, kayaking and diving.

Pou Herenga Tai refers to the carved poles along the trail that draw inspiration from both Maori and Pakeha heritage. As Far North mayor John Carter puts it: 'Be prepared for an amazing experience from sweeping and unspoilt vistas to a historic journey that embraces the origins of New Zealand's nationhood.'

Twin Coast Cycle Trail Pou Herenga Tai

SUMMARY

Start point Opua, Bay of Islands
End point Horeke, Hokianga Harbour
Distance 86 km
Likely time 2 days
Grading Grade 2 (Easy) to Grade 3 (Intermediate)
Surface Mostly smooth gravel
Bike type Mountain bike or comfort/hybrid bike
Map and trail website www.twincoastcycletrail.kiwi.nz

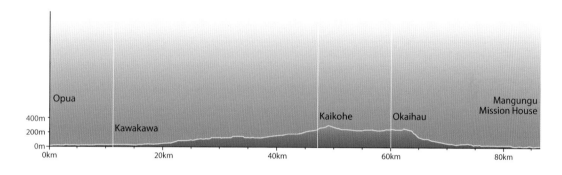

In emergencies There is cellphone coverage along most of this trail. Call 111. Some of the gates on this trail have GPS coordinates on a small red plaque, which help emergency services locate you

Bike hire Top Trail, 39 Rankin St, Kaikohe (bike hire as well as transport and accommodation), phone 0800 TOP TRAIL or 0274 535 176, www.toptrail.co.nz

Getting there From Auckland, follow SH1 north for 216 km to Kawakawa, then head down SH11 for 12 km to Opua

Trail transport To arrange transport to any part of the trail, contact Top Trail

Taumarere Station to Kawakawa Station For details on the times and fares, contact the Bay of Islands Vintage Railway, phone 09 404 0684 or 021 171 2697, www.bayofislandsvintagerailway.org.nz

ROUTE DESCRIPTION

Opua to Kawakawa

11 km, 2–3 hours, Grade 2 (Easy)

The trail starts from a car park behind the boat yards at the end of Baffin Street. Opua has a general store for last-minute supplies and a lovely cafe for a pre-ride coffee. It's a great spot to sit back and observe people and boats coming and going.

The start of the trail is well signposted and has been laid down on top of the old railway tracks. The Bay of Islands Vintage Railway Trust plans to restore this line and may then run vintage trains from the station in Kawakawa most of the way to Opua. For now, the first 7 km is a scenic cycle trail.

The railway station and cafe at Kawakawa.

Easy rail trail riding from Kaikohe to Okaihau.

Ride from Opua along the trail to the longest operational curved railway bridge in the Southern Hemisphere. At the eastern end of the bridge, behind Taumarere Station, the trail continues on to Kawakawa township.

Kawakawa is a lovely small town, famous for the amazing technicoloured toilets designed by Austrian-born architect Friedensreich Hundertwasser. There are a few cafes, the most popular being Gillies Street Cafe and the Station Cafe.

Kawakawa's main street reflects the ad hoc nature of some pioneer town planning. First the railway line was built in 1875, and then some horse tracks developed on both sides. These tracks both became main roads, and are now SH1, with the railway line down the centre.

Kawakawa to Kaikohe
35 km, 4–5 hours, Grade 3 (Intermediate)

From Kawakawa Station, go to Station Road, next to the Caltex petrol station. The trail starts 100 metres down Station Road. Follow the gravel path for 5 km to Pembroke Road where you can nip out to the Moerewa shops 300 metres to your right.

Continue following the rail trail from Pembroke Road onto Otiria Road, which becomes Ngapipito Road. Over the next 20 km, parts of the trail follow the railway line and parts of it are completely new. This 20-km section was finished in late 2016.

There are two truss bridges along here, crossing Orauta Stream. One of them is close to the site of Kawiti Station, named after Te Ruki Kawiti, an ally of Hone Heke. This site has huge historical importance as the place where the descendants of Te Ara Kepeka placed their dead in puriri trees on a nearby hill. When the flesh had completely gone from the body, the bones were taken to special caves nearby. The railway line was only able to come through this site with the agreement of local Maori, who knew that they would be able to find employment with the railway.

The railway line climbs from Ngapipito Road up a steep section called Jacobs Ladder to a crossing of Mangakahia Road next to the Kaikohe aerodrome. The rail trail from there to Kaikohe has been open for a couple of years. It is smooth and flat, and tree-lined along many stretches, making it popular for walking as well as cycling.

Follow the railway line to the main road (SH12), which is on the edge of Kaikohe. Turn right for the centre of town and food and accommodation.

Kaikohe to Okaihau
14 km, 1.5–2.5 hours, Grade 1 (Very easy)
Kaikohe — the hub of Northland — is a good base for the night, with the Mid North Motor Inn offering a warm welcome to cyclists. The town has an interesting museum of early settlement, a great coffee house (Cafe Malaahi) and the rustic Ngawha Springs hot pools (6 km east of the town).

Opened in 2011, the section from Kaikohe to Okaihau is easy rail trail.

From the shops in the centre of Kaikohe, head west on the main road. When you are 500 metres past the Mid North Motor Inn, you will see the trail signposted on your right.

Squeeze across a narrow cattlestop and follow the smooth gravel path across farmland, through a curved tunnel, and past Lake Omapere before a fun descent through Two Punga Park to Okaihau. This small town was the railway terminus for decades and thrived as a result. It's seen better days, and looks like it could do with some cycle-trail tourism.

PAUL MCARDLE

Warning! Northland horses do eat bike seats.

Luckily it has a great little cafe. When you reach the main street, the Village Cafe is 50 metres away, on your left. There are public toilets in the park right beside the trail, and a dairy and pub nearby.

Okaihau to Horeke, Hokianga Harbour

24 km, 2–3 hours, Grade 3 (Intermediate)

This section had only just finished construction at the time of writing. Much of the trail has been built down the Utakura River by the local landowners themselves. It is a beautiful valley, with pockets of diverse native forest, and there are plans to plant more native trees. This is the hilliest section of the Twin Coast Cycle Trail.

From Okaihau the trail runs beside Horeke Road for 3 km, before turning left across farmland and dropping to Utakura Valley. In late 2015, the trail ended at Mangataraire Road (15 km from Okaihau). From there the trail runs parallel with Horeke Road, and leads to the small village of Horeke, one of the oldest towns in New Zealand. Mangungu Mission House is 2 km further on via a gravel road.

There are public toilets and limited accommodation at Horeke. Meals are served on the waterfront at New Zealand's oldest tavern (established in 1826). This is a quiet town, so making advanced bookings is advisable.

From Horeke, you can arrange a shuttle with Top Trail back to any town on the trail.

Alternatively, if you enjoy cycle touring, organise for a boat to take you across the harbour to Rawene or Kohukohu, and pedal on. One of the New Zealand Cycle Trail routes goes down to Auckland via the Kauri Coast Cycle Trail and the Kaipara Missing Link (see www.kennett.co.nz for further details).

TRAIL TALES

The Northland region was sculpted by the eruptions of two volcanic fields: one around Whangarei and the other the Kaikohe–Bay of Islands volcanic field. The latest volcanic activity took place around 1300–1800 years ago and formed the Ngawha Springs just out of Kaikohe. Maori travelled to the springs to salve wounds and aching limbs in the soothing sulphur waters. In the late nineteenth century, miners were also attracted to the area by cinnabar, the red ore that is the basis of liquid mercury or 'quicksilver', and also by the coal deposits at Kawakawa.

From 1864, Kawakawa quickly became one of the best suppliers of coal in the country. A horse-drawn tramway was developed to transport the coal to barges on the Kawakawa River, 4 km away, and from there it was barged down to ships waiting at Opua. The tramway was soon replaced with a railway line — the first in the North Island. However, as the coal had to be loaded three times — into trains, then barges, then ships — the railway

Pioneering days at Kawakawa.

line was pushed on to Opua. This took seven years and involved building the longest curved wooden railway bridge in the Southern Hemisphere. Opua then developed into a deep-sea port, from which coal and then agricultural products were shipped. It is now mostly used by recreational boaties.

The next large town on the cycle trail is Kaikohe. This began as a small Ngapuhi settlement called Opango. In the early nineteenth century, a rival Maori tribe raided the village and the Ngapuhi residents were forced to flee. While hiding, they fed off the berries of the kohekohe groves on Tokareireia (Kaikohe Hill). As a result, the village became known as Kaikohekohe (meaning 'food of the kohekohe') but was later shortened to Kaikohe.

During the New Zealand Wars, this area was the site for a number of clashes. At the end of the wars, Maori chief Hone Heke, famous for cutting down British flagpoles, settled in Kaikohe. He died there in 1850, and there is a tribute to him at Monument Hill, close to the Taheke Road entrance to the trail.

The town remained a small settlement until 1914, when the rail line was pushed through from Auckland with the goal of reaching Kaitaia. Dairy farming then developed in the area. The line continued north, reaching Okaihau in 1923. Okaihau, meaning 'feast of the winds', was named because of its position on an exposed ridge. A settlement was established by a group of Canadians in 1862. Extending the line beyond Okaihau continued at a slower pace, and in 1936 it stalled completely at Rangiahua, 12 km west as the kereru flies. However, mounting costs saw the section north of Okaihau removed, and Okaihau regained its fame as New Zealand's northernmost railway terminus.

At the end of the trail is Horeke, the second oldest town in New Zealand. The town sprang up almost overnight when an Australian firm established the first commercial shipyard there in 1826. Only a few ships were actually constructed, but Horeke became the heart of the Hokianga for the next decade. Some Horeke buildings were built over water because of the scarcity of land for sale. In February 1840, more Maori chiefs signed the Treaty of Waitangi at Mangungu Mission House than at Waitangi. And in May that year Horeke shared the honours with the Bay of Islands for establishing the country's first postal service.

FOOD AND ACCOMMODATION

Paihia Popular tourist town with lots of places to eat and stay at: www.bay-of-islands.co.nz

Opua Plenty of accommodation and a few shops: Opua Motel, phone 09 402 7632 or 0800 666 835, www.opuamotel.co.nz; Pine Lodge Bay of Islands, phone 09 402 7808, www.pinelodgebayofislands.co.nz; Pukeko's Nest, phone 09 403 7951

Kawakawa Plenty of shops, accommodation and the Hundertwasser toilets. Try Centrepoint Motel, phone 09 404 1175, www.kawakawamotel.co.nz

Kaikohe Plenty of accommodation and shops: www.kaikohe.co.nz. The closest accommodation to the trail is the Mid North Motor Inn, phone 09 405 3160, www.midnorthmotorinn.co.nz

Okaihau Two dairies, a good cafe, a takeaway shop, a pub and even a hardware store.

Horeke Food and accommodation, shuttle and bike hire: Horeke Hotel (limited opening hours), phone 09 401 9133; Riverhead Guest House (book in advance, no credit card or Eftpos facilities), phone 09 401 9610 or 021 814 562, www.riverhead-guesthouse-horeke.co.nz

SHORTCUTS AND DETOURS

Bay of Islands Short Ride The 7-km section from Opua around the coast, across bridges and through a tunnel to Taumarere Station is the best short ride in the region.

The Kauri Coast From the Hokianga Harbour, the New Zealand Cycle Trail has predominantly on-road trails extending north to Cape Reinga and south to Auckland via the west coast. The trip through Waipoua Kauri Forest is regarded as the best stretch of road riding in the country. For more information see www.kennett.co.nz

Off Yer Bike Highlights include exploring the beaches and islands by boat of any size; getting in touch with New Zealand history at the Waitangi Treaty Grounds; or heading for the country's best diving location — Poor Knights Islands.

ormed along historic railway lines laid down from Thames to Paeroa, Waikino and Te Aroha, the Hauraki Rail Trail is one of the easiest and most popular trails in the country. It is an area rich in cultural heritage, which is reflected in the architecture and design of the small towns along the trail. The highlight for most is the Karangahake Gorge, with its scenic forest and fascinating history. It is worth parking your bike in the middle of the gorge for an hour to do the intriguing Windows Walk, where shallow tunnels have been carved beside canyon walls with windows punched through along the way.

Most riders start from Thames, a diverse town with a few museums and many small shops. From the southern end of town, the trail heads across the Hauraki Plains, on the same formation steam trains once powered along, billowing smoke and blowing their whistles. Could any of the drivers have imagined that one day the public would come from far and wide to pedal their way along the tracks?

There are several small cafes and pubs within coo-ee of the cycle trail, all especially welcoming to those that have worked up a healthy appetite. The first small town, Paeroa, is famous for its L&P (Lemon and Paeroa) soft drink, but is also an antique lovers' dream.

From Paeroa, the trail forks and most people head east through the Karangahake Gorge. The trail goes to Waikino Station, where you can back-track to Paeroa, or continue to Waihi by riding on the trail or catching a vintage train.

Back at Paeroa, the trail heads south to Te Aroha, another historic small town that is renowned for its hot pools and restorative soda spas.

In 2017 the trail was extended by 36 km from Kopu, near Thames, to Miranda. There are also plans to extend this trail from Te Aroha to Matamata (35 km) in 2018. Check the New Zealand Cycle Trail website for updates on these developments.

SUMMARY ●

Start point Thames, Paeroa or Waihi

End point Waihi, Te Aroha or Thames

Distance 119 km for the full trail; 54 km straight from Thames to Te Aroha; and 22 km for the Karangahake Gorge to Waihi section

Likely time 3 days for the full trail; a half-day for Karangahake Gorge only

Grading Grade 1 (Very easy)

Surface Wide, smooth gravel path

Bike type Mountain bike or comfort/hybrid bike

Map Trail maps available from www.haurakirailtrail.co.nz and i-SITEs in Thames, Paeroa, Te Aroha or Waihi

Trail website www.haurakirailtrail.co.nz

In emergencies There is cellphone coverage on most of this trail. Call 111

Hauraki Rail Trail

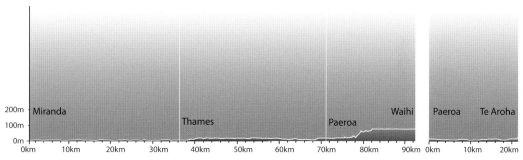

Bike hire Jolly Bikes, Thames, phone 07 867 9026 or 021 0816 5000, www.jollybikes.co.nz; Waihi Sports and Cycles, phone 07 863 8418, www.waihibicyclehire.co.nz; Hauraki Cycle Trail, phone 027 203 9719, www.haurakicycletrail.co.nz, (bikes in Paeroa, Waihi and Te Aroha); Paeroa Sportsworld, phone 07 862 6480

Getting there Miranda is 80 km (1 hour) southeast of Auckland and Te Aroha is 55 km (45 minutes) from Hamilton. The Waihi end of the trail is 60 km (50 minutes) from Tauranga

Trail transport For transport around the trail, contact the Sherpa Bus (bookings essential), phone 027 203 9719, www.haurakicycletrail.co.nz/sherpa-shuttle;

Coasting towards the Karangahake Gorge.

Blue Tui Shuttles and Tours, phone 07 872 2404, www.bluetui.co.nz

Karangahake Gorge Train For a timetable and fares, phone 07 863 9020, or check out www.waihirail.co.nz

ROUTE DESCRIPTION

Pukorukoru (Miranda) to Thames

36 km, 3–5 hours, Grade 1 (Very easy)

This section was finished in April 2017. There is a parking area 400 metres from Pukorukoru (Miranda) up East Coast Road. Ride south from the parking area and turn left onto the new path. Most of it follows stopbanks around the bottom of the Firth of Thames.

After 3 km you will pass the entrance to the Miranda Hot Springs and Holiday Park. From there the path is beside the road to Waitakaruru (9 km from the start). There is a small cafe and store a few minutes further on. At about the 24-km mark you will cross Piako River on a clip-on path beside the highway. There is a cafe across the road but it is not safe crossing the highway. The trail heads back out to the Firth and after 34 km rejoins SH25 to cross the Waihou River Bridge to Kopu. Turn left (north) to ride to Thames a few kilometres away or right to head down to Paeroa.

Thames to Paeroa

34 km, 3–5 hours, Grade 1 (Very easy)

The Thames i-SITE and most shops are on Pollen Street, which runs parallel to the highway and the coast. There are plenty of good cafes, a bakery, a fruit shop and a good bike shop. A market day is held on Saturday mornings at the end of Pollen Street.

A convenient place to meet up is at the Brew Cafe and Gallery on the corner of Pollen and Richmond streets. From there you can ride two blocks down Richmond Street to a wide coastal path, and turn left to get to the wharf.

The official trail start is at a small car park next to the wharf (opposite the corner of SH25 and Grey Street). There is a cool little cafe there and a takeaway store.

From Wharf Cafe, the trail heads south beside the highway for 10 minutes, then crosses farm paddocks and dips through a tunnel under the main highway to Auckland. After 12 km, there is a sign inviting you to visit the Cheese Barn Cafe, 200 metres off the trail at Matatoki. It's an appetising destination for your first rest.

From the Cheese Barn, ride back to the trail and continue south for 10 km to Hikutaia, where there is another popular cafe, the Convenient Cow. It is on the opposite side of the busy highway — take care.

It is now 12 km to the world-famous-in-New-Zealand L&P soft-drink town of Paeroa. If it's been a while between drinks, you must reacquaint yourself with the uniquely Kiwi flavour of L&P (it's harmlessly forgettable). Paeroa is the hub of the Hauraki Rail Trail. There is a large L&P cafe right next to the Paeroa information centre.

Pay careful attention to the trail signs as you pass through Paeroa — apparently people can get lost here. The giant L&P bottle is beside SH2, only 60 metres from the bridge you will cross on the way out of town, but it is hidden from view by a tree.

Paeroa to Waihi

22 km to Waihi, 2–4 hours, Grade 1 (Very easy)

This is the most popular section of the trail and over summer it can become crowded. For ease of transport, and because this section is so darned good, you may want to ride it there and back.

From the Paeroa information centre, cross the road and follow the trail south along the stopbank to a road bridge. Cross the bridge on the pedestrian path. The far side of the bridge is where the trail also branches off to Te Aroha.

Once you are across the Ohinemuri River bridge, cross SH26 to follow the path left down Rotokohu Road. The path runs beside the road and then across flat farming land before entering the Karangahake Gorge.

Just before crossing a double-decker bridge that leads into the long railway tunnel, stop and take a look at the map board beside the track. This is where you can branch off to

Don't forget some gold coins for fresh treats along the way.

the right for 800 metres to reach a picnic area next to a cafe and to a few short walks, including the famous Windows Walk (see page 47).

Alternatively, go straight ahead and stay on the Hauraki Rail Trail. It crosses the bridge and goes through a 1.1-km-long lit tunnel, before crossing another bridge and then following the river to the Victoria Battery processing site. Interpretation boards show the massive scale of the operation. One last bridge and a short section of trail leads to the lovingly restored Waikino Station, with its scrumptious cafe.

The vintage train, which takes bikes, runs from Waikino to Waihi at 2.30 p.m. over summer and during holidays. Alternatively, back-track to the bridge and follow the main trail for 8 km to Waihi (it is Grade 2 in places).

Paeroa to Te Aroha
21 km, 2–3 hours, Grade 1 (Very easy)
From the far side of the bridge on the outskirts of Paeroa, turn right onto the trail and head south. You can't get lost. It is flat and straight. When you are 7 km from Paeroa you'll see a sign advertising Devonshire tea. It's served by a delightful couple in a lovely garden.

Other than Devonshire tea, and two public toilets, this is a fairly forgettable section of the trail. It ends at the old railway station in Te Aroha, two blocks from the main street.

Te Aroha is a friendly old town, well worth getting to know. All the shops are on the main street, and include antiques, cafes, an information centre and the coolest bike racks in the world! It also has a museum, a domain and lots of mountain-bike tracks. If this is your first bike ride in years, the best destination will be the hot pools. First there are the exclusive mineral spa baths, which claim to be the best in the world due to the restorative qualities of the silky soda water, and where each couple/group gets a private spa of their own (bookings are advisable). Twenty metres from the spa pools are the public leisure pools, also hot, but much cheaper because they use common tap water (for commoners).

TRAIL TALES

In November 1769, Captain Cook sailed to the head of a large inlet now called the Firth of Thames and up the Waihou River. He found the banks of the river lined with towering kahikatea, behind which endless forests dominated the view. Cook named the river the Thames, after the River Thames of his homeland, and the name stuck to the town, but not the river.

Maori had inhabited this area for around 500 years before Cook's arrival, and had a large pa 3 km west of where Paeroa lies today. The attraction was the 32,400-ha Kopuatai Swamp, which was a rich food basket at this time. Most of this swamp has since been drained for farmland; however, 10,000 ha has been protected as an ecological reserve.

The Maori settlement was also on the main route south from Hauraki to the Bay of Plenty. Travellers paddled waka along the Waihou and Ohinemuri rivers to Paeroa. From here they tramped through the Karangahake Gorge and across the Waihi Plains to the Tauranga Harbour, from where they could continue by boat once more.

Just over a century after Cook sailed into the Hauraki Gulf, European traders and missionaries began to settle in Thames and Paeroa. The first major discovery of gold was made in the area on 10 August 1867 by a prospector named William Hunt, in a waterfall in the bed of a stream just north of Thames. It led to the first in a series of gold-mining booms in the region. Towards the end of the 1800s, Thames was the largest town in New Zealand with a population of 18,000 and well over 100 hotels.

Gold mining was not the only large industry for the area at the turn of the century. Early settlers quickly recognised the value of kauri timber for buildings, bridges, wharves, railway wagons, and even street paving. From the 1870s the valley east of Thames was logged extensively until, by 1928, all but the most inaccessible kauri had been felled. Not until 1970 were the remaining native forests of the Kauaeranga Valley protected as part of the Coromandel Forest Park.

In the 1930s, when the gold-mining and kauri-logging industries had both dwindled, settlers began draining the wetlands of the Hauraki Plains for farming.

Further to the southeast, in the Karangahake Gorge, mining for gold began in March

1875. However, the gold was hidden deep underground, in quartz rock. The quartz had to be dug out, crushed and treated before any gold could be extracted, and many early companies went bust before enough gold could be extracted to cover costs. The process improved dramatically in 1889 with the introduction of the MacArthur-Forrest cyanide process and, by 1909, output from the Karangahake quartz mines made up 60 per cent of all the gold mined in New Zealand. Five large batteries were built between Paeroa and Waihi, and millions of tons of ore were dug up and crushed.

The Waihi Gold Mining Company built the largest crushing factory of all — the Victoria Battery — in 1897 to process ore from the Waihi Martha Mine. With 200 stampers operating 24 hours a day, it was capable of crushing up to 800 tons of ore in one day. The ore was carried to the site along a narrow-gauge railway (the rakeline).

With the gold processing in full swing, the government passed legislation allowing companies to dump waste into the Ohinemuri River. The cyanide-laced sludge soon killed all river life and left behind a contaminated dead-zone. The dumping continued until 1954, a year after the last processing plant, at Waikino, closed.

Just as the Karangahake Gorge had been a major trail for Maori, so it was for Europeans, who built a road and then, from 1900 to 1905, a railway (the East Coast Main Trunk Line) from Waihi to Paeroa, then north to Thames and south to Te Aroha and beyond.

The 1.1-km Karangahake tunnel was lined with concrete and up to five layers of brick. But the tunnel had its problems. Smoke from the engines caused health problems for the train drivers. Also, shortly after the railway line opened, it became evident that an extra road bridge was needed over the railway because horses were being spooked by trains popping out of the tunnel and were refusing to cross the lines.

The settlement of Karangahake, circa 1916.

The Karangahake Gorge railway line was also susceptible to rock fall and finally, in the 1970s, it was bypassed by a new line — the Kaimai Deviation. The gorge section of railway line, from Paeroa to Waihi, was finally closed in 1979, and the area was then developed for recreation and tourism. In 2014, the government granted consent for mining to resume in Karangahake Gorge.

FOOD AND ACCOMMODATION

Miranda Hot Springs Accommodation, food, hot pools: Miranda Holiday Park, phone 0800 833 144, www.mirandaholidaypark.co.nz

Waitakaruru Cafe and store.

Thames Accommodation, shops, food: www.thamesinfo.co.nz; Sunkist Guesthouse, phone 07 868 8808, www.sunkistguesthouse.nz

Matatoki The Cheese Barn, open seven days, www.thecheesebarn.co.nz

Hikutaia Thames Valley Homestay, phone 07 862 4827 or 027 437 6458, www.thamesvalleyhomestay.co.nz

Paeroa Plenty of accommodation, shops, food: www.paeroa.org.nz

Karangahake Gorge Accommodation, a winery and a cafe.

Waikino The railway station has a lovely cafe.

Waihi Food, accommodation and a bike shop: www.waihi.org.nz

Tirohia Devonshire tea at the Depot Garden, 1685 Paeroa–Tahuna Road, phone 07 862 8738 or 021 079 8393.

Te Aroha Food, accommodation and hot pools: www.tearohanz.co.nz

SHORTCUTS AND DETOURS

Karangahake Gorge The best half-day ride on this trail is clearly from Paeroa to Waikino Station and back. It's 28 km return, and includes the most interesting history and best scenery. Make sure you check out the Windows Walk (see below).

Windows Walk, Karangahake Gorge This is one of the most interesting 1-hour walks in the country. Take a torch because parts of it are through small tunnels, with windows looking out over the gorge. You'll hardly believe it's New Zealand. It starts from the end of an 800-metre side branch of the Hauraki Rail Trail (veer off the main trail, just west of the double-decker bridge in Karangahake Gorge).

Te Aroha Mountain Bike Trails There is a good 1–2 hour, Grade 3 (Intermediate) mountain-bike trail in the hills behind Te Aroha. Pick up a map of the trails at the information centre. The trail starts from Te Aroha Domain where the hot springs are.

WAIKATO RIVER TRAILS

The Waikato River Trails explore a part of New Zealand's longest river, which was once a highway for Maori travelling by waka.

Nicknamed the 'hidden trail', it reveals a series of hydro lakes and dramatic volcanic landscapes as it passes through forest and farmland.

The trails are full of surprises. Some are easy, gravelled paths, with long boardwalks or swing bridges. Others are bumpy mountain-bike tracks, complete with tight switchbacks and steep hills. There are five distinct sections, so if you've only ever ridden a rail trail before, choose carefully or be prepared to push your bike. There are plenty of challenges — and rewards — along this relatively remote journey.

There are only three villages along the 105-km route. At the northern tip, the trail begins beside Lake Karapiro, 27 km southeast from Cambridge. At the southern end of the trail, there is a car park by Atiamuri, 40 km north of Taupo. While the remoteness is something to relish, you must be reasonably self-sufficient or arrange for a shuttle to meet you at set places with food, and possibly take you to accommodation off the trail.

Like many of the cycle trails, this one is dynamic. Since it was opened in 2011, there have been two major upgrades improving over a quarter of the trail, and over 70,000 native trees have been planted. More improvements are planned, and local businesses are offering more services to cyclists every year. As there is little difference in elevation from one end of the trail to the other, it rides just as well in either direction.

SUMMARY

Start point Pokaiwhenua Stream (near Cambridge) or Atiamuri (near Taupo). There are
    shorter options — most people just ride the northern or southern section
End point Either of the above
Distance 105 km
Likely time 2–3 days for the full trail, or 2–3 hours for short sections
Grading Grade 2+ (Easy) to 4 (Advanced)
Surface Mostly off-road gravel path with some sections of forestry road and sealed
    road. More off-road sections are being built
Bike type Mountain bike to ride the whole trail, or a comfort bike to just do the
    northernmost section (Arapuni to Pokaiwhenua)
Map Available from www.waikatorivertrails.co.nz, or a pamphlet map is available from
    i-SITEs and businesses around the trail (in Cambridge, Putaruru and Tokoroa)
Trail website www.waikatorivertrails.co.nz
In emergencies Outside the small towns of Arapuni, Mangakino and Whakamaru, there
    is little to no cellphone coverage on the trail. If that worries you, take an emergency
    personal locator beacon (PLB)

L. Karapiro

Horahora Rd

1

Tirau

5

P

Pokaiwhenua Bridge

1

Little Waipa Res.

Putaruru

Arapuni

Darby Rd

Lake Arapuni Rd

Jones Landing

Waotu

Jim Barnett Res.

Waotu South Rd

L. Arapuni

road ends

1

TOKOROA

Waikato R.

Waipapa Dam

L. Waipapa

32

Maraetai Dam

Lakefront Res.

KINLEITH FOREST

1

Mangakino

L. Maraetai

Dunham Pt Res.

L. Atiamur

30

L. Whakamaru Res.

P

Mangakino Strm

Whakamaru Dam

Atiamuri

1

to Pureora

32

Whakamaru

30

L. Whakamaru

Waikato R.

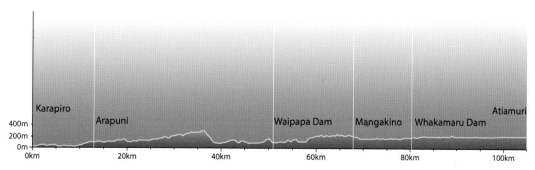

Karapiro

Arapuni

Waipapa Dam

Mangakino

Whakamaru Dam

Atiamuri

400m
200m
0m

0km   20km   40km   60km   80km   100km

A secluded stretch of the Waikato River, near Atiamuri.

Bike hire Waikato River Trails, phone 07 883 3720, www.waikatorivertrails.co.nz;
    Rhubarb Cafe, Arapuni, phone 07 883 5722; Blue Tui Shuttles, phone 07 872 2404,
    www.bluetui.co.nz
Getting there Most people drive to and from various stages of the trail or arrange
    shuttle transport with the Waikato River Trails Trust. The Pokaiwhenua Stream end
    is 27 km southeast of Cambridge via SH1 and Horahora Road (only 10 km north of
    Arapuni). The Atiamuri end is 40 km north of Taupo via SH1

ROUTE DESCRIPTION

The Waikato River is dissected by several hydro dams, each forming a lake behind it.
Each stage of the trail is named after the lake it follows. All stages can be ridden in both
directions.

Karapiro (Pokaiwhenua Bridge to Arapuni)
13 km one way, 1.5–2.5 hours, Grade 2+ (Easy)
Those riding the whole trail will want to start at the Pokaiwhenua Bridge car park,
whereas those just out for a half-day ride usually start at Arapuni and ride north towards
the bridge, and then back again.

The Pokaiwhenua Bridge is on Horahora Road, 4 km south of SH1. It is well signposted from the highway, and the car park is on the south side of the bridge.

From the car park, follow the Waikato River Trails south, sometimes beside Lake Karapiro, at other times beside Horahora Road. The first place worth stopping is 5 km down the gravel trail, at Little Waipa Reserve. Here there are toilets and a grassy picnic area. The next 8 km to Arapuni is much more enjoyable. The trail has stunning views of the river, and at one point you'll glide along a 500-metre boardwalk, over the Huihuitaha Wetlands. There are a couple of short steep hills that are easier to walk than bike.

At Arapuni, make sure you check out the amazing Arapuni suspension bridge — the longest in the country. This bridge is 100 metres off the trail on your right — ride the bridge there and back. From the bridge, turn left and ride 80 metres out to the main street of Arapuni, at the corner of Arapuni Road and Rabone Street.

Turn left down the main street to ride a few hundred metres to the superb Rhubarb Cafe. Phone ahead to be certain they are open.

Arapuni (Arapuni to Waipapa Dam)

34 km, 4–6 hours, Grade 3+ (Intermediate)

The first 5 km of this section (Arapuni south to Jones Landing) used to suit expert mountain bikers but was upgraded to intermediate in 2015. It is signposted from the Arapuni suspension bridge to the landing, which is a popular reserve beside the river. Alternatively, from Arapuni take Arapuni Road south for 1 km, then turn left onto Darby Road and follow this for 2 km before turning right and heading down Lake Arapuni Road for 4 km. You will then be at the turn-off to Jones Landing (200 metres away).

From Jones Landing, the trail largely follows sealed roads for 15 km. Continue south on Lake Arapuni Road for 8 km, at which point the road curves to the right and becomes Wiltsdown Road. After another few hundred metres, turn right onto Waotu South Road and follow a 600-metre-long path to Jim Barnett Reserve, a welcome highlight — the trail heads off-road through a small patch of forest for 1.5 km. It rejoins the road at the main entrance to the reserve, where there is information on the history of the forest. You can also camp here.

About 22 km from Arapuni, you will reach the end of the sealed road on Waotu South Road. The trail dives down to the river via a series of 37 tight switchbacks. At the bottom, the riding radically improves as the trail passes through regenerating forest and across a huge swing bridge. About 2 km from the Waipapa Dam, near the end of the stage, is a grunty little climb followed by a flight of wooden steps down a steep gully.

Waipapa Dam is a good spot to rest and regroup.

Waipapa (Waipapa Dam to Mangakino Lakefront Reserve)

20 km, 3–4 hours, Grade 3+ (Intermediate)

From Waipapa Dam, continue south on a section of trail running beside Waipapa Road for almost 2 km. The trail then branches away from the road and heads through forest, on a mix of old forestry roads and new cycle trail.

The trail rejoins Waipapa Road near Maraetai Dam, and stays on-road to Mangakino Lakefront Reserve, 3 km away at the end of Lake Road. Here there are toilets, a cafe, and camping areas.

Maraetai (Mangakino Lakefront Reserve to Whakamaru Dam)

13 km, 1.5–2.5 hours, Grade 3– (Intermediate)

This is one of the easier stages of the Waikato River Trails, with only a few short steep hills, a wide gravel path, and a long swing bridge affording great views. Many people ride it both ways.

From the lakefront reserve, ride south past the golf course, and after a few kilometres you'll cross the long Mangakino Stream bridge. When you reach Whakamaru Dam, turn

Riders on the Arapuni to Waipapa section.

right and travel a few hundred metres to the shops, which include a cafe and a pizzeria. Alternatively, turn left and cross the dam to ride the final section of the trail.

Whakamaru Dam to Atiamuri

25 km, 2–4 hours, Grade 3– (Intermediate)

This is the longest section of the trail, and is rated very highly by mountain-bike clubs looking for a relatively easy trip.

The trail starts on the northern side of Whakamaru Dam. You will see a trail signboard near the end of the dam, from where the trail heads into the trees. To start with, the trail follows a gravel road as it passes a popular camping reserve. About halfway along this section, you must bypass the 'Stairway to Heaven' by riding on SH30 for 300 metres. From there, the trail branches well away from the highway, following close to the river's edge.

The rumbling of vehicles on SH1 heralds the end of the trail. A left-hand switchback leads up to a nondescript parking area beside SH30 (Ongaroto Road), only 200 metres from SH1. A new highway bridge was built here in 2013 and has a cycle path on it. Eventually the trail will continue to a new car-parking area near Atiamuri Village, 1 km away. No accommodation or food was available at Atiamuri in 2017.

TRAIL TALES

The country's longest river, the Waikato, runs 425 km from the central North Island volcanic plateau to the Tasman Sea at Port Waikato, just south of Auckland. It was largely formed by a massive volcanic eruption 1800 years ago.

However, Maori legend gives another account of its origin. One day, Taupiri, a mountain in the southern Waikato, fell ill and sent a servant and his dog to the central plateau to fetch the renowned curative waters from her friend Tongariro. When Tongariro heard about Taupiri's illness, he called to the gods for help. The gods responded by creating a spring of water that gushed out of a rock and poured down the mountain. The water quickly flowed northwards towards Hauraki, and the servant and his dog had to hurry to guide it back towards Taupiri. Eventually, the waters reached Taupiri and broke through the Hakarimata Range to form the Taupiri Gorge.

Freshwater mussels and eels were once plentiful in the Waikato River, and were a staple of the local Maori diet. In the nineteenth century, the river was a major travelling route, and European boat owners planted poplars, birch, willow and alders along its banks as a ready source of easy-burning fuel for steamships.

Since 1914, eight dams have been constructed on the Waikato River between Hamilton and Lake Taupo. This area was chosen because the narrow river valley was easy to dam and allowed for the creation of long lakes that stored water for hydro-electric generation.

Slow progress on the construction of the Arapuni Hydro Electrical Station, circa 1931.

The first dam on the river, Horahora, was commissioned by the Waihi Mining Company and was built near the northern end of the Waikato River Trails. It generated power from 1914 to 1947 when the Karapiro Dam was completed and formed a huge lake that submerged the Horahora power station. In order from north to south, the remaining dams are: Karapiro, Arapuni, Waipapa, Maraetai, Whakamaru, Atiamuri and Ohakuri.

Arapuni power station was commissioned in 1929, and is the oldest surviving dam on the river. The youngest is Waipapa power station, which was completed in 1971.

Arapuni also boasts the longest suspension footbridge in the country. The 152-metre bridge in the bush-lined gorge at Arapuni was built in the mid-1920s to enable workers staying at Arapuni Village to access the power station construction site quickly and easily.

The Jim Barnett Reserve, just south of Arapuni, boasts an equally impressive history. Over 26,000 years ago, the Taupo volcano erupted violently, creating Lake Taupo and destroying everything for miles around. At Waotu, however, a low hill diverted the more serious outfall from the eruption. When Maori finally arrived in the area, they discovered a narrow strip of intact first-generation native forest among a sea of scrub, flax and toi toi. They named the forest Te Waotu tahi nga rakau — the tall forest that stood by itself. It quickly became a favoured settlement area, first by Ngati Kahupungapunga, then, from the sixteenth century, by Ngati Raukawa and finally by Europeans. By the end of the 1800s, farming was well established and logging had begun in the ancient forest. About 90 per cent (900 ha) of that original bush had been logged by the 1920s. Jim Barnett Reserve and an adjoining block of covenanted land make up the largest remaining tract of original forest. The reserve was purchased from the Barnett family in 1992 to be maintained by Forest and Bird, Putaruru Rotary, Putaruru Walking Group, the South Waikato District Council and the Waotu community.

In 1946, as the Karapiro Dam neared completion, the Crown established a township to the south. Mangakino was originally developed to house the hundreds of workers needed for the next proposed dams. The town was only ever meant to be a temporary settlement, and in that first year the Mangakino Primary School was just a large hut containing one teacher and 13 pupils. By 1954, however, Mangakino District High School had been built and held the record for the largest student population in the country. In its heyday Mangakino boasted a cinema, library, concert hall, gymnasium, bowling club and extensive sports fields, some of which still exist today. Mangakino's population in 1960 was recorded as 5588 residents, but by 1963, following the completion of Maraetai II Dam, it had halved.

In 2002, the South Waikato Economic Development Trust pledged to build a 100-km 'Forest and River Trail' from Horahora in the north to Atiamuri in the south. In February 2006, the Waikato River Trails Trust was formed as a charitable organisation to develop, promote and maintain the river trails. They have improved the environment by

Boardwalk across the Huihuitaha Wetland.

working with volunteers to plant over 70,000 native trees beside the river, with thousands more planned for future planting efforts.

To help raise funds for the trail upgrades, there is an annual race held in early November called The Taniwha, with options for walking, running or biking from 7 to 83 km.

Further down the Waikato River, another trust is constructing Te Awa, the Great River Ride. This is a 70-km trail between Lake Karapiro, Cambridge, Hamilton and Ngaruawahia.

FOOD AND ACCOMMODATION

Waikato River Trails To book accommodation and meals, phone 07 883 3720, or go to www.waikatorivertrails.co.nz

Pokaiwhenua Bridge Accommodation (here and at Arapuni) and bike hire, phone 0800 287 448, www.lakedistrictadventures.co.nz

Arapuni Food, bike hire and guided tours: Rhubarb Cafe, 6 Arapuni Road, phone 07 883 5722 or 027 4317 207 (open Wednesday to Sunday). Accommodation: Arapuni Backpackers, phone 021 178 9332 or 07 883 5759, www.arapuni.co.nz. There is camping along the trail at Jim Barnett Reserve, Little Waipa Reserve on Horahora Road and Jones Landing on Lake Arapuni Road, www.southwaikato.govt.nz

Near Arapuni Out in the Styx Guesthouse, phone 0800 461 559, www.styx.co.nz

Mangakino Shops and accommodation: Mangakino Hotel, phone 07 882 8800, www.mangakinohotel.co.nz. Lake Maraetai Lodge, phone 0800 882 282, www.lake-maraetai-lodge.co.nz. Camping is available at Mangakino lakefront, Lake Road.

Whakamaru Food: That Dam Cafe, Fred's Pizzeria, Whakamaru Store. Accommodation: Arataki Farm, phone 07 882 8857; That Dam Lodge, phone 07 882 8292 or 021 0272 5567, www.thatdamlodge.co.nz

SHORTCUTS AND DETOURS

The Rhubarb Ride The most popular short ride of this trail is from the Rhubarb Cafe up to Little Waipa Reserve and back. That's only 12 km return, which takes 2 hours at a leisurely pace. It's mostly easy, but there are a few short hills that are often walked. All the same, it is a satisfying workout, with the pleasant destination of the Rhubarb Cafe.

Connectors to other Great Rides There are recommended connecting routes from the Waikato River Trails to Te Awa in Cambridge; Te Ara Ahi-Thermal by Bike heading to Rotorua (see pages 60–69); and the Timber Trail in Pureora Forest Park (see pages 80–91).

Post-ride treats await at Arapuni.

Maungatautari Guided Walk Situated 10 km west of Arapuni, Maungatautari is the largest ecological mainland island in the North Island, and home to several rare and endangered species. Guided tours are offered in the sanctuary, from $25 per person. See www.sanctuarymountain.co.nz for more details.

TE ARA AHI — THERMAL BY BIKE

Te Ara Ahi, which means the pathway of fire, explores a landscape where the earth's molten core seethes just below the surface and occasionally breaks through. The most recent major eruption was in 1886, and it buried a village, destroyed a mountain and created lakes.

The trail passes eight unique geothermal areas ranging from steaming volcanic craters and active geysers to soothing hot pools, now popular for soaking in. Other attractions include Maori cultural shows, a world-class mountain-bike park, and the North Island's main tourist centre — Rotorua.

Te Ara Ahi-Thermal by Bike is a mixed trail, with some sections much more popular than others. Few people ride the whole length. From Rotorua, it follows an interesting gravel path around Sulphur Point, then various on- and off-road sections to Te Puia cultural institute on the edge of town. From Te Puia, a mountain-bike track takes you through Hemo Gorge to the Whakarewarewa Mountain Bike Park where there is a cafe. From there, the trail is mostly on a smooth concrete path beside the Rotorua–Taupo highway, and some quiet country roads, to Waimangu — a stunning volcanic area with a cafe, walks and tours.

The route follows country roads from there to Rainbow Mountain, where conditions suddenly become much tougher as you skirt around the mountain, past Te Ranga Stream (Kerosene Creek) and on to Waiotapu. The rest of the trail is all on road and ends at a hot pools site (with camping). There is an optional extra to continue to Lake Ohakuri, a remote but scenic area where a thermal stream flows into a small bay.

If you are short on time, then I recommend catching a morning shuttle from Rotorua up to Waimangu for a walk around the thermal sights before refuelling at the cafe and then riding back to Rotorua. That's mostly downhill, and only takes 5 hours return.

SUMMARY

Start point Rotorua
End point Lake Ohakuri
Distance 47 km
Likely time 1–2 days
Grading Grade 2 (Easy) from Rotorua to Waimangu; Grade 3 (Intermediate) from
    Waimangu to Waikite Valley Thermal Pools
Surface A mix of gravel path, concrete path and sealed road
Bike type Mountain bike or a comfort/hybrid bike
Map A pamphlet map is available from the Rotorua i-SITE
Trail website www.nzcycletrail.com
In emergencies There is cellphone coverage on most of this trail, except near the
    southern end

Lake Rotorua

ROTORUA

Sulphur Bay Res.

Hemo Gorge

Whakarewarewa
Te Puia

Whakarewarewa MTB Park

L. Okareka

Tikitapu (Blue Lake)

Lake Tarawera

L. Rotokakahi
(Green Lake)

Tamaki Maori Village

Highlands Loop Rd

Waimangu Rd

Earthquake Flat

Waimangu

Okaro Rd
L. Okaro

Waikite Valley Thermal Pools

Waikite Valley Rd

Waikite Valley Rd

P

Rainbow Mtn

Kerosene Ck
(Te Ranga)

Waiotapu

thermal
area

Te Kopia Rd

Whirinaki Strm

PAEROA RANGE

to Taupo

ake Ohakuri

optional
extra section

Te Kopia Rd

Waihunuhunu Strm

Lake Ohakuri

Te Ara Ahi – Thermal by Bike

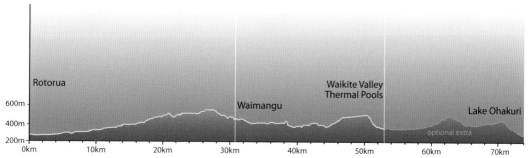

Rotorua

Waimangu

Waikite Valley
Thermal Pools

Lake Ohakuri

600m

400m

200m

optional extra

0km   10km   20km   30km   40km   50km   60km   70km

Bike hire There are more bike shops in Rotorua than any other town of its size and most of them hire bikes: Outdoorsman Headquarters, phone 07 345 9333, www.outdoorsman.co.nz; Mountain Bike Rotorua, phone 0800 682 768, www.mtbrotorua.co.nz

Getting there Rotorua is 240 km (3.5 hours) from Auckland and 450 km (6.5 hours) from Wellington. Rotorua Airport is 5 km (20 minutes) east of town. Once you are in Rotorua there are a couple of transport options. To get from Rotorua to Waimangu Volcanic Valley, try the Thermal Land Shuttle, phone 0800 894 287, www.thermalshuttle.co.nz or go to South-star Adventures, phone 027 654 3038, www.southstaradventures.com

Special considerations Carefully check the temperature of the water before getting into a hot pool or stream; some can be almost boiling hot. Do not put your head below the surface of the water as there is a possibility of contracting a disease called amoebic meningitis

Early morning at Lake Rotorua.

ROUTE DESCRIPTION

Rotorua to Waimangu Volcanic Valley

31 km, 3–5 hours, Grade 2 (Easy)

If this is the only section you have time for, then I recommend doing it in reverse by catching a shuttle to Waimangu and riding back to Rotorua, as it is mostly downhill in that direction. Otherwise, follow the directions below.

From the Lake Rotorua i-SITE on Fenton Street, head one block down Arawa Street to Princes Gate. From beneath the giant trellis arches you will find the official start of the track. Tune in to the blue markers and follow them carefully along a maze of paths.

The first point of interest, 200 metres away, is the large neo-Tudor building on Queens Drive, which is the Rotorua Museum. A few minutes later, you'll pass the Polynesian Spa (great for the end of the ride) and then weave across the bizarre Sulphur Bay reserve. There are some interesting interpretation boards along this steamy trail. Follow the blue markers to Sala Street, passing under the state highway at Puarenga Stream.

When you are about 6 km out of town, you will see a few shops down a side street (Tryon Street) on your left. Here is the entrance to the Whakarewarewa Maori village and thermal area.

From Whakarewarewa Village, the trail continues south, past Te Puia, a much larger cultural centre, and on to a new off-road track that leads through Hemo Gorge to the Whakarewarewa Forest mountain-bike tracks. The main entrance and car-parking area is to your left when you reach a large grassy field. It has a cool cafe nestled in an area throbbing with bike culture. You could easily get diverted into the 160-km maze of mountain-bike tracks, or just kick back with a flat white and enjoy the vibe.

From the park entrance, head towards SH5, a stone's throw away, and you'll roll on to a concrete cycle path that glides south beside the highway. It's easy cycling for several kilometres before you nip onto Highlands Loop Road. This soon brings you back to a separate cycle path and then leads you away from the highway to Waimangu Road. A few kilometres along this road, you'll reach the entrance to Waimangu Volcanic Valley, which has a cafe, self-guided walks, tours and even a boat trip. It is open from 8.30 a.m. to 5 p.m. seven days a week and is highly recommended.

Waimangu Volcanic Valley to Waikite Valley Thermal Pools
22 km, 2–4 hours, Grade 3 (Intermediate)
From Waimangu, head down Okaro Road, past Lake Okaro picnic area, to a T-intersection at SH38. Cross the highway and take the off-road cycle track that leads around Rainbow Mountain (Maungakakaramea) to Te Ranga Stream (Kerosene Creek), which is popular for its free hot pools. From the creek, the trail heads to Waiotapu, where there is an old-school Kiwi pub (with cheap accommodation), a petrol station and a cafe/store attached to a large honey factory. The popular Wai-O-Tapu Thermal Wonderland is only 2 km away down Waiotapu Loop Road, and is famous for the Lady Knox Geyser. It is open from 8.30 a.m. to 5 p.m. seven days a week. On the way you pass the Waiotapu mud pool, which is free to visit and is New Zealand's largest bubbling mud pool.

Ride west from the pub along Waikite Valley Road for 6 km to the Waikite Valley Thermal Pools. The pools are open from 10 a.m. to 9 p.m. daily with a cafe, camping ground and short walks. This is a great destination for families.

Optional extra: Waikite Valley Thermal Pools to Lake Ohakuri

21 km, 2–3 hours, Grade 3 (Intermediate)

Continue west from the pools on Waikite Valley Road for about 3 km, then turn left into Te Kopia Road and head mostly downhill past the impressive Paeroa thermal bluffs, which are largely bush-covered, but also venting steam. DOC plans to build a short track into the forest here. Watch for new signs.

When you have travelled 18 km down Te Kopia Road, you will see a turn on your right that leads down to Lake Ohakuri (commonly known as Paradise) and the end of the trail. It wasn't signposted at the time of writing.

TRAIL TALES

Rotorua is New Zealand's oldest tourist destination, attracting visitors for almost two centuries. The Maori story of the region begins over 600 years ago, when a waka named *Te Arawa* arrived on the East Coast of the North Island. *Te Arawa* carried a number of notable chiefs, including Ngatoroirangi, the waka's tohunga (spiritual expert). Once they had landed, Ngatoroirangi left the waka to begin a survey of the region, making his way over time to the summit of Tongariro. However, Ngatoroirangi was unprepared for the bitter weather on the upper reaches of the mountain and felt himself freezing to death. Recognising how close he was to dying, he called to his sisters Te Pupu and Te Hoata to save him. From far off in the spiritual homeland they came to his rescue, travelling beneath the earth as fire. Wherever they rose to the surface, they left behind fire, thus creating the active geothermal system of the region.

On 31 May 1886, the renowned Maori guide Sophia Te Paea Hinerangi took a group of tourists across Lake Tarawera to view the 'eighth wonder of the world', the silica hot springs of the Pink and White Terraces. The group returned later that day with reports of a phantom war canoe seen gliding silently across the lake. People speculated that this was a waka wairua (spirit canoe) bringing warnings of death.

Eleven days later, on 10 June 1886, Mount Tarawera erupted so violently that a 17-km rift formed, disgorging ash, steam and mud. To the south, Lake Rotomahana exploded to 20 times its original size and the Waimangu Volcanic Valley geothermal system was created. Millions of tons of ash and debris covered the area, destroying villages, killing over 100 people, and destroying the Pink and White Terraces. The eruption lasted six hours, but the geothermal area has remained active to this day.

In 1917, Frying Pan Flat, at Waimangu, exploded. Within two weeks, the subsequent crater had been filled by Frying Pan Lake, becoming the largest hot-water spring in the world. In 2011, scientists announced the rediscovery of parts of the Pink and White Terraces, buried under 2 metres of mud and 60 metres of water in Lake Rotomahana.

However, the Waimangu Volcanic Valley is not the only geothermal attraction of the area. Wai-O-Tapu Thermal Wonderland dates back about 160,000 years and is now a protected scenic reserve. In the 1890s, inmates from the local prison discovered a clearing with a hot-water spring. When they went to wash themselves and their clothes in the hot water, the soap made the spring erupt into a spectacular geyser. The spring was named the Lady Knox Geyser and has been 'soaped' for tourists since the 1900s.

A depiction of the Mount Tarawera eruption, 1886.

With the destruction of the Pink and White Terraces, the famous Maori guide Sophia Hinerangi moved to the edge of Rotorua and began a tradition of guiding at Whakarewarewa.

Whakarewarewa, on the outskirts of Rotorua, had been devastated by the Tarawera eruption and the land around it was bare of trees, except for a small pocket of native bush on the top of the highest hills above the Blue Lake and a random scattering over other small areas. In 1898, recognising how slowly the native trees were growing, the government set up a nursery to research the best exotic species for commercial forestry. Seeds were imported from around the world, and, in 1899, New Zealand Forest Service staff and prison labourers planted out the first of 170 different species. Californian coast redwoods were put in the ground in 1901 and have since grown to be among the tallest trees in New Zealand. In 1925, the redwood grove was declared a memorial to commemorate New Zealand Forest Service staff who had died in World War I.

TE ARA AHI-THERMAL BY BIKE

Viewing platform at the Waiotapu mud pool.

In 1993, local mountain biker Fred Christensen worked with community service workers in the forest to build the first mountain-bike park in the country. This is now one of the most popular mountain-bike destinations in the Southern Hemisphere.

In 2009, the vision of Te Ara Ahi-Thermal by Bike, a cycle trail that would explore 'the pathway of fire', was created. The trail was completed in 2013.

FOOD AND ACCOMMODATION

All the geothermal areas are well established with a wide range of amenities such as cafes, souvenir shops, toilets and bike-storage facilities.

Rotorua A range of shops, accommodation and cultural tours: www.rotoruanz.com

Whakarewarewa Forest Waipa Cafe, bike hire, phone 0800 682 768,
www.mtbrotorua.co.nz

Waimangu Volcanic Valley Cafe, tours, phone 07 366 6137, www.waimangu.com
Waiotapu Food, accommodation, hot pools, Waiotapu Tavern (budget rooms),
    phone 07 366 6640, www.waiotaputavern.co.nz
Wai-O-Tapu Thermal Wonderland Cafe, phone 07 366 6333, www.waiotapu.co.nz
Waikite Valley Thermal Pools Cafe and camping, phone 07 333 1861, www.hotpools.co.nz

The fence beside Princes Gate, Rotorua.

SHORTCUTS AND DETOURS

Whakarewarewa Forest mountain-bike tracks This hugely popular mountain-bike park
    has over 160 km of trail built for pure fun. The tracks range from Easy to Extreme,
    and most have the magical element of 'flow'. There are maps available at the car park
    and good signage throughout the park.
Best short ride Pack in the most attractions in the shortest distance by riding from the
    Princes Gate, 200 metres from the Rotorua i-SITE, out past Sulphur Bay and through
    Hemo Gorge to the Whakarewarewa Mountain Bike Park, 8 km away. There is a cafe
    there, and entry to the park is free. After having a look around, head back the same
    way — it's mostly downhill on the return trip to town.

Now that the Bay of Plenty has three fabulous cycle trails, it is an excellent destination for a biking holiday. The Motu Trails can be ridden individually, or combined into one long loop for cycling enthusiasts. The bay also has great bush walking, beach-combing and boating. There is something for everyone.

The Dunes Trail is an easy all-weather path, with iconic coastal scenery. Most people do it as a there-and-back ride, making the cafe at Tirohanga Holiday Park their destination. There are views out to smoking White Island (New Zealand's most active volcano) and inland to the bush-clad peaks of the Raukumara Range.

Motu Road, the original coach road from the Bay of Plenty to Gisborne, is ideal for those with an appetite for exercise. It is a narrow gravel road with large hills and excellent scenery. In places, the native trees meet overhead, and on our trip we even saw a wild deer trotting along the road.

For experienced mountain bikers, the Pakihi Track provides the icing on the cake. It's a historic stock route, weaving through the beautiful Urutawa Conservation Area. This forest is home to many species of native birds, native bats, and the endangered Hochstetter's frog.

SUMMARY ························

Start and end point Opotiki
Distance Dunes Trail 10 km each way; or the full 90-km
    loop including Motu Road and the Pakihi Track
Likely time Dunes Trail takes 1 hour each way; the full
    loop takes 8–10 hours or can be done over 2 days
Grading Dunes Trail, Grade 2 (Easy); Motu Road, Grade 3
    (Intermediate); Pakihi Track, Grade 4 (Advanced)
Surface Dunes Trail: wide gravel road; Motu Road: a mix
    of sealed and gravel road; Pakihi Track: narrow rock-
    and-dirt track
Bike type Any bike with medium-width tyres is fine for
    the Dunes Trail and Motu Road; a mountain bike is
    best for Pakihi Track

Motu Trails

Omarumutu
35
End of Dunes Trail

Waiaua

Motu Rd

Waiaua R.

RAUKUMARA RANGE

Motu Coach Road

Meremere Hill

Takaputahi R.

Pakihi Road

Toatoa

Pakihi Road end

Pakihi Track

Papamoa Hill

Pakihi Track

Pakihi Strm

Whitikau

bridge

Pakihi Hut

Pakihi Track

Pakihi Track/Motu Rd Junction

Motu Rd

Onukuroa

Motu

Motu R.

Motu Falls

Motu Rd

Rere Falls Trail
to Gisborne

Matawai

2

to Opotiki

to Gisborne

Map A pamphlet map is available from the Opotiki i-SITE on Bridge Street. For more
    detail, use 1:50,000 topomaps, NZTopoBE41 Opotiki and BF41 Oponae
Trail website www.motutrails.co.nz
In emergencies The Motu Road and Pakihi Track are remote and have no cellphone
    coverage. Consider taking an emergency personal locator beacon (PLB) from Opotiki
    i-SITE
Bike hire and shuttles Motu Trails Ltd (bike hire, shuttles, secure parking), phone
    0800 668 887 or 07 315 5864, www.motucycletrails.com; Bushaven (bike hire,
    shuttles and accommodation), phone 07 929 7564, www.bushaven.co.nz
Getting there Opotiki is 350 km (4.5 hours) from Auckland on SH2

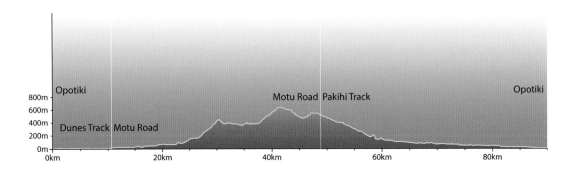

ROUTE DESCRIPTION

Dunes Trail

11 km one way, 1.5–2.5 hours, Grade 2+ (Easy)

This easy gravel path rolls along the sand dunes of the Bay of Plenty coast. There are no big hills, and the gravel surface is smooth but a little loose in places. This is an excellent trail for families. Part of it is on a 'sand ladder' across the beach.

From the centre of Opotiki, cycle north to the end of St John Street and cross the celebrated Pakowhaiki–Otutaopuku Bridge (it's huge — you can't miss it).

The Dunes Trail heads east, weaving among the sandhills to the Tirohanga Holiday Park (an ideal base for cyclists). To get to the cafe, ride through the park to the petrol station out on the highway.

The trail continues past the holiday park and finishes at the main highway, opposite Jackson Road. Head back from here, or follow the directions below to try out the Motu Road and Pakihi Track.

There are a few motorbike barriers on the Dunes Trail that also stop fully loaded cycle tourers.

The Dunes Trail.

Motu Road to Pakihi Track

38 km, 3–5 hours, Grade 3 (Intermediate with big hills)

From the end of the Dunes Trail, carefully cross the highway and ride up Jackson Road for 860 metres. Just before the road starts to climb, take a left onto a minor track, which leads to a new cycling bridge. The Motu Road is on the far side. It was the original coach road to Opotiki.

The Motu Road leads all the way to Matawai township and passes the Pakihi Track on the way. There are two big hills to climb.

The first is Meremere Hill (447 metres), which passes through Meremere Scenic Reserve. The top half of this climb is steep enough to leave you wondering how the horse-drawn coaches ever managed.

From the top of Meremere Hill there is a short descent to Toatoa — just enough for you to regain your composure before the road starts to climb into Toatoa Scenic Reserve. This hill is almost as steep, but nowhere as long. It tops out at 625 metres. Toatoa has a public shelter.

Only 12 km beyond Toatoa, you will reach a large sign and a shelter and toilet at the top of the inviting Pakihi Track entrance. This is 38 km from the Dunes Trail. If resting at this spot, just go 10 metres down the Pakihi Track to best appreciate the forest.

From here you can follow the Pakihi Track and on to Opotiki, or continue riding the Motu Road to Matawai. It is 17 km to Motu Village, and the Motu Road almost climbs right over Onukuroa (780 metres). The last 14 km from Motu to Matawai is virtually flat and passes unusually scenic farmland.

The Pakihi Track.

Pakihi Track to Opotiki

41 km, 3–5 hours, Grade 4 (Advanced)

The Pakihi Track has virtually no uphills, and the surface is generally easy. The main reason for its Grade 4 ranking is the vertical drops along the sides of the track, which in the second half is quite narrow in places.

From the Pakihi Track signpost beside the Motu Coach Road, dive off into the mature native forest. A benched single track descends to Pakihi Hut, 10 km away. The Pakihi Hut is about 100 metres down a side track, on a terrace above the Pakihi Stream. It is a basic DOC hut with six bunks, mattresses and a small firewood stove. There is no charge to stay in this hut.

Almost 1 km past the hut, cross the river on a new suspension bridge and continue down the valley, carefully following the single track, which has many dangerous drop-offs on your right. Ride well within your abilities and walk if prudent to do so.

About 9 km from Pakihi Hut, you will reach the road end next to a second swing bridge where there is another toilet and shelter.

Most people ride from here back to Opotiki, although you can arrange for a shuttle to pick you up. The first 7 km is gravel, with plenty of potholes to dodge. Then it's gently downhill on the sealed Otara Road. Turn right when you reach Te Rere Pa Road, then after 500 metres head left onto the stopbank. It leads back to the swing bridge at the start of the Dunes Trail, on the edge of Opotiki.

The Pakihi Track was built as a stock route to Opotiki and, according to rural myth, took more dynamite per metre to build than any other track in the country. It is prone to slip damage after major storms.

TRAIL TALES

One of the first ancestors of the Opotiki area was Tarawa, who swam to the Bay of Plenty from across the sea, supported by supernatural fish, which he called his 'potiki' (pets or children). Tarawa left these potiki in a spring, which became known as 'O potiki mai tawhiti' (of the children from faraway), and so the district gained the name Opotiki.

Europeans were rather hesitant to venture into the Opotiki region after some of the first missionaries from Tauranga arrived in 1828, just in time to witness the tail-end of a particularly bloody battle between two warring tribes.

It was not until December 1839 that Reverend John A Wilson of the Church Missionary Society established a mission on the hill above the present-day golf clubhouse, and three months later the Roman Catholics followed. At this stage a large Maori village, Pa Kowhai, extended along the riverbanks from King Street to the site of today's A&P showgrounds. However, more blood was to follow.

In 1864, unrest was developing in the area as the Maori King movement gathered momentum and the German-born missionary Carl Sylvius Völkner was urged to leave Opotiki. He took his wife to Auckland but then returned alone to continue his church duties. During his absence, the more militant Hauhau had moved to the region. Some believed that Völkner had returned to spy on them, and, on 2 March 1865, he was captured and hanged from a willow tree near his church, and the mission was sacked.

The government retaliated with military force. The First Waikato Regiment

Four men widen the Motu Track, 1903.

set up a garrison in the area and its soldiers were encouraged to settle there in order to retain a military presence. Many of the trails and roads were developed or improved for military activities. Military campaigns increased in intensity when Te Kooti, a famous Maori chief, escaped from the Chatham Islands in 1868 and made his way to the Opotiki area. Major battles occurred on the sand dunes at Opotiki Harbour entrance; at the entrance to the Waioeka Gorge on the western side of the Waioeka Straight; and at Maraetai in the gorge itself. Te Kooti escaped all these clashes, though his followers suffered heavy casualties.

The Motu Road shadows a pre-European track called Te Kowhai Track. Until the early 1900s, this track was the only land route linking the Bay of Plenty to Poverty Bay. Word spread among Europeans of this crucial link between the two areas and, in 1889, four men began widening the track to improve access for horses.

The Motu Coach Road was finally completed in 1919. However, it was only passable by coach in the summer months, with planks and ropes constantly needed to help vehicles get through, and one travel guide warned of many sheer drops along its length. Even to this day it is a high-maintenance road, temporarily closed after most major storms.

The upper reaches of the Motu River Valley remained untouched until the 1890s when European settlers began to clear the land. Predominant trees in the area included rimu, matai, kahikatea and tawa. Millions of tons of timber were chopped down and milled for housing, and land was also burned to clear for farming.

The first sawmill in Motu opened in 1901 and, by 1920, the area had three mills, producing 14,390 tons of timber a year, the majority of which was sent by rail to Gisborne. In total, seven mills were built in the area; but by 1940, most of the easily accessible trees had been cleared, the mills began to close and many people moved away.

Toatoa (the valley of the clouds) developed as a key watering stop for horses along the Motu Coach Road. In the early 1900s, a group of local dairy farms set up a cooperative cheese-making factory there, which garnered some acclaim for its fine cheeses.

The stunning and remote Motu Road.

In late 1919, six men and a dog made the first trip down the Motu River by boat. The adventure took them 10 days, and afterwards they agreed that the dog had had the right idea in leaving them at the first rapid, only to meet them again at the coast. These days, with modern equipment, the Motu is considered one of the premium five-day rafting adventures in New Zealand.

FOOD AND ACCOMMODATION

Opotiki Plenty of food, accommodation and shops: www.opotikinz.com

Tirohanga Cafe, petrol, accommodation: Tirohanga Beach Motor Camp, phone
   07 315 7942, www.tirohangabeachmotorcamp.co.nz

Toatoa Accommodation: Toatoa Farmstay (accommodation, bike hire, shuttle and secure
   parking), phone 07 315 8340, www.toatoaaccommodation.co.nz

Motu Accommodation: Motu Community House, phone 06 862 8736,
   email rakanui@xtra.co.nz. Cafe: Motu-vation (open Fri–Sun), phone 06 863 5045.

Bushaven (near the Pakihi Track) Accommodation, bike hire and shuttle: phone 07 929 7564,
   www.bushaven.co.nz

Pakihi DOC hut, www.doc.govt.nz/parks-and-recreation/places-to-stay/

Matawai Cafe, store, accommodation: Matawai Campground (sells basic food items), phone
   06 862 4830.

For more accommodation options see www.motutrails.co.nz

SHORTCUTS AND DETOURS

Rere Falls Trail Those keen on cycle touring down very quiet and scenic country roads will
   love this 103-km, 1–2-day ride from Matawai to Gisborne. There are options to stay
   at Motu, Matawai and Eastwoodhill Arboretum. It is signposted as a New Zealand
   Cycle Trail route. For more information, refer to *Classic New Zealand Cycle Trails* or
   www.kennett.co.nz

Hukutaia Domain Just over 8 km south of Opotiki, on Woodlands Road, this 95-year-old
   domain is famous for its diversity of native plants, and a puriri tree that was used to
   hide the bones of the 'distinguished dead'. It is a pleasant ride on a sealed country road
   from sea level to 80 metres' elevation. From Opotiki, head west down Bridge Street,
   and take the first left after crossing the river — that's Woodlands Road. The entrance is
   signposted just before the end of the road.

THE TIMBER TRAIL

ince it was opened in March 2013, the Timber Trail has become the new favourite among those who love the outdoors, but typically shy away from the hardships associated with tramping or mountain biking. At last, here is a remote yet relatively easy ride, through stunning forests with a fascinating history. There is a lovely lodge to stay at halfway, and you can even arrange to have your bags transported and meals supplied.

From Pureora, 55 km southeast of Te Kuiti, the trail heads south, weaving through tall rainforest where 800-year-old rimu and kahikatea tower 50–60 metres above the trail. Kereru (wood pigeon) and kaka can be seen swooping through the forest, and if you

are lucky (and get up early) you might hear the haunting call of the rare kokako, more commonly seen on the back of a New Zealand $50 note.

The trail climbs around the flanks of Mount Pureora, through cloud forest, with an optional 2-hour side trip to the top and back. The views are magnificent on a fine day.

From the trail's high point near the 14-km marker post, a fantastic, well-graded downhill leads to massive swing bridges and more beautiful forest before finally breaking out into an area of recently clear-felled pine plantation. The cutover area doesn't look so great right now, but is slowly reverting to native forest, and should be stunning again in a hundred or so years.

The Timber Trail

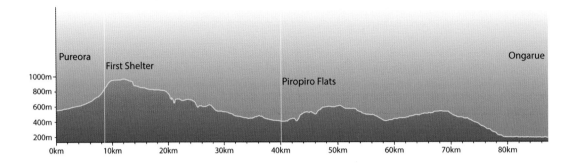

Near the halfway mark you can choose between staying at the Black Fern Lodge or there are camping and lodge options at Piropiro Flats. Black Fern Lodge is famous for its excellent food and accommodation, and its whio (blue duck) recovery programme.

On the second day, the trail soon enters original forest again and crosses one of New Zealand's longest suspension bridges, which offers breathtaking views of the forest. From there, a 3-km hill provides a challenge for those who haven't done any cycling for a while, but it is followed by a long and easy downhill run on a historic bush tramway that was built almost a century ago. DOC has provided fascinating interpretation panels describing the timber-milling industry that was prolific at this end of Pureora Forest and was based out of Ongarue, now just a small settlement at the end of this fantastic two-day cycle trail.

SUMMARY ··

Start point Pureora
End point Ongarue
Distance 85 km, plus 14 km if staying at Black Fern
    Lodge
Likely time 2 days
Grading Grade 2 (Easy) to Grade 3 (Intermediate)
Surface Mostly volcanic ash, all off-road
Bike type A mountain bike is best, although a few
    riders are using hybrid bikes
Map A DOC pamphlet is available at Te Kuiti and
    Pureora Field Base, phone 07 878 1050
Trail website www.thetimbertrail.com
In emergencies There is no cellphone coverage on
    most of this trail. Call 111 if you can get coverage.
    An emergency personal locator beacon (PLB) is
    recommended

The Maramataha Bridge.

Bike hire Bikes can be hired from all four transport companies listed below

Getting there From Auckland to Pureora is 260 km (3.5 hours). Drive to Te Kuiti, then follow SH30 for 51 km southeast before turning off at the Timber Trail sign, and driving a further 3 km to DOC's Pureora Field Base. From Taupo to Pureora is 78 km (1 hour). From Wellington to Ongarue is 385 km (5 hours, 40 minutes)

Trail transport The two ends of the trail are 54 km apart via slow, windy roads. Various transport options are available. If travelling from Auckland, park at Pureora and get Pa Harakeke (phone 07 929 8708 or 027 207 1500, www.paharakeke.co.nz) to pick you up after the ride and take you back to Pureora; Timber Trail Shuttles operate from Ongarue and Black Fern Lodge. You can park your car safely at Ongarue, shuttle to Pureora, ride the trail and pick your car up whenever you are ready (phone 027 496 1764 or 021 153 2179, www.timbertrail.net.nz or email info@timbertrail.net.nz). From Taupo, you can shuttle to Pureora with Tread Routes (phone 07 377 8319 or 027 446 2408, www.treadroutes.co.nz). Also see Blue Tui Shuttles and Tours (phone 07 872 2404, www.bluetui.co.nz)

Towering trees near Pureora.

ROUTE DESCRIPTION

Pureora to the first shelter

8.5 km, 1–2 hours, Grade 3 (Intermediate)

This first section is ideal for those looking for a short there-and-back ride. From the DOC Pureora Field Base, ride 200 metres east and you will see the Timber Trail signposted beside the road (opposite a large picnic and camping area).

Follow the signposts and you can't go wrong. Every intersection is signposted, and there are distance posts at every kilometre of the trail.

The trail weaves through towering native forest, saved by a famous battle for its conservation, and now part of an ecologically significant area. After 3.4 km there is a signposted intersection to a historic bulldozer, a few minutes down a side track.

Shortly after the bulldozer turn-off, the Timber Trail passes through a mix of tall, exotic trees and regenerating native forest. The gentle gradient gives way to slightly steeper sections as it climbs towards Mount Pureora. At the top of the regenerating scrub, just 5 metres off the track, is a small red shelter, from where there are expansive views of the area.

A group of local farmers enjoy the trail, at the Ongarue end.

First shelter to Piropiro Campsite (or Black Fern Lodge)

31.5 km, 3–5 hours, Grade 3 (Intermediate)

From the first shelter the trail enters cloud forest, and on average becomes a degree or two steeper as it climbs to the highest point on the trail at the 14-km mark. With loaded bikes, some riders may have to walk a few short sections, but never for more than a minute.

The intensely green and twisted cloud forest is both a photographer's dream and, due to low light levels, a nightmare.

Before the top of the climb a rough tramping track (at the 11-km mark) leads up to the top of Mount Pureora, 2 km away. The track is unrideable and takes 40–50 minutes to walk each way. The last few hundred metres is above the bush line and, on a fine day, you will be rewarded with a 360-degree panorama of the central North Island from Lake Taupo to Taranaki and beyond. This side trip, including lunch on the top, took our group 1.5 hours, and is not included in the riding time given above.

Back on the Timber Trail, you will soon notice the gradient easing off, and beyond the 14-km mark the downhill is long and effortless. There is cellphone coverage between the 14- and 16-km marker posts. Eight marker posts will have whizzed by before you reach a massive suspension bridge. Unless you suffer from vertigo, it is worth stopping in the

Black Fern Lodge.

middle to appreciate the forest views, and consider for a moment how many kilometres this 115-metre 'flyover' has saved you.

The forest here is part of an ecologically significant area, where predators such as stoats and weasels are trapped. This makes the habitat viable for rare species such as tiny native frogs, secretive bats and the exquisite kokako.

After crossing a few more suspension bridges, you'll reach a rest area at Harrisons Creek, with a toilet and a small shelter. Another 5 km and the trail enters a large patch of recently logged forest that is only just starting to revert to native. It still looked ugly in 2017, but will improve year by year. Most of the trail through the cutover area follows old forestry roads, with short sections of purpose-built cycle trail here and there.

After 35 km, you'll reach the turn-off to the highly recommended Black Fern Lodge (6.7-km side trip). From here, it is a further 4.8 km to the turn-off to Piropiro. Just across a small bridge is a large camping area, 100 metres off the Timber Trail. Above Piropiro is the new Timber Trail Lodge and nearby is a 'glam camping' area.

Piropiro to Ongarue

47 km, 3–6 hours, Grade 2+ (Easy, with the exception of a 3-km hill)

From Piropiro campsite, follow the markers along Piropiro Road for 2 km before riding between two concrete bollards and into tall native forest on a new section of purpose-built trail. Just over 5 km from Piropiro is the largest suspension bridge on the Timber Trail (and the third longest in the country), spanning 141 metres across the Maramataha River Valley.

On the other side, a 3-km climb passes massive rimu and totara trees, and later a striking stand of tawa forest (tawa is sometimes called New Zealand willow).

Shortly after the top of the climb (47-km marker post) you will cross a large clearing, which is the historic bush tramway terminus. The trail now follows historic railway lines most of the way to Ongarue. Impressive cuttings, more bridges, old huts and fascinating interpretation signs make this one of the most interesting cycle trails in the country. Take plenty of time to enjoy it. At the Ongarue Spiral the track loops around and underneath itself by a bridge and a tunnel. You could easily spend 20 minutes reading the interpretation boards at this one spot alone.

A few kilometres from the end, the trail runs beside a deer fence before ending at a side road. Turn left, then 100 metres later, right onto Ngakonui-Ongarue Road. It is a very easy ride from here down the flat sealed road to Ongarue Village, where there is a park at the village green. A cafe and flashpackers has been built, with more accommodation on the way.

From Ongarue, you can ride to Taumarunui 24 km away on the quiet Ongarue Back Road (half-gravel, half-sealed). Alternatively, if driving, head out to SH4.

TRAIL TALES

Pureora Forest Park is one of the largest and most diverse conservation areas in the North Island. It is home to a multitude of forest types, from tawa low down to kamahi around the highest reaches of the Timber Trail, but it is the podocarps that dominate. These formidable trees, which can grow to 40–60 metres tall, include kahikatea, rimu, matai, miro and New Zealand's tallest totara. Hundreds of other plant species live below, and on, these forest giants. This impressive rainforest provides a valuable habitat for some of our rarest animal species: the kokako and kiwi, frogs and skinks, and native fish.

It was this biodiversity of both plants and animals that attracted the first humans to the area. Maori from several tribes, including Te Awara, Tuwharetoa and Ngati Raukawa, visited these forests for centuries to gather food at different times of the year. To the west of Pureora Forest Park lies Maraeroa, the land of the Rereahu people, whose ancestors travelled to New Zealand around 800 years ago in the *Tainui* canoe. Parts of the Timber

Locomotives at the Ongarue Spiral, Pureora Forest, 1923.

Trail cross Maraeroa land, and we recommend you visit Pa Harakeke to learn more of their history and their present-day plans and aspirations.

European interest in Pureora focused on timber first and foremost. The tall forests of New Zealand provided enough trees to see timber milling develop as a major pioneering industry. At Pureora, the impact was minor until the Main Trunk Line reached Ongarue in 1901. With the railway came farmers and loggers. Loggers cleared the land of the big trees, and farmers cleared everything else, if the land was farmable. The first mill built at Ongarue was run by Maori and was simply called the Maori Mill. It operated for a few years from 1900. Trees were felled and their branches removed in preparation for the huge trunks to be transported out to the mill at Ongarue, where they were sawn into thick slabs and loaded onto trains. In the beginning, the trunks were transported by bullock teams, but this was slow and difficult. As logging progressed, most of the early mills in New Zealand built small railway lines called bush tramways to reach further and further into the forest. At one time, over 1000 bush tramways existed around the country, and they were the main method of moving timber out of the forests until the 1940s, when trucks took over.

In 1914, a large milling company by the name of Ellis and Burnard Co. built its own mill at Ongarue and by 1922 had started constructing a bush tramway into the forest. Much of the southern end of the Timber Trail follows the company's main tramway, which included the impressive Ongarue Spiral. In 1958, the tramway was closed due to flood damage and superseded by forestry roads and trucks. The Ongarue mill closed in 1966. Forest was still being cleared but, by the 1960s, techniques had changed. Rather than selectively extracting the best timber and leaving the rest, which recovered very quickly to a large extent, the new method of clear felling was far more destructive. Using chainsaws, bulldozers and large trucks, forests were completely stripped at an alarming rate. The scoured land would be converted to farms or pine plantations, leaving no habitat for native animals. Exotic tree plantations were first planted at Pureora in 1949. Much of the Timber Trail passes through areas where exotic forests have been selectively logged since 2000 and are now being left to revert to native forest.

In 1978, conservationists led by Stephen King (not the author) waged a daring campaign to stop the logging at Pureora. They formed what journalists called 'Suicide Squads' because they chained themselves to trees and camped out in the forest canopy. Logging of native trees stopped permanently in 1982. DOC has recognised four areas of ecological significance, where they actively monitor rare species and trap introduced pests. You will see many wooden boxes beside the trail. These are DOC200 traps, which kill rats, stoats and weasels. As a result of this protective stance, many of the forest's bird species are enjoying a safe habitat. The forest now has its voice back.

FOOD AND ACCOMMODATION

There were no shops at Pureora or Ongarue in mid-2015, though there are plans to develop some. The nearest facilities to the Pureora trail head are at Benneydale (17 km away) and Mangakino (55 km away), and the nearest facilities to the Ongarue end are at Taumarunui (24 km away). Most accommodation around the trail is listed at www.timbertrailaccommodation.co.nz. A full package of food, transport and accommodation can be booked through www.timbertrail.com.

Te Kuiti Several places to eat and stay, go to www.waitomo.govt.nz

Benneydale Cafe and accommodation: Art Doc Sleepout, phone 07 878 4780, www.artdoc.co.nz; Wooden Heart Cafe and Benneydale Lodge, phone 07 878 4708, www.benneydale.co.nz

Pureora Cabins and campsites, www.thetimbertrail.com; Pa Harakeke chalets and cafe and
    secure parking, phone 07 929 8708 or 07 878 4879, www.paharakeke.co.nz
Piropiro (end of Stage 2) Timber Trail Lodge, phone 0800 885 6343,
    www.timbertraillodge.co.nz; Epic Cycling Adventures for camping, bike hire and bag
    shuttle, phone 022 023 7958, www.thetimbertrail.nz
Waimiha Black Fern Lodge, phone 07 894 7677, www.blackfernlodge.co.nz; Timber Trail
    Farmstay, phone 07 894 5829 or 021 153 2179, www.timbertrail.net.nz
Ongarue Food, accommodation and camping: Flashpackers, phone 027 321 6274,
    www.timbertrailhub.co.nz and The Timber Trail Centre, www.timbertrailcentre.co.nz
Taumarunui Good shops and accommodation: www.visitruapehu.com or call the Taumarunui
    i-SITE, phone 07 895 7494.

A historic hut at the No. 11 Camp.

SHORTCUTS AND DETOURS

Tractor Loop This is a great 6-km loop for family groups. From Pureora, ride the first 3 km of the trail and turn left at the tractor sign. From the historic tractor, continue out to Perhams Avenue (gravel) and turn left for an easy, downhill ride back to Pureora.

Top of the World Starting from Ongarue, the Timber Trail Shuttle (www.timbertrail.net.nz) takes groups by ATV through private land to the Top of the World, 980 metres high, in Pureora Forest. From there you ride 33 km back to Ongarue on historic tram tracks (Grade 2–3).

Pureora to Whanganui If you are looking for an extended cycling holiday, a great idea is to link the Timber Trail with the Mountains to Sea trail by riding Ongarue to Taumarunui (24 km) and Taumarunui to Whakahoro (67 km). Another great option is to ride from Ongarue to New Plymouth via the Forgotten World Highway.

GREAT LAKE TRAIL

Taupo is the Great Lake, and this Great Ride dips in and out of bays on the lake's northern half, sidling from the Western Bay Road to Whakaipo Bay, near Taupo township. The trail has a unique feel because it has been designed every metre of the way by curmudgeonly old bikers who wouldn't rest until they got it right. They forced everyone working on the trail to ride it regularly, so the whole team knew exactly what they were doing. As a result, everything they built rides well, attracts thousands of people and leaves the venerable trail designers to complain, tongue in cheek, that there are too many bloody people on the tracks.

The trail passes through a landscape formed by two huge volcanic eruptions. It weaves above and below rhyolite cliffs towering up to 100 metres high. Around the cliffs the land is cloaked in low regenerating forest, consisting mostly of kanuka and five finger, although there are some larger trees (celery pine/tanekaha and maire) taking hold and offering promise of a substantial forest in the future.

Taupo is popular for many adventurous pastimes, some as fleeting as bungy jumping, others as meditative as trout fishing. It is home to New Zealand's largest road cycling event, and several fantastic mountain-bike trails. The best of all, though, is the Great Lake Trail.

Great Lake Trail

SUMMARY ••

Start point Waihaha Bridge, Western Bay Road
End point Whakaipo Bay
Distance 55 km
Likely time 1 day
Grading Grade 3 (Intermediate)
Surface Pumice-based soil
Bike type A mountain bike is best
Map Drop into any bike shop in Taupo to buy a trail map (see Bike hire on the following page)
Trail website www.biketaupo.org.nz

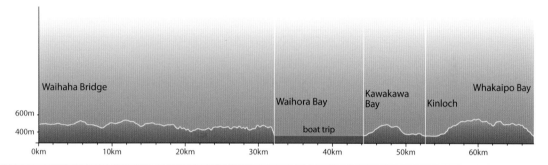

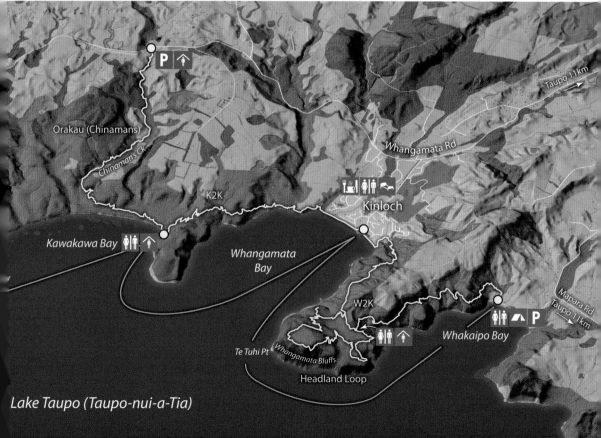

Lake Taupo (Taupo-nui-a-Tia)

In emergencies Cellphone coverage is intermittent on this trail

Bike hire See www.greatlaketaupo.com for nine operators

Getting there Taupo is 280 km (3.5 hours) from Auckland and 370 km (5 hours) from
    Wellington. The trail starts at Waihaha Bridge, 54 km from Taupo. Head north out of
    Taupo for a few hundred metres, and turn left at Poihipi Road (there is a giant bicycle
    sculpture on the corner). Turn left again at Whangamata Road, and left again 39 km
    from Taupo onto SH32. Another 14.5 km down the road, the trail car park is on the
    southern side of Waihaha Bridge, on the lake side of the road

The Orakau/Chinamans Track.

Trail transport Tread Routes (www.treadroutes.co.nz), Great Lake Shuttles
    (phone 021 656 424, www.greatlakeshuttles.co.nz) and Adventure Shuttles
    (www.adventureshuttles.co.nz) can take you to the start of the trail

Waihora Bay to Kawakawa Bay Chris Jolly Outdoors, phone 0800 470 079,
    www.chrisjolly.co.nz, can take up to 11 riders and also offers guided tours. Cost is
    approximately $75 per person from Waihora Bay to Kawakawa Bay. Bookings essential.
    Minimum cost of two people

ROUTE DESCRIPTION

Western Bay Road to Waihora Bay

31 km, 3–6 hours, Grade 3 (Intermediate)

Bike Taupo crews finished this section in March 2014. From Taupo, drive 54 km to the Waihaha Bridge on Western Bay Road. There is a small car-parking area near the south side of the bridge.

From the car park the track heads down valley, through a squeeze barrier and across the Waihaha River on a swing bridge. In the first 14 km there are several small climbs and descents, but mostly it is pretty much flat. Some of the corners are off-camber and can be slippery when wet. Otherwise, this is a fun track that runs beside a valley of regenerating forest and tall volcanic cliffs.

Taupo's giant bike.

The next section descends to Waihora Bay (where Kotukutuku Stream joins the lake) and has more bridges and switchbacks than any other section. There is a waterfall, shelter and toilet at the lake.

From Waihora Bay, a pre-booked water taxi will take you to Kawakawa Bay to continue the Great Lake Trail from there. Otherwise you have a long ride back to Western Bay Road!

Kawakawa Bay to Kinloch

8 km, 1 hour, Grade 3 (Intermediate)

Kawakawa Bay is a popular destination for rock climbers, who walk in from Kinloch and often camp at the bay. You may see a few boaties as well, although the camping and picnic area is not large. It has a shelter and toilets.

From Kawakawa Bay, the Bike Taupo pixies have upgraded an old tramping track to Kinloch, re-routing everything that was too steep. It used to be tough going; now it's an easy 3-km climb to a magnificent rocky lookout followed by a sweeping downhill ride. When you reach the shores of the lake, just ride along the flat towards Kinloch, ignoring all the turn-offs heading away from the lake. Within a few minutes you will reach the Kinloch shops and recreation area.

If you aren't able to do the boat trip from Waihora Bay to Kawakawa Bay, you can still ride this section on its own (see Shortcuts and Detours).

W2K: from Kinloch to Whakaipo Bay

15 km, 1.5–3 hours, Grade 3 (Intermediate)

This section has been open since 2008, and it's just got better with age! From Kinloch Domain, carefully follow the W2K (Whakaipo to Kinloch) marker posts through the marina and out of the village. Climb gently for about 7 km onto the shoulder of Te Tuhi Point. At a signposted intersection, turn right to do the Headland Loop or go straight ahead to fly down to Whakaipo Bay, 8.5 km away.

The Headland Loop (see page 101) is 10 km long and rejoins the W2K track, where signposts make it clear to turn right to carry on to Whakaipo Bay.

Whakaipo Bay is a quiet, beautiful place, about 12 km from Taupo via Acacia Bay. Either arrange for a shuttle or, after a swim and a picnic, ride out via Mapara and Acacia Bay roads.

The Waihaha section of the trail.

TRAIL TALES

Lake Taupo, New Zealand's largest lake, is the water-filled crater of a supervolcano. Taupo began erupting about 300,000 years ago, and has been the site of two of the world's most violent eruptions. The first was the Oruanui eruption, about 26,500 years ago, which was responsible for shaping the current lake. Most of New Zealand was affected by ash-fall from that eruption, which was deposited as far away as the Chatham Islands.

The next great eruption occurred about 1800 years ago, and is famed as the most violent eruption recorded in human history. This eruption enlarged Lake Taupo, and its plume extended 50 km into the air. All of New Zealand was covered in volcanic material, from 1 cm of ash to more than 100 metres of fiery gas and rock flow.

It is believed that ash from this eruption resulted in the red sunsets recorded by the Romans and Chinese of the time.

One thousand years later, around the thirteenth century, Maori arrived in the country and made their way to the Taupo region by the end of the fifteenth century. While the eruption-scarred landscape provided meagre food options, the pioneers were attracted to the thermal waters around the lake.

The area remained poor in resources, although obsidian rock left over from the eruptions was important for trading with South Island tribes for pounamu (greenstone).

The Ngati Kapawa hapu (sub-tribe) of the Ngati Tuwharetoa iwi (tribe) lived at the eastern end of Whakaipo Bay where the cycle trail now ends. They developed tiered gardens at the clay cliff of the point, one of a few such gardens created in New Zealand during pre-European times. The white clay cliff acted as a solar panel for the gardens, providing tropical temperatures perfect for growing kumara. The residents also set up a wananga (training ground) for warriors in the middle of the bay.

Europeans, mainly missionaries seeking converts, trailed the Maori from around 1840. At this time, Taupo was known as Tapuwae-haruru, meaning 'resounding footsteps', which relates to the hollow sound made when walking heavily on some areas of pumice land.

Taupo was strategically positioned at the crossroads of the North Island. Maori tracks from around the central North Island converged there, forming a communication network. With fears of a Maori uprising, the government decided it would be advantageous to control this route. In 1867, the armed constabulary arrived to set up a post, but nothing much else developed for almost a decade.

The first shops began to appear in 1876. At some stage, the settlement took the name Taupo from Taupo-nui-a-Tia, meaning the 'great cloak of Tia', who Maori believe discovered the lake. During the 1870s, holidaymakers made their way by paddle steamer up the Whanganui River and then by horse-drawn coach as far as Tokaanu at the southern end of the lake. After staying at the Tokaanu Hotel, they would steam across the lake.

Kinloch, Whangamata Bay, Lake Taupo, April 1964.

There was no road around the lake shore, and the steamer ran well into the 1920s.

Due to volcanic activity, the soil around Taupo was deficient in nutrients and unsuitable for farming. It was only after 1950 that serious efforts were made to clear and fertilise the land. From that point, Taupo flourished as a farming and forestry district.

Kinloch (from Scottish Gaelic 'Ceann Loch') began its life as an isolated sheep station. Then in the 1950s, Keith Holyoake, a National Party MP (and later, prime minister) became instrumental in developing the area into a holiday resort. Holyoake later counted this as his 'proudest achievement', but the development raised much debate when it was discovered that he had arranged to buy land at Kinloch from local Maori, with the inside knowledge that the government (under his influence) was about to build a road to the

The Waihaha River at the western end of the trail.

previously isolated area. To do so, a long-standing piece of legislation that prevented Maori from making such sales had to be lifted. 'Kiwi Keith' made a fortune, and created a grievance that has yet to be resolved.

More recently, over 8000 native trees have been planted at Whakaipo Bay by volunteers including rugby legend Colin Meads, with 5000 of these trees planted during the Rugby World Cup in 2011.

The idea of a mountain-bike trail around the lake originated as far back as 20 years ago, with local cyclists advocating the idea and working with DOC on the planning. It then germinated when the W2K track from Whakaipo Bay to Kinloch was built in 2007–2008. Finally, when Bike Taupo were granted $2 million in 2010 from the New Zealand Cycle Trail project, their dream started becoming a reality, but is still a long way from being fully realised.

Track builder Mike Saunders (in purple) test rides his handiwork.

FOOD AND ACCOMMODATION

Taupo Plenty of accommodation and shops: www.greatlaketaupo.com
Kinloch General store, cafe and a small range of accommodation options:
    www.kinloch.org.nz

SHORTCUTS AND DETOURS

Orakau/Chinamans Track This 10-km branch track is officially part of the Great Lake Trail.
    Drive or ride to a small car park beside Whangamata Road, 8 km west of Kinloch. From
    there, a fun Grade 3 (Intermediate) trail descends to Kawakawa Bay. Then just follow
    the Great Lake Trail markers over the hill to Kinloch, a further 8 km away.

Kawakawa Bay A popular ride among the locals is to start from Kinloch and ride over to
    Kawakawa Bay, 8 km away, for a swim or a picnic, and then return the same way.

The Headland Loop This section has been open for a few years now, and it's just got
    better with time! From Kinloch Domain, carefully follow the W2K marker posts
    through the marina and out of the village. Climb gently for about 7 km onto the
    shoulder of Te Tuhi Point. At a signposted intersection, turn right to do the Headland
    Loop. It is 10 km long, and there are two good lookout spots along the way. When
    you rejoin the W2K track, turn left and fly back down to Kinloch. That 24-km trip
    takes 2–3 hours.

MOUNTAINS TO SEA

From the side of Ruapehu, this multi-day adventure leads you on a journey along a cobbled coach road, down quiet country lanes, and into the Whanganui National Park on a rough track to the iconic Bridge to Nowhere. This large concrete road bridge was abandoned within just a few years of being built and is now surrounded by wilderness.

From the Bridge to Nowhere, the journey takes a break from pedalling as the track ends on the banks of the Whanganui River right in the middle of . . . nowhere. You must take to the river, by canoe or jetboat, and travel down a route that was paddled by Maori for centuries. You must arrange transport down the Whanganui River before you leave on your trip. Upon reaching the small village of Pipiriki, the cycling resumes, only this time it is on a quiet road down valley to Whanganui city. The last 10 km to the Tasman Sea are mostly on smooth cycle paths, allowing you to unwind at the end of the trip.

Mountains to Sea has more variety of trail type than any other New Zealand Cycle Trail. This makes it a challenge to be taken seriously, but with careful planning, good equipment and reasonable weather it's guaranteed to be the trip of a lifetime.

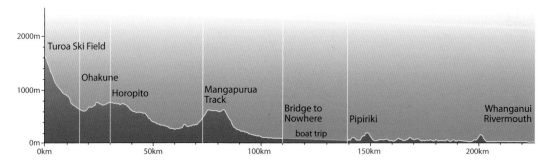

SUMMARY ●●●

Start point Ohakune or National Park

End point North Mole, Whanganui

Distance 226 km (including 28 km on the river)

Likely time 4 days (shorter options available)

Grading Grade 2+ (Easy) to Grade 4 (Advanced)

Surface 55% sealed road, 25% off-road trail, 8% gravel road, 12% river

Bike type A mountain bike is essential

Maps Take Kiwimap Taranaki–Ruapehu for the big picture, then a DOC pamphlet
    Mangapurua/Kaiwhakauka Tracks for more detail. If you are going to paddle the
    Whanganui River we also recommend you take NZTopo50-BJ32 Pipiriki Map

Trail websites www.mountainstosea.co.nz and www.doc.govt.nz

Mangapurua / Kaiwhakauka Track

In emergencies There is very little cellphone coverage on most of this trail.
An emergency personal locator beacon (PLB) is recommended (available from
Bridge to Nowhere Tours, 0800 480 308)

Bike hire In Ohakune from TCB, 06 385 8433, www.tcb.nz; or Mountain Bike Station,
06 385 9018 or 0800 BIKING, www.mountainbikestation.co.nz

Getting there Ohakune is 360 km (4.5 hours) from Auckland and 285 km (3.5 hours)
from Wellington. Instead of driving you can catch the Northern Explorer train to
Ohakune and bus back from Whanganui

Ohakune Old Coach Road

Optional start If you feel it's not a real mountains-to-sea adventure unless you start above the tree line, then you can ride up the Ohakune Mountain Road to Turoa Ski Field on the south side of Ruapehu. At just over 1000 vertical metres, it is New Zealand's biggest sealed road climb. To save your knees, pop into Mountain Bike Station in Ohakune and talk with them about getting a lift up the mountain

Bridge to Nowhere to Pipiriki You must book a jetboat or canoe to meet you at Mangapurua Landing before you leave. There is no cellphone coverage at the landing — no shops, no buildings, nothing. Contact either Bridge to Nowhere, phone 0800 480 308, www.bridgetonowhere.co.nz; or Whanganui River Adventures, 0800 862 743, www.whanganuiriveradventures.com

ROUTE DESCRIPTION

Ohakune Mountain Road: Optional Start

16 km each way, 2–3 hours up, 30 minutes down, Grade 3 (Intermediate)

This is by far the most extreme start to a cycle trail. If you are mega fit, ride from Ohakune up, up, up the Ohakune Mountain Road. It is sealed all the way to Turoa Ski Field car park, and you will pass various vegetative strata on this scenic road through Tongariro

National Park. Be warned though, with 1000 metres of elevation to gain, this is one of the toughest road climbs in New Zealand!

Alternatively, contact Mountain Bike Station (details under Bike hire) in Ohakune and arrange a shuttle to the top. It is a wild place to start this wonderful journey.

Ohakune Old Coach Road to Horopito

14 km one way, 2–3 hours, Grade 2+ (Easy)

Ride northwest from Ohakune Station under the huge New Zealand Cycle Trail sign and across a new cycle-trail bridge. From there, the route runs beside Old Station Road and Marshalls Road for about 10 minutes before crossing a small bridge on your right and heading up into the hills. The track surface is rocky in places — remnants of the century-old cobbled coach road. There are several fascinating interpretation panels along the way, many massive rimu to admire and, just off the main trail, two huge viaducts. The Hapuawhenua Viaduct is 45 metres high.

The last stretch to Horopito follows farm roads. If you choose to turn back to repeat the ride to Ohakune, the return trip will be much faster as it is mostly downhill. Otherwise continue on to Whanganui National Park.

Horopito to Mangapurua Track

43 km, 3–4 hours, Grade 3 (Intermediate)

From Horopito, ride southwest beside SH4 for 800 metres, then turn right to follow Middle Road to Ruatiti Road, 14 km away. Turn right and follow Ruatiti Road to Ruatiti Domain where there is free camping allowed beside the Manganui o te Ao River. It is mostly downhill — fast fun on a sealed road. Then the road narrows and morphs into gravel and the start of the Mangapurua Track. Just 3 km before the track is Ruatiti Backpackers (phone 06 385 4266) or you can stay at Mellonsfolly Ranch, which is 4.4 km past the start of the Mangapurua Track, down Crotons Road. You can request a pick-up when booking your accommodation.

Mangapurua Track to Bridge to Nowhere

38 km, 3–5 hours, Grade 3+ (Intermediate)

From the start of the 4WD Mangapurua Track, head left through a gate and cruise up a well-graded 4-km climb (this can be very muddy after heavy rain). When you reach a second gate near the top of the hill, take a look back; the views are breathtaking on a clear day. This is the only real climb. After an hour, you'll reach a letterbox and see a National Park sign ahead.

About 2 km after entering the national park, you will reach a Y-intersection with a signboard and a large pou (carved pole). Veer left (to the right is the Kaiwhakauka Track).

The Hapuawhenua Viaduct, Old Coach Road.

Continue rolling along the ridge, and you'll soon pass a steep walking track (signposted on your left) that goes up to the Mangapurua Trig. The trig is overgrown, so just go up to the first clearing (another minute) for some stunning views.

The track is all downhill from here, but it is slowly becoming more and more rutted by quad bikes, and when wet, parts of it become Grade 4 (Advanced). Depending on your skill level, allow 2–4 hours to reach the Bridge to Nowhere.

About half an hour from the trig track, after descending right into the valley, you'll reach Johnson's Clearing, which is a good place for a rest and regroup.

The track follows the valley gently downhill all the way to the bridge; so gently, it's almost flat. There are many narrow swing bridges, a few bluffs and several large clearings en route. DOC has erected signs advising you to walk across each bluff. At least three cyclists have fallen off the side while trying to ride them. When you see the bluffs, you will agree that it's amazing that not one of those cyclists died. Just walk them and you'll be fine.

Exploring one of the Whanganui River's side streams.

The bridge itself, quite aptly, appears out of nowhere. Opened in 1936, it had become overgrown by 1948. DOC has restored this iconic structure and installed fascinating interpretation signs. Give yourself plenty of time to enjoy it.

There is a lookout track 100 metres on from the bridge and then toilets a few hundred metres further on again. The ride down to Mangapurua Landing and the Whanganui River takes about 15 minutes. There is a shelter 200 metres before the landing (not a bad place to camp if required).

Bridge to Nowhere to Pipiriki
28 km, 1.5 hours to jetboat, 8 hours to canoe
From the Mangapurua Landing, 15 minutes from the Bridge to Nowhere, there are a few options for travelling down the Whanganui River.

The Combo Catch a jetboat (or paddle a Canadian canoe) down to the Bridge to Nowhere
    Lodge about 5 km away. Stay the night in comfort and enjoy a big dinner and
    breakfast. The next day, jetboat (1 hour) or paddle down to Pipiriki (6 hours).
The Express Catch a jetboat all the way down to Pipiriki in one go (1.5 hours). You can

Battleship Bluff, on the Mangapurua Track.

also arrange to paddle the last 10 km into Pipiriki, which is a great way to get a feel for the Whanganui River.

The Nature Lover Paddle the whole way (8 hours), staying at the Bridge to Nowhere Lodge or a DOC campsite along the way.

The paddle down the river takes about 5 hours from the lodge if you allow plenty of time for photos. Much of the river is like a long narrow lake with hardly any flow at all, but there are several Grade 2 rapids to negotiate with waves up to 1 metre high. These require a moderate amount of canoeing skill. You can portage them if you like.

Pipiriki is a small quiet town with a holiday park where you can camp, stay in cabins or a studio unit, and get basic food supplies, ice creams, coffee, etc.

Pipiriki to Whanganui and the sea

87 km, 6–8 hours, Grade 3 (Intermediate because of traffic only)

From Pipiriki, follow the Whanganui River Road down valley. After 8 km there is a short climb to a great lookout spot.

Jerusalem, 12 km from Pipiriki, is famous for a number of reasons. It is the site of a historic Maori village, a Catholic nunnery, and poet James K Baxter moved there in 1969 and is buried there. The settlement has a stunning church, and quiet accommodation is available there (bookings essential).

Almost 5 km on from Jerusalem, the gravel ends as you roll into London (Ranana), which has the Kauika Campsite at the far end, just next to a large marae.

Next stop should be at Kawana Flour Mill, on your right, 4.6 km from London. It was built in 1854, and beautifully restored in 1980. The mill is 50 metres off the road. After checking it out, continue for just over 1 km and you will reach a cafe just past Hikumutu. It has a large model of the *River Queen*, a boat that starred in the Vincent Ward movie of the same name. It is open on weekends only.

From the cafe it is 8 km to Corinth (Koriniti), where there is a cottage and a luxury lodge to choose from for accommodation. The road meanders south, across tributaries and past bush remnants

A Catholic church at Jerusalem.

and limestone cliffs for another 25 km before tackling the formidable Gentle Annie Hill. There are a couple of fantastic lookout/recovery platforms at the top. This is a great place to recover before flying down the far side, to a shelter and interpretation boards 10 minutes away (and 63 km from Pipiriki).

For those who don't like biking on busy roads, this is a good place to end your ride. The next 2 km is along the highway, which has no shoulder and is used by many heavy trucks. Ride in single file and keep well left.

If continuing to the official end of the ride, follow the highway south, past Upokongaro to Whanganui. By now you will have noticed small green trail markers. These posts direct you into Whanganui, across the Dublin Street Bridge, down beside the river, past the i-SITE and out through an industrial area to the coast at North Mole (one of two large breakwaters). The markers aren't very obvious, so you need to keep your eyes peeled.

The i-SITE is 8 km before the coast, right beside the trail, and has a cafe that serves delicious hot chocolate. At the coast you will find a Mountains to Sea signboard beside a dramatic section of coastline.

Hot tip: Take some breadcrumbs for finding your way back along the last few kilometres. The route is well signposted heading down to the sea but not in the other direction.

The Whanganui River, from the lookout near Pipiriki.

TRAIL TALES

Just as the Mountains to Sea trail has three distinctly different stages, so does its history — the Ohakune Coach Road, the Mangapurua Track and the Whanganui River.

The Ohakune Coach Road began as just one of many tracks in the area that had been used by Maori for centuries. The arrival of Europeans and their horses saw it stamped into a bridle trail by the 1880s. At this time, as rail was developing in importance, there were two significant railway lines in the North Island; one from Auckland down to Te Awamutu and the other from Wellington to Marton. In June 1883, the government sent renowned surveyor John Rochfort to the central plateau to survey a line that could link the two.

Rochfort was met with some resistance from Maori who objected to the government taking their land. Many survey markers 'disappeared' as a form of silent protest. Despite this, Rochfort finished his survey and officially recommended the line for a rail route in February 1884.

While the Main Trunk Line was being constructed, the Ohakune 'bridle trail' provided the only link across the unfinished section and so it was upgraded to a 4-metre-wide dray and cart road, paved with cobbles to provide a firm surface and good grip for horses pulling coaches up the steep grades — and, by 1906, the Ohakune Coach Road as we know it was formed.

At the start of 1908, there was still a gap between Ohakune and Horopito, and the government became impatient and offered the chief engineer a £1000 incentive to close the gap in time for a special parliamentary trip from Wellington to Auckland later that year.

Workers doubled their efforts to meet the goal. A 'test train' with the workers' families on board went through shortly before the deadline. There was still ballast missing from under some of the sleepers, and at one narrow cutting, the train hit the sides and had to back up and wait while the cutting was widened using picks and shovels.

A boat carries Prime Minister Joseph Ward down the Whanganui River, circa 1908.

However, the job was finished in the nick of time, and the Parliamentary Special made it through on 7 August 1908. After that, the Ohakune Coach Road was redundant and gradually became overgrown and forgotten.

In October 2002, local people rediscovered and began uncovering the Old Coach Road, and researching its origin. In 2010, they gained funds from the New Zealand Cycle Trail project to repair it and open the trail through to Horopito.

Horopito started life as a temporary camp for the railway workers, and then grew into a major sawmilling town. After the native forest had been cleared, the town was abandoned and later became known as the location of a large scrap-metal car yard used in 1981 for the classic Kiwi film *Smash Palace*.

Further along the Mountains to Sea trail, the Mangapurua Track is a famous example of a failed government initiative, which left behind the iconic Bridge to Nowhere. In 1917, the government opened the Mangapurua Valley for farming, granting land to servicemen returning from the Great War (as if they hadn't been through enough already). The grand plan was to build a road connecting Raetihi with the Whanganui River via the Mangapurua Valley. At the height of settlement, there were 30 farms and a school in the Mangapurua Valley.

Access to the Whanganui River was at first quite dangerous and the government promised to improve it. The Bridge to Nowhere was started in January 1935. The 34-metre-long bridge was made from 105 cubic metres of concrete mixed by hand and 15 tons of steel bent and cut on site. It was built by the Raetihi firm of Sandford and Brown and was eventually opened in June 1936.

But the area was prone to erosion, making farming difficult, especially as slips kept closing the road. Demoralised settlers started abandoning their farms as early as the mid-1920s, and the few hardy souls remaining were forced to leave in 1942 when the government refused to maintain the road and officially closed the valley.

From the Mangapurua Landing, the trail has a rich history all the way down the Whanganui River to the sea. For centuries, Maori used the Whanganui River and its tributaries for trade and travel between Wellington, the Waikato, Taranaki, Taupo, and the Bay of Plenty regions. By 1891, the majority of the difficult rapids had been dynamited out of the river, and a regular riverboat service was set up to carry passengers, mail and freight to settlers between Whanganui and Taumarunui. As a consequence, tourism flourished in the region. However, the main riverboat trade dwindled in the 1920s due to improved roads, the completed Main Trunk Line and tourist attractions in other areas demanding attention. Then, in 1934, the River Road between Pipiriki and Whanganui was completed, and the writing was on the wall for the riverboat service. It closed in 1958.

Many Whanganui River marae were also affected by the construction of the River Road. Most had been set up on the far bank of the river — the true right. There they were protected from the elements and enjoyed the warm morning sun. However, the River Road was on the true left, and, over time, most marae shifted to the road side of the valley.

Pou at the meeting of the Kaiwhakauka and Mangapurua tracks.

Whanganui National Park was established in 1986. Most of the park is cloaked in lowland native forest. Tawa makes up 70 per cent of the trees, with black beech the dominant species on the ridge tops. The park is home to kiwi, North Island robin, bellbird, tui, and the shining and long-tailed cuckoo (pipiwharauroa and koekoea).

The first people to mountain bike the Mountains to the Sea were probably the Kennett brothers. In early 1988, my brothers Paul and Simon and I caught the night train to Ohakune, dismounting at 1 a.m. and sleeping under a nearby tree. It took us two days to ride to the Bridge to Nowhere on what was then a rough track with many short unrideable sections. At the river, we built a raft with rope and truck-tyre tubes that we had carried in; it took 14 hours to float and paddle down the river to Pipiriki. From there, with only one muesli bar left between us, we cycled down the River Road to Whanganui and on to Marton to catch the train home.

After much upgrading work, the official Mountains to Sea trail was opened in early 2012. In 2017, further upgrades at the Whanganui city end were under way.

FOOD AND ACCOMMODATION

Ohakune Plenty of cafes, restaurants and accommodation: www.ohakune.info

Horopito Luhar Farm Log Cabin, phone 06 385 3384 or 027 651 5377 for accommodation in Horopito and Ohakune.

Raetihi Cafes and restaurants, grocery store, accommodation: www.raetihi.com; Raetihi Holiday Park, phone 0800 408 888, www.raetihiholidaypark.com

Ruatiti Valley (end of day 1) Ruatiti Backpackers for budget accommodation and meals, phone 06 385 4266, www.ruatitibackpackersandcamping.co.nz, email ruatitibtnw@farmside.co.nz; Mellonsfolly Ranch for accommodation and meals, phone 027 702 3158, www.oldwesttown.co.nz

Whanganui River (near Mangapurua Landing) To organise transport and accommodation, contact Bridge to Nowhere, phone 0800 480 308, www.bridgetonowhere.co.nz
For other operators on the Whanganui River, www.whanganuiriver.co.nz/operators

Pipiriki Camping, accommodation, basic food supplies and river transport: Whanganui River Adventures, phone 0800 862 743, www.whanganuiriveradventures.com

Jerusalem (Hiruharama) Accommodation beside the church, phone 06 342 8190, email info@jerusalem convent.co.nz

London (Ranana) Kauika Campsite, just rock on up.

Hikumutu Cafe open in the weekend.

Koriniti The Flying Fox lodge, dinner, bed, breakfast and packed lunch, phone 06 927 6809, www.theflyingfox.co.nz

Whanganui Plenty of supermarkets, shops, cafes, restaurants, takeaways, accommodation: www.visitwhanganui.nz; bike shop The Bike Shed, corner Ridgway and St Hill streets, phone 06 345 5500, www.bikeshed.co.nz

National Park Plenty of accommodation and a good cafe at the railway station: www.nationalpark.co.nz

Whakahoro DOC camping ground and cabin in the old school, www.doc.govt.nz; Blue Duck Station has several options from backpacker to luxury, as well as a cafe, phone 07 895 6276, www.blueduckstation.co.nz

SIMON KENNETT

ALTERNATIVE START: FISHERS TRACK AND KAIWHAKAUKA TRACK

This alternative start to the Mountains to Sea trail begins in National Park and follows 48 km of scenic backroads connected by 26 km of off-road tracks to the Mangapurua Track. Both National Park Village and Whakahoro are small holiday destinations.

Remains of a doomed settlement.

National Park to Whakahoro

53 km, 3–5 hours, Grade 3 (Intermediate)

From the back of National Park, follow Fisher Road west into the wilderness. Most of this 'track' is a narrow gravel road, with 5 km of grassy historic track still existing. It is mostly downhill for 17 km. At Upper Retaruke Road, turn right and pedal down to Oio Road and then turn left and continue down valley to Whakahoro, where you will find a cafe and accommodation on a terrace above the Whanganui River. This is a great place to stop and explore. There is a DOC campsite, which has a cabin with 10 bunks in the old school house, or, for you comfort seekers, the Blue Duck Station has a cafe and several accommodation options ranging from backpackers up to a spacious lodge.

Whakahoro to Bridge to Nowhere

38 km, 5–8 hours, Grade 4 (Advanced)

From Whakahoro, the Kaiwhakauka Track provides a link to the Mangapurua Track. The start is clearly signposted, and the Kaiwhakauka Track was upgraded in 2012, but not very well. The first 6 km to the Whanganui National Park boundary is on a farm track that was further upgraded in 2017. This is followed by several kilometres of rough and narrow Grade 4 (Advanced) single track. The last 5 km climbs up a farm track to the Mangapurua Track. Skilled mountain bikers will love it in dry weather, whereas cycle tourers will struggle, especially if it has been wet.

At the top (3–4 hours from Whakahoro), you will reach the Mangapurua Track. Turn right to ride past Mangapurua Trig and down to the Bridge to Nowhere, 2–4 hours away.

SHORTCUTS AND DETOURS

Bridge to Nowhere Loop   The bridge is an icon that you really should see, even if you only have a day or two to spare. Most people do this as a round trip starting from Raetihi by riding into the bridge, down to Mangapurua Landing and then jetboating or canoeing down to Pipiriki and riding (or getting shuttled) back up to Raetihi. Self-propelled the whole way, this takes a fit group 2–3 days. With jetboat and shuttle-bus support it can be done in a day (see www.bridgetonowhere.co.nz).

Turakina and Hunterville Loop   Have a rest day in Whanganui and then pedal back to Ohakune via the Turakina Valley. Take a side trip to Hunterville if you want to split it into two days. This would make a great week-long loop trip for cycling enthusiasts!

The start of the Mangapurua Track.

MURRAY DRAB

HAWKE'S BAY TRAILS

Hawke's Bay is the closest you can get to a European cycling holiday in New Zealand. The cycle paths are wide, smooth and mostly flat, inviting all ages of rider on all sorts of bikes. The climate is almost Mediterranean. Most of the vineyards and wineries adhere to central European architecture, and many produce world-renowned wines. Even some of the landscaping has a Tuscan feel. In this region, as in Europe, cycling is an everyday activity for everyday people.

The Hawke's Bay Trails is a 200-km network linking most of the special attractions in Napier, Hastings and Havelock North. The top five rides are detailed here. Those keen to explore will find many more options.

The Coastal Ride running from Napier south towards Cape Kidnappers is the most popular. It is the easiest cycle trail in this book and has great scenery. The destination is the Clifton Cafe, or even Cape Kidnappers itself if you are happy to do a tour out to the gannet colony.

The Water Ride (northern end) heads up the coast for an hour, past cafes, playgrounds, and swimming and picnic spots to Bay View before weaving around a few wetlands and back to Napier.

The Puketapu Loop is the best ride for those really hot summer days, as it has lots of trees, and the destination is the Puketapu tavern. Some people call this the 'Pub Run'.

The Wineries Ride passes 11 vineyards with cafes and cellar doors. It is also completely flat and easy.

The antidote to all the fine wine and food offered in Hawke's Bay is the Tukituki Loop. It is the only ride with enough hills to guarantee more calories will be burnt than consumed at the cafe en route.

SUMMARY

Start point Several starting points in Napier, Taradale, Hastings and Havelock North

End point As above, plus Clifton

Distance Rides range from 18 to 47 km

Likely time 2–4 hours per ride

Grading Grades 1 (Very easy), 2 (Easy) and 3 (Intermediate)

Surface Mostly smooth limesand, also some concrete paths, and two rides have some sealed road

Bike type Comfort bike, mountain bike, road bike — anything with two wheels

Map A pamphlet map is available from all i-SITEs in Napier, Hastings and Havelock North and many businesses in Hawke's Bay

Trail websites www.nzcycletrail.com and www.iway.org.nz

In emergencies There is cellphone coverage on most of this trail

Hawke's Bay Trails

to Taupo, Wairoa

Rorookuri

Bay View

Water Ride

Napier
Airport

Ahuriri Estuary

Westshore

Ahuriri

Port

NAPIER

Puketapu
Domain

Puketapu

bridge

Tutaekuri R.

Puketapu Loop

Swamp Rd

Otatara Pa

bridge

Taradale

Fernhill

Ngaruroro R.

Roys Hill Res.

Omahu Rd

Wineries Ride

Oak Ave

bridge

Coastal Ride

bridge

Clive

Tukituki R.

Haumoana

Black Bridge

Whakatu

Te Awanga

Flaxmere

Triangle
Cellars

gatarawa
Vines

Hastings
Golf Club

Hastings

Moore Rd

Clifton

to Cape Kidnappers

Maraekakaho Rd

eni Estate

Bridge Pa

Chalk and
Cheese

Havelock North

Te Mata Rd

Tukituki Loop

Tukituki Rd

Waimarama Rd

to Waipawa

Red Bridge

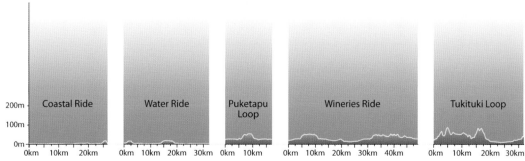

| | Coastal Ride | Water Ride | Puketapu Loop | Wineries Ride | Tukituki Loop |

Bike hire and tours Fishbike (bike hire and coffee close to the Napier i-SITE), phone 0800 131 600 or 06 833 6979, www.fishbike.co.nz; Takaro Trails (one of the country's best cycle-guiding companies, also hires bikes and offers self-guided tours of all types), phone 06 835 9030, www.takarotrails.co.nz; Good Fun Bike Rides, phone 06 650 7722 or 021 777 964, www.goodfunbikerides.co.nz; On Yer Bike Winery Tours, phone 06 650 4627, www.onyerbikehb.co.nz; Napier Bike Hire, phone 0800 245 344, www.bikehirenapier.co.nz

Getting there Napier is 315 km (4 hours) from Wellington and 140 km (2 hours) from Taupo. There are also daily flights from Auckland and Wellington to Napier. Once you are in Hawke's Bay, you can take your bikes on the public buses from Napier to Taradale, Hastings and Havelock North

Family time on the Coastal Ride.

ROUTE DESCRIPTION

The Coastal Ride

27 km, 2–3 hours, Grade 1 (Very easy)

Most people start this ride from, or near, the Napier i-SITE, which is on the coast (Marine Parade), two blocks from Napier's shopping centre. From the street-front entrance of the i-SITE, go around the left side to find a wide concrete path following the Pacific coastline. Head south towards Cape Kidnappers. Within 10 minutes you will pass a kids' road skills area and a large concrete pump track.

After 9 km, you will cross the mouths of two rivers, the Tutaekuri and the Ngaruroro. At the 11-km mark, duck under the Clive River Bridge and then cross it on a pedestrian footpath. At the far end, the Clive shops are just 100 metres down the main road. There is a dairy and a cafe.

If you don't need to go to the shops, just duck under the bridge again and continue along the main path towards Cape Kidnappers. Before long, you will ride beside the East Clive Wetlands, a habitat restoration project already inhabited by many coastal birds.

After riding 17 km from Napier, you'll reach another major bridge (Black Bridge) and will have to repeat the ducking process to safely cross via a pedestrian path before continuing south towards the cape. When you reach houses, take care to follow the pathway signs or you will get lost. This section passes the Haumoana General Store.

The path ends at a shingly beach with a clear view of Cape Kidnappers. The Clifton Holiday Park is right next to the beach, and the Clifton Cafe (open 9 a.m. to 5 p.m.) is a stone's throw away. Another popular destination is the Clearview Winery (signposted 3 km before the end of the trail), which welcomes cyclists.

If you have never been to the gannet colony at Cape Kidnappers before, then this is a must-do. The best time of the year is from early November to late February. Arrange to join a tour through the i-SITE before you start your ride.

The Water Ride (north end)
33 km, 2–4 hours, Grade 1 (Very easy)

Starting from Napier i-SITE on Marine Parade, head north on the coastal path, past the port and through West Quay Wharf, where the path disappears for 200 metres. At the far end of the wharf, ride past Ahuriri (it has a great playground for kids next to a cafe for adults). Cross a major road bridge and follow the signs down a couple of short streets to the Westshore cycle path. This is the highest-quality cycle path in the country — a wide, smooth, concrete ribbon, with great coastal views and picnic tables with cycle racks.

Just before Bay View, there is an option to branch off to the Snapper Park Cafe 1 km away. This is a popular destination for local riders.

The next section, across the flats north of the airport, is most scenic after rain, otherwise it can look a bit nondescript.

The cycle trail leads across SH2 and onto a limesand path that weaves around a hill called Rorookuri, also known as Quarantine Island, although it hasn't been an island since the 1931 earthquake lifted the surrounding ground above sea level. There is also a wetland that is being restored, and a huge wooden beacon that is used to guide ships along the coast.

After passing the airport, the trail skirts around a larger wetland and ducks under the highway onto an old road bridge. Ride along the old bridge, and when you're 100 metres north, turn right onto another limesand path that leads back to Ahuriri. From there, you rejoin the path you started on and retrace your tyre tracks back to Napier.

The Puketapu Loop
18 km, 2–3 hours, Grade 1 (Very easy)
On a hot summer's day, this is the best ride in Hawke's Bay because it is weaves through graceful old trees. Also, parking is easy, and the destination involves good food and drink.

Start from Pettigrew Green Arena (Gloucester Street, Taradale). From the stopbank path beside the car park, turn right and simply follow the path up valley all the way to Puketapu, 8 km away. Take care on two road crossings near Puketapu.

Puketapu has a tavern called The Puketapu, which has won awards for being the best country restaurant in the region. It also has a good store with plenty of snack food, and almost 1 km from the store down Dartmoor Road is a large domain with toilets, trees and a playground. It's ideal for a family picnic.

After a break, follow signposts to Vicarage Bridge. At the far end, hang a sharp left and follow the limesand path back to Pettigrew Green Arena. This is one of the best sections of trail in the bay.

The Wineries Ride
33–47 km, 2–4 hours, Grade 2 (Easy)
This easy ride around the famed Gimblett Gravels wine region is a dream for connoisseurs of fermented grape juice. The wineries also serve food and non-alcoholic drinks, and some of the settings are absolutely stunning.

Where to start this loop ride? Three of the wineries hire bikes (see Bike hire), or, if you have your own bike, you could start from Roys Hill (near Fernhill) or the Hastings Golf Club (they welcome cyclists and have a cafe, bike racks and toilets). Triangle Cellars is another good starting point.

Roys Hill is only 20 metres high but offers good views of the wine region. The Wineries Ride is mostly on limesand paths right beside the road. Take care when you're crossing as most of the roads have a 100 kph speed limit. As you can see from the map, it is a 5-km dog-leg out to Sileni, but Sileni is one of the best wineries to visit, with great architecture, a cellar door and a gift shop selling wine, cheese, chocolates, olive oil and kitchenware; just perfect for anyone who loves cooking. Other highlights are Oak Avenue (planted in 1876) and riding the stopbank path beside the Ngaruroro River.

If you don't do any of the side trips then this is a 33-km loop. If you ride all the side trips then it is 47 km long. It is all flat, except for the option of riding up Roys Hill for the view.

You guessed it — the Wineries Ride.

The Tukituki Loop

33 km, 2–4 hours, Grade 4 (Advanced)

This is the only one of the Hawke's Bay Trails with hills, so if you're looking for some exercise, look no further. Half the ride is on the road, and half is on limesand paths.

The car park at Black Bridge (on Mill Road, 2 km south of Clive) is a popular starting point. But if you don't mind riding an extra 4 km, you could start from a cafe in the centre of Havelock North, and head down Te Mata Road.

Black Bridge is on the Coastal Ride and crosses the Tukituki River, 16 km south of Napier. From Black Bridge, follow the wide limesand track along the stopbank on the western side of the river. After 8 km it leaves the stopbank and weaves through trees to River Road. Follow River Road away from the Tukituki River for 800 metres to Waimarama Road.

Turn left at the intersection at Waimarama Road to continue up valley. The trail is a mixture of on- and off-road from here to Red Bridge, 5 km away. On the way you must ride the 'Mad Mile' — a section of Waimarama Road with no shoulder space and lots of traffic. Ride single file and keep as far left as possible.

Cross Red Bridge (pushing the 'Cyclists Active' warning sign first) and turn left again. Follow Tukituki Road for 9 km down valley before turning left onto Moore Road for 900 metres and hooking into another limesand path. Follow this path right back to Black Bridge.

The Tukituki Loop with Te Mata Peak behind.

TRAIL TALES

In the 1300s, the first humans arrived in the Hawke's Bay. They had paddled from the north, landing at Wairoa, Te Taha (Westshore) and Waimarama. They noted the fish-hook shape of the land and designated it the sacred jawbone that Maui had used to fish up the North Island.

Te Mata was an important location for Maori on their arrival in the region. There is evidence of well-developed karaka 'orchards', especially in the circular arrangement of the trees in upper Te Hau Valley, which are believed to be more than 200 years old. There are also numerous archaeological sites of moa bones and pa.

Likewise, the Otatara Pa Historic Reserve in Taradale is a significant archaeological site. The reserve comprises over 44 ha and includes two historic pa. In centuries past, there were several pa around Te Whanganui a Orotu, a huge tidal lagoon that was a bountiful source of food.

Over the centuries, sediment washing down to the sea filled the lagoon. Then the devastating earthquake that struck the Napier region in 1931 lifted an area of over 3000 ha by 1.5 metres, leaving half the lagoon exposed and most of the remainder as

A petrol tanker toppled in the Napier earthquake, 1931.

shallow patches of brackish water. This area has since been drained and utilised for agriculture and settlement.

What remains today, Ahuriri Estuary, is still a critical destination for migrating wading birds. Visitors include royal spoonbills, black-fronted dotterels, wrybills, variable oyster-catchers, white herons, Caspian terns, bar-tailed godwits, golden plovers, red knots and ruddy turnstones.

In 1769, around four centuries after Maori arrived in the area, Captain Cook sailed the *Endeavour* into the bay and anchored offshore. While never actually stepping on the land, Cook named the bay for Sir Edward Hawke, First Lord of the Admiralty, then named Cape Kidnappers after an incident that took place during his visit. Local Maori coming to trade with the ship noticed Cook's Tahitian cabin boy and, believing him to be a prisoner, decided to rescue him. As the Maori paddled the lad to shore in their waka, the crew of the *Endeavour* opened fire, and the cabin boy jumped out and swam back to his ship.

The first European landings were left to whalers, who set up coastal stations. Graziers and land speculators joined them around 1836.

In 1838, a group of French missionaries arrived in New Zealand and, in 1851, established a Marist mission station at Pakowhai, near the Ngaruroro River between Napier and Hastings. In 1858, the missionaries moved to Meeanee and established a major community, including planting a vineyard to produce both sacramental and table wine. And so New Zealand's oldest winery was established. The first record of a commercial sale dates back to 1870. In 1897, there was a disastrous flood, and the missionaries realised that they needed to move the vineyard to higher ground; thus, the 800-acre Mission Estate was purchased from the Tiffen family and the Marist brothers travelled each day from Meeanee to work the new land. Then, in 1909, the mission community moved to its present site.

Hawke's Bay's future as a farming region was set in motion in 1848 when James Northwood and Henry Tiffen leased 50,000 acres of land for grazing in Central Hawke's Bay. The next year, 3000 merino sheep arrived, driven up the coast from Wellington by Henry's brother Fred.

The Puketapu Loop.

Puketapu, on the Puketapu Loop ride, was once a major crossroads and staging point for stagecoaches, mail coaches and horse and bullock trains travelling to Taihape, Taupo, Wairoa and Gisborne. The Puketapu Hotel and Pheasant's Nest, now the tavern, was established in 1885 by Mr Frederick Thomas Bradley.

The Puketapu area takes its name from the small hill situated on the banks of the Tutaekuri River. The name translates to Sacred Hill — puke meaning hill, tapu meaning sacred. One day, the local Maori at Waitangi near Clive noticed the river running red with blood. They investigated, only to find that a massacre had taken place on this hill and the blood of those killed had run down and into the river, and so they set a tapu on the hill.

On Tuesday 3 February 1931 at 10.47 a.m., a magnitude 7.9 earthquake struck the bay, killing 257 people and devastating the region. There are still few buildings in Hawke's Bay taller than five storeys, and because most of the rebuilding took place in the 1930s when art deco was fashionable, Napier is regarded as one of the finest art deco towns in the world.

In 2001, the mayor of Napier, Barbara Arnott, began a partnership with local Rotary groups and over the following 10 years they built 60 km of cycle trail. Other councils around the region then received several million dollars to build more cycle trails as part of the New Zealand Cycle Trail project and in Hastings as part of iWays, a nationally led transport initiative to encourage people to travel by healthy means (walking and cycling). The region now has over 200 km of cycle paths and lanes.

FOOD AND ACCOMMODATION

Napier Full range of fabulous food and accommodation: www.napiernz.com; or go to the Napier i-SITE on Marine Parade.

Hastings Plenty of food and accommodation: www.visithastings.co.nz, or drop into the Hastings i-SITE on the corner of Russell Street South and Heretaunga Street East.

Havelock North A smaller range of lovely food and accommodation places: www.havelocknorthnz.com

Puketapu General store and tavern with an award-winning restaurant, The Puketapu, phone 06 844 7206, www.thepuketapu.co.nz. There is also the Puketapu Domain (picnic site, playground and toilets) just 1 km from the signposted loop.

Pettigrew Green Arena, Taradale Subway takeaway (open 7 days) and toilets.

SHORTCUTS AND DETOURS

200 km Network The Hawke's Bay Trails is a network ideally suited to shortcuts and detours. Take a look at the cycle trails map and make up an itinerary to suit your location and travel plans.

Otatara Pa Walk About 2 minutes' ride along the Puketapu Loop there is a turn-off on your right to a 10-minute walk to Otatara pa for panoramic views and Maori history.

Cape Kidnappers For reasons unknown, Australasian gannets started nesting at Cape Kidnappers in the 1870s, and their population has grown to over 6000 pairs, making it the largest mainland gannet colony in the world. Its future is looking good as volunteers and DOC are restoring the vegetation, and in 2006–07 a 10.5-km long, coast-to-coast fence was built to keep predators out of the cape.

RIMUTAKA
CYCLE TRAIL

The Rimutaka Cycle Trail follows riverside cycle paths, a historic rail trail, quiet country roads and a coastal route used by drovers in the 1840s. From Wellington Harbour, the trail circumnavigates the Rimutaka Range — a mountainous forest park dividing the lower North Island into the Wellington and Wairarapa regions.

The ride starts at the Petone foreshore, incorporating the Hutt River Trail, a very easy cycle path that runs beside the Hutt River. Both the beach and the river are popular for swimming in summer. The second stage of the ride crosses the top of the Rimutaka Range via a railway formation with tunnels and bridges that were built in the pioneering days when rail was king. The route then hugs the range and passes the expansive Lake Wairarapa en route to Palliser Bay.

From Palliser Bay, the final leg follows a rocky and wild coastline past Windy Point and Turakirae Head to one of the country's older farms, Orongorongo Station. Elephantine rocks are dotted throughout a landscape of low coastal vegetation and, on a fine day, the ocean seems an impossibly rich shade of blue.

A recommended option is to branch off to Martinborough, the region's wine-growing capital, for a night or two.

SUMMARY

Start point Wellington or Petone Wharf

End point Orongorongo Station, South Coast

Distance 115 km

Likely time 2–3 days

Grading Grade 2 (Easy) to 3 (Intermediate)

Surface Mostly sealed and gravel paths, with some sections on road

Bike type Mountain bike or touring bike with fat tyres

Map Maps of the Hutt River Trail and the Rimutaka Rail Trail are available at the Wellington i-SITE or download them from www.gw.govt.nz. There are map boards along both trails. For the route around the coast, take Kiwimap Rural Roads Wellington Wairarapa

Trail website www.nzcycletrail.com

In emergencies There is good cellphone coverage in the Hutt Valley but not along the rest of the trail

Bike hire Green Jersey Cycle Tour Company, Wairarapa (for full tour packages, including bike hire and transport), phone 06 306 6027 or 027 245 3489, www.greenjersey.co.nz and Cycle Rimutaka, Eastbourne, phone 027 570 0108, www.cyclerimutaka.com

Getting there Wellington is 770 km from Auckland and 200 km from Whanganui (the end of the nearest Great Ride). There are also dozens of flights a day into Wellington.

Rimutaka Cycle Trail

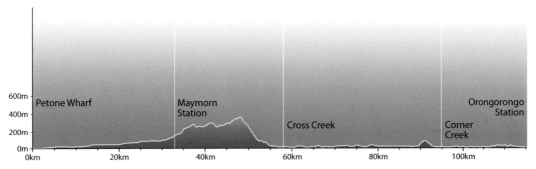

From Wellington city you can catch the East by West ferry to Petone — check out the timetable at www.eastbywest.co.nz. Alternatively, catch a commuter train to Petone. Some people prefer to skip the Hutt River Trail and start with the Rimutaka Rail Trail from Maymorn Station, by catching the Wairarapa line train. For train times, go to www.metlink.org.nz and phone 0800 801 700 to tell them that you have bikes. Check that the trains have not been replaced with buses, which can't take bikes

Trail transport Arrange a shuttle from Orongorongo Station back to Wellington: Green Jersey Cycle Tour Company (see Bike hire); Rimutaka Shuttles, www.rimutakashuttles.com, phone 06 308 9007 or 021 047 2082 or Cycle Rimutaka (see Bike hire)

Special considerations The summit tunnel on the Rimutaka Rail Trail is 580 metres long, so take a light to guide you through

Cross Creek Road, near the Rimutaka Rail Trail.

ROUTE DESCRIPTION

Hutt River Trail: Petone to Maymorn Station

33 km, 3–5 hours, Grade 2 (Easy)

Ride east along the Petone esplanade, at the head of Wellington Harbour, and cross the mouth of the Hutt River on the busy road bridge (there is a footpath on the southern side). At the eastern end, ride clockwise around and underneath the bridge to start following the Hutt River Trail north. The first 6 km is sealed and then it becomes smooth gravel.

At the 15-km mark, the trail ducks under the main road, and at the 24-km mark you are faced with a choice. The official trail becomes a bit rougher as it continues following the Hutt River. If you prefer road riding and don't mind a short steep hill, then there is a good shortcut here that takes you to Maymorn Station (see below).

If you stick to the official trail, ride to Harcourt Park and past the back of the Kiwi Holiday Park. From there, continue along the signposted trail to the Te Marua Dairy (30 km from Petone on SH2). Parts of this trail are a bit rough and ready. After an ice cream or Devonshire tea just up Plateau Road, say goodbye to the Hutt River Trail as you head up Plateau Road for 300 metres before turning right and climbing Maymorn Road to Maymorn Station.

For the shortcut option at Maoribank, 24 km from Petone, take a 50-metre zig-zag path up to a set of traffic lights on SH2. Cross the highway and take Mangaroa Hill Road and Parkes Line Road left to Maymorn Station. This is 5 km on the road, compared to 8 km on the trail.

Optional start: If you are short on time, catch the Wairarapa train in the morning north as far as Maymorn Station.

Rimutaka Rail Trail: Maymorn Station to Cross Creek
25 km, 3–4 hours, Grade 2+ (Easy)
From Maymorn Station, go under the small railway overbridge and turn left down a dead-end country lane. After 1 minute, you'll reach a locked gate at the trail head. Squeeze

The eastern end of the Rimutaka summit tunnel.

around the gate and onto the gravel road. There is a short hill to tackle early on, but then it is easy all the way to a long tunnel. At the far end is the large picnic area at Tunnel Gully, set among well-spaced gum trees.

Follow the narrow public road through Tunnel Gully Recreation Area for 400 metres, and when it curves left, you need to go straight ahead. Squeeze around another gate to continue following the original railway line. Just over 2 km later, at a T-intersection, turn left (the shortcut to the right is hilly). Squeeze around the next gate and turn right to coast down the old SH2. At the bottom of the hill, just before hitting the new highway, turn right and follow signposts to the Rimutaka Rail Trail car park.

From the car park, the trail is well signposted up to a great picnic area and shelter at the summit tunnel. Built in 1877, this is the longest of four tunnels and is 580 metres long. Don't forget your lights. The downhill on the far side is called the Rimutaka Incline — it is steeper than normal railway lines, and special Fell engines were needed to run the locomotives up and down this section. Partway down there is a 200-metre walk down into and then up the other side of Siberia Gully, infamous for severe winds. In 1880, a train was blown off the tracks here, killing three people.

When you reach Cross Creek Shelter, turn right, cross a bridge and follow a single track for 2 km to a car-parking area at the end of Cross Creek Road.

From here a shuttle can be arranged to take you to Martinborough 27 km away. Martinborough is the capital of the Wairarapa's wineries and has plenty of accommodation and several great cafes and restaurants.

Cross Creek to Ocean Beach

37 km, 2–3 hours, Grade 3 (Intermediate)

Ride 1 km down Cross Creek Road to Western Lake Road. Turn right and head southwest, past Lake Wairarapa. This is a scenic road but it is open to the public, so it pays to make yourself visible with a bright jacket or a flashing rear light.

About 40 minutes from Cross Creek Road, you will reach a public shelter on the shores of Lake Wairarapa, the largest wetland in the lower North Island.

Near the coast (33 km from Cross Creek), there is a short, sharp climb over to Ocean Beach. Just before the top (at a yellow letterbox on your left), stop and look back at the great views of Lake Onoke and Palliser Bay. Drop down a sweeping road to Ocean Beach and follow a gravel road to the right along the coast for 4 km. There, nestled among low forest, you will find the cosy Corner Creek Campground (DOC) with tables, toilets and a shelter.

Turakirae Head: The Wild Coast

20 km, 3–5 hours, Grade 3 (Intermediate)

From the campground, you will be following a historic farm track around a wild, rocky coastline.

There are some short hills along the way (steep enough for you to have no shame in walking them) and the occasional stream with rough fords where the old track has been washed out. The world's flattest memorial is only 3 km from the campground — a tribute to the early drovers who regularly ran sheep and cattle between Wellington and the Wairarapa.

Continue southwest, over Mukamuka Stream, past Windy Point and over the rugged shingle fans of Kotumu Stream to Barney's Whare, where there is a picnic table. This was once the hideout of Frank Barnes, a reclusive maritime painter, and it can now be rented through Orongorongo Station. Much of this section was upgraded in 2017.

From there, the track hugs the base of the Rimutaka hills, past the southernmost point of the ride, Turakirae Head. You have to make a 1-km diversion to get to the actual headland, which is a seal colony over winter and a rock-climbing playground during summer. Otherwise, continue following the main 4WD track and signs to the Orongorongo River.

Cross the Orongorongo Bridge to a car park on the far side at the end of the trail and the end of Coast Road.

Arrange transport to meet you here and take you to Wellington, which is 43 km away via Wainuiomata and Petone.

The Wild Coast, near Mukamuka Stream.

TRAIL TALES

Up to 150 years ago, the Heretaunga (Hutt Valley) was covered in dense forest, interlaced with significant waterways and swamps that teemed with bird and fish life. For centuries, these waterways were the transport 'highways' used by Maori, who had three settlements along Pito-one (Petone) Beach. At the eastern end, where the main river flowed into the harbour, was Hikoikoi pa. At the opposite end of the beach lay the Pito-one and Tatau-o-te-po pa.

In 1839, the first New Zealand Company ship, the *Tory*, arrived in Wellington Harbour. William Wakefield landed at Pito-one pa to discuss settlement options with chiefs Honiana Te Puni Kokupu and Te Wharepouri. These three men negotiated for European settlers to live around the harbour, and early the following year, the first settlement ship, the *Aurora*, arrived. Basing themselves on Pito-one Beach, the settlers quickly established the country's first bank and newspaper.

Many settlers gravitated inland, founding a small town called Britannia on the banks of the Heretaunga, which Wakefield had renamed Hutt River in honour of the founder of the New Zealand Company. However, within months the area was flooded, and Wakefield encouraged the settlement to re-establish at Thorndon on the southern side of the harbour.

A few settlers remained at Pito-one, risking both flooding and escalating conflict with Maori to farm the fertile river plains. Then, in 1855, a major earthquake pushed up land in the valley, draining much of the swampland and making the area more attractive for settlement. But flooding still remained a problem, and in the 1890s settlers began building a stopbank along the river edge.

The stopbank proved popular for weekend strolls, and almost a century later, in 1985, PEP (Project Employment Programme) workers built a concrete path along it, and the bank was opened to bikes as

A Fell engine and carriages ascend the Rimutaka Incline.

the Riverside Cycleway. During the 1990s, the Hutt Valley Rotary clubs and Greater Wellington Regional Council teamed up to continue building paths and developed the Hutt River Trail right up to Te Marua.

Further north, the origins of the trail date back to the 1870s when the Wellington railway line was extended from Upper Hutt to Kaitoke and then over forested hills to the Wairarapa.

This was no mean feat. While a suitably gentle grade was mapped out on the Hutt Valley side of the Rimutaka Range, the rugged Wairarapa side took a steeper grade than conventional railways could follow. And so the Fell locomotive was called into service.

Englishman John Fell invented a simple locomotive braking system that used a set of four horizontal wheels to grip a raised central rail. Each wheel applied about 6 tons of pressure to the central rail. Such friction could haul an engine uphill and break its speed on the downhills.

Four Fell engines were ordered from England. They were built and trialled there and then dismantled into 8000 parts each and shipped to the rail workshops in Petone to be reassembled.

In 1955, the old Rimutaka Incline was superseded by a more direct railway line to the Wairarapa and its rails were lifted. In 1984, the New Zealand Forest Service reopened

The steam engine graveyard, Rimutaka Rail Trail.

access to Cross Creek at the Wairarapa end, and in 1987, the Rimutaka Rail Trail opened along the original line. Its fascinating history is told with interpretation panels at points beside the trail and at the museum in Featherston.

Centuries before, the Maori explorer Haunui scaled the Rimutaka Range, and from the top saw a lake glistening far below. He named the lake Wai Rarapa, which means 'glistening water'.

Covering about 7800 ha, Lake Wairarapa is a shallow lake, never more than 2 metres deep, and the biggest wetland in the lower North Island. It drains into the tidal 650-ha Lake Onoke on the coast near the settlement of Lake Ferry.

Originally Lake Onoke had a mouth at its eastern end that opened and closed depending on weather, tides and shifting sands. This resulted in unpredictable flooding, and European farmers decided to open the mouth permanently to protect their farms. Local Maori were unhappy, fearing that this would affect their fishing in the lake. In May 1892, the farmers set about digging an opening. Maori protested, forming a chain around the diggers, grabbing their shovels and effectively stopping the work.

A century later, in 1989, both Lake Onoke and Lake Wairarapa were placed under a conservation order to protect their natural flora and fauna.

The first European to set foot in the Wairarapa is thought to have been William Deans. He walked around the coast from Wellington with a Maori guide in 1840. Deans assessed the Wairarapa Plains as being ideal for farming, and so, following in his footsteps, farmer Charles Bidwill ran his sheep around the southern coast in 1844. At Mukamuka, the sea ran hard against the hills, and Bidwill was forced to carry each sheep through the surf to prevent them from drowning. His flock made it through safely, but subsequent drives lost stock to the sea. Then the 1855 earthquake struck, raising the coastline and creating easy passage.

The effect of the earthquake, which was magnitude 8 on the Richter scale, is most obvious at Turakirae Head, the southernmost point on the trail, where the Rimutaka Range ploughs into Cook Strait; here the quake raised the beach by 2.5 metres.

Turakirae Head is now a scientific reserve managed by DOC and valued for its variety of rare plants. It is best known for its winter colony of mostly juvenile male kekeno (fur seals) and in summer is often visited by *Homo sapiens* rock climbers, attracted by its large boulders.

The last property on this ride is Orongorongo Station, farmed by the Riddiford family for 140-odd years. Sandwiched between Rimutaka Forest Park and the exposed coastline of the southern North Island, Orongorongo Station has withstood the 1855 earthquake, two fires, and, in 1939, a landslide. What was once a very private station now provides holiday accommodation to visitors.

One of several stream crossings on the Wild Coast.

FOOD AND ACCOMMODATION

Accommodation options are listed on www.nzcycletrail.com and www.wairarapanz.com

Petone, Lower Hutt and Upper Hutt A range of places to stay and eat as well as several bike shops: www.huttvalleynz.com

Harcourt Park Wellington's Kiwi Holiday Park is a popular destination right beside the trail, phone 04 526 7400, www.wellingtonsholidaypark.co.nz. There is a dairy and takeaway store nearby at the Brown Owl shopping centre.

Featherston and Martinborough Accommodation, shops and cafes: www.wairarapanz.com

Orongorongo Station Self-catered accommodation, phone 04 568 6466 or 027 478 7177, www.holidayhouses.co.nz

SHORTCUTS AND DETOURS

Rimutaka Rail Trail This is a popular day trip. Drive or catch the train to Maymorn Station. Follow the directions through Tunnel Gully and the Rimutaka Rail Trail to Cross Creek. At Western Lake Road, turn left and ride 10 km to Featherston. There are daily trains in the evening or morning to take you back to Maymorn or all the way to Wellington.

Martinborough wineries There are several wineries to visit within 20 minutes' cycling of Martinborough Square. Drop into the Wairarapa i-SITE to find out more about their wineries tour. The Green Jersey has a hundred bikes to hire in Martinborough, and can provide maps and a support vehicle if needed (see Food and Accommodation above).

SOUTH ISLAND

QUEEN CHARLOTTE TRACK

No other track in New Zealand has the unique combination of adventurous mountain biking during the day and the comforts of modern living at night. The journey begins with a boat trip along Queen Charlotte Sound, one of the Marlborough Sounds' sunken valleys. Hopping off the boat, onto the long jetty at Ship Cove, you'll know the adventure has begun. The wall of coastal forest ahead looks wild and remote, and yet it hides one of the most historic sites in the country: the place that explorer Captain Cook visited five times in the 1770s.

From Ship Cove, the track follows a series of trails, some ancient, others relatively new. Some sections climb steeply to a saddle, others skirt around the coast. There are several

Queen Charlotte Track

Crail Bay

Kenepuru Sound

Mahau Sound

Portage

Black Rd

Torea Saddle

Te Mahia

Te Mahia Saddle

Mistletoe Bay

Onahau Bay

Lochmara Bay

Torea Bay

Kumutoto

basic

Davies Bay

Anakiwa

Grove Arm

Momorangi Bay

Queen Charlotte Dr.

The Grove

Anakiwa Rd

PICTON

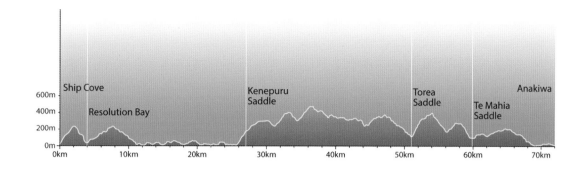

Ship Cove

Resolution Bay

Kenepuru
Saddle

Torea
Saddle

Te Mahia
Saddle

Anakiwa

600m
400m
200m
0m

0km   10km   20km   30km   40km   50km   60km   70km

Miners Camp   Endeavour Inlet

Furneaux Lodge

Ship Cove

Camp Bay

Endeavour Inlet

Resolution
Bay

Kenepuru
Saddle

Punga Cove

Endeavour Inlet

Kenepuru
Head

Bay of Many Coves

Bay of
Many Coves

Ruakaka
Bay

Blackwood
Bay

Queen Charlotte Sound

Arapawa Island

Tory Channel

resorts along the trail, offering great food and accommodation. You can get your luggage delivered to each night's destination, leaving you free to enjoy the track unencumbered. Water taxis service the track throughout the day, so you can also be flexible with your itinerary and choose to do as much, or as little, of the Queen Charlotte Track as you wish.

The top third of the track is only open to mountain bikers from 1 March to 30 November, and you will need to buy a track access pass to cross private land (see Summary for details).

SUMMARY ··

Start point Picton (then boat to Ship Cove)

End point Anakiwa (or ride on to Picton)

Distance 72 km

Likely time 2–3 days

Grading The track has five sections, consisting mostly of Grade 3 (Intermediate) and Grade 4 (Advanced) trail; there is one Grade 5 (Expert) section at the start which will be upgraded in 2018

Surface 100% natural surface; some clay sections are very slippery when wet

Bike type A mountain bike is essential

Open season The top third of the track, from Ship Cove to Kenepuru Saddle, is only open to bikes from 1 March to 30 November. March, April, May and November are the best months to ride the full track

Track access pass You will need an $18 four-day pass to cross the private land on the Queen Charlotte Track. You can purchase the pass from the Picton i-SITE or any business along the track, listed at www.qctlc.com

MARTIN LANGLEY

Ship Cove — the adventure begins.

DOC has placed excellent maps and signs along the track.

Maps A pamphlet map is available at all local businesses associated with the track and the Picton, Nelson and Blenheim i-SITEs. For more detail, purchase the NewTopo Queen Charlotte Track map

Trail website www.qctrack.co.nz

In emergencies Cellphone coverage is available along parts of the trail (mostly the ridge tops), but not all. An emergency personal locator beacon (PLB) is recommended

Bike hire Wilderness Guides (who also do transport and accommodation), phone 0800 266 266, www.wildernessguidesnz.com; Marlborough Sounds Adventure Company, phone 0800 283 283, www.marlboroughsounds.co.nz; Sea Kayaking Adventures, phone 0800 ANAKIWA (262 5492), www.nzseakayaking.com

Getting there Ferries run from Wellington to Picton several times a day and take around 3.5 hours. Try Bluebridge (www.bluebridge.co.nz) or the Interislander (www.interislander.co.nz). Driving from Christchurch to Picton via SH1 is 340 km, and takes 4.5 hours.

Trail transport From Picton there are several small ferries servicing the track: Beachcomber, phone 0800 624 526 or 03 573 6175, www.beachcombercruises.co.nz

ROUTE DESCRIPTION

Ship Cove to Resolution Bay
4 km, 1 hour, Grade 5 (Expert) in 2017

This is the steepest and roughest section on the track, so you may want to consider starting from Resolution Bay instead, which is just around the corner. However, Captain

Cook spent almost six months at Ship Cove (Meretoto), so it is rich in history. There are interpretation panels, a shelter, sculptures, a great lookout, and it is, after all, the start of the track. You are also very likely to see weka here. These inquisitive flightless birds will try stealing anything up to the size of a bike helmet.

If you do start at Ship Cove, expect to walk most of the first hill (35–45 minutes). There are plans to build a new section of track which will make this section Grade 3 (Intermediate) from mid-2018.

Resolution Bay to Kenepuru Saddle (or Camp Bay)
23 km, 2–4 hours, Grade 3 (Intermediate)
The first climb follows a track built by DOC in 2011 and is perfectly graded up to a great lookout spot. The downhill to Endeavour Inlet follows a rough historic bridle track, worn with decades of use; but with gravity on your side, you will soon be skirting around the coast to Furneaux Lodge (cafe, restaurant, accommodation).

One of the two shelters perched on the ridge high above Queen Charlotte Sound.

Follow the coast to Miners Camp, where you can buy snacks from a tiny track-side stall. Not far past there, veer right, away from the coast. The next significant intersection is a few kilometres later where you can go left to Camp Bay and Punga Cove for the night or continue right up to Kenepuru Saddle.

Note: The track from Ship Cove to Kenepuru Saddle is closed to bikes over summer (1 December to 28 February).

Kenepuru Saddle to Torea Saddle and Portage

24 km, 2.5–5 hours, Grade 4 (Advanced)

From Kenepuru Saddle, the track is much hillier. Some riders choose to avoid this section and take the road from the saddle to Portage. If you stick to the track, be aware that it's exposed in places (but has breathtaking views) and drinking water is scarce, though there are water tanks at two DOC shelters along the way. Following the road will take 1–2 hours, while the track will take 2.5–5 hours.

Boardwalk above Waterfall Bay.

On this challenging section, the track climbs up and down to a three-sided shelter high above the Bay of Many Coves (1–2 hours). It has water, a toilet and great views.

After a rest, continue climbing to the highest point on the track at almost 500 metres altitude. It is 1–2 hours from the first shelter to the second, Black Rock Shelter, which also has water and a toilet.

Both shelters have curious weka living nearby — don't feed them or let them steal your food. They can move at lightning speeds.

Most of the track follows the main ridge that bucks its way between Kenepuru and Queen Charlotte sounds. This next section is 20–40 minutes long and ends with an exhilarating descent to Torea Saddle. The track pops out onto Torea Road, right next to a war memorial for 21 local men killed in the 'war to end all wars' (World War I). It had another eight names added after World War II.

The coastal village of Portage is 500 metres off the track, down the sealed Torea Road. The Portage Resort Hotel is the perfect place for a well-deserved cold drink on the veranda.

Torea Saddle to Te Mahia Saddle

9 km, 1.5–2.5 hours, Grade 4+ (Advanced)

From the grey war memorial at Torea Saddle, change into your lowest gear and sweat your way up a 400-metre climb. Even the fittest whippets will have to walk parts of this first section, but the views make it all worthwhile. Some of the downhills are steep and occasionally rutted, but nothing to worry about if your brakes are working well.

This section is tough, especially when wet. Alternatively, take Kenepuru Road to

Te Mahia Saddle — it is much flatter and you could easily cover the distance in half the time while still enjoying fine scenery.

Te Mahia Saddle to Anakiwa
12 km, 1.5–2.5 hours, Grade 3 (Intermediate)
This section to Anakiwa is biking at its best. After skirting across the hill above farmland, the sweet single track weaves through beautiful native beech forest. There are a couple of gentle climbs, but the trail mostly glides downhill.

Anakiwa is a coastal settlement, best known for the Outward Bound education centre that was set up here half a century ago. At the track end there is an information kiosk, and sometimes over summer a coffee caravan. It's a great spot for a picnic.

Optional section: Anakiwa to Picton
24 km, 1.5–2 hours, Grade 3 (Intermediate)
From Anakiwa, Anakiwa Road and Queen Charlotte Drive lead to Picton. They are part of the broader New Zealand Cycle Trail network, and are both quiet with stunning scenery.

For the first 4 km, either follow Anakiwa Road, or a new cycle path beside the road. When you reach Queen Charlotte Drive, turn left, passing through The Grove before rolling over a small hill to Momorangi Bay (8 km from Anakiwa). It is a classic Kiwi camping spot with a holiday park and shop and cafe right beside the road.

After refuelling, carry on along Queen Charlotte Drive to Ngakuta Bay. From there, you can either stay on the road or follow the LINK Pathway most of the way to Picton. Both are great riding options, and a fine way to finish this biking adventure.

TRAIL TALES

The Queen Charlotte Track follows the coastline and ridges between two drowned river valleys of the Marlborough Sounds — Kenepuru Sound and Queen Charlotte Sound. The Maori name for the Marlborough Sounds is Te Tau Ihu o Te Waka a Maui — 'The Prow of the Canoe of Maui'. Legend has it that Maui was fishing with his brothers one day when he pulled up a gigantic fish, which became the North Island. His brothers were jealous of the feat and capsized the waka, which then became the South Island, and the detailed carving on the prow formed the Marlborough Sounds.

Archaeological records show that Maori settled the sounds in the fourteenth century. The first European to see the sounds was Abel Tasman, who spent Christmas there in 1642, but neither he nor any of his crew set foot ashore.

Explorer Captain James Cook anchored the *Endeavour* in Ship Cove, at the start of the trail, on 15 January 1770 to restock water, food and wood supplies. The ship needed maintenance and repairs, so he set up a long-term camp on shore, planting vegetable gardens and building an enclosure for pigs. Cook wrote in his journal on 6 February 1770: 'The number of inhabitants hardly exceeds 3 or 400 people, they leive dispers'd along the shores in search of their daly bread, which is fish and firn roots for they cultivate no part of the lands.'

An engraving of a Maori settlement in Queen Charlotte Sound by an early French navigator.

Cook returned to this sheltered cove another four times between 1770 and 1777. He also discovered a plant (Cook's scurvy grass) that had enough vitamin C in it to cure the scurvy among his crew. The cove is now marked by a monument, shelter, toilets and interpretation boards.

Two weeks after landing at Ship Cove, Cook climbed to the top of the nearby Motuara Island, raised the flag and claimed British sovereignty.

Later, the area was frequented by early whalers, but it was farming that became the major livelihood of the pioneers, who cleared most of the forest in the sounds. From 1864, the land at Anakiwa was farmed by Cradock and Harriet Beauchamp, great-uncle and -aunt to Katherine Mansfield. Farming the steep slopes had marginal success, however, and as the soil fertility dropped, the battle with gorse increased. Most of the land around the track has since reverted to low manuka forest, a natural stage in forest regeneration. A few patches of tall beech forest remain, most notably just north of Anakiwa.

The Beauchamps built a guest house at Anakiwa, which operated until 1962, when it was purchased by Outward Bound New Zealand, an outdoor education centre that has since run courses attended by tens of thousands of people.

Portage gained its name because Maori are said to have dragged their canoes over Torea Saddle to avoid a long and dangerous journey between Queen Charlotte and Kenepuru sounds. Maori had many settlements in the sounds as the sheltered waters made for easy travel and offered an abundance of kai moana (seafood). Early European pioneers even considered building a canal through Te Mahia Saddle to transport wool and livestock from Kenepuru Sound to Picton.

Queen Charlotte Track evolved over a century. In the 1880s, settlers built several short walking tracks between bays that were subsequently upgraded to be suitable for horses.

Double trouble on the Queen Charlotte Track.

It wasn't until January 1981, however, that these 'connectors' were merged into a single continuous run from Ship Cove to Anakiwa. The final section was the work of Outward Bound, who put in around 10,000 work days on the track. Mountain bikers ventured onto the track as early as 1986.

However, DOC budget cuts in the late 1980s led to a lack of maintenance, and the gorse soon closed parts of the track. In the early 1990s, local DOC staff decided to reopen the track and give it one name — the Queen Charlotte Walkway. But they needed help.

In the summer of 1992–93, the Royal New Zealand Air Force provided 120 volunteers over a two-week period. They camped near the trail and did shifts with 60 workers at a time. Local landowners, particularly Rod Eatwell, also helped by providing land, and track-clearing expertise. Since it was reopened and rebranded as the Queen Charlotte Track, the number of people using the track has grown, and in March 2013, the track was added to the New Zealand Cycle Trail network. The track is mostly used by walkers.

FOOD AND ACCOMMODATION

Picton Loads of shops and accommodation: www.visitpicton.co.nz

Camp Bay Punga Cove Resort, phone 03 579 8561, www.pungacove.co.nz; Mahana Lodge, phone 03 579 8373, www.mahanalodge.co.nz; Noeline's Homestay, phone 03 579 8375, www.thevilla.nz/homestay

Portage Debretts Pelorus, phone 03 573 4522, www.debretts-pelorus.com; Portage Resort Hotel, phone 0800 762 442 or 03 573 4309, www.portage.co.nz; Treetops Backpackers, phone 03 573 4404, email staytreetops@xtra.co.nz

Mistletoe Bay Eco Village, with basic food supplies, phone 03 573 4048, www.mistletoebay.co.nz

Te Mahia Bay Te Mahia Bay Resort (1 km off the track, but highly recommended), phone 03 573 4089, www.temahia.co.nz

Anakiwa Anakiwa 401 accommodation and Green Caravan cafe, phone 03 574 1388, www.anakiwa401.co.nz; YHA Anakiwa Lodge, phone 03 574 2115, www.anakiwa.co.nz

Momorangi Bay Momorangi Bay Campground and cafe/takeaways, phone 03 573 7865, www.doc.govt.nz or email momorangi.camp@xtra.co.nz, www.doc.govt.nz

SHORTCUTS AND DETOURS

Anakiwa Track Those short on time can drive to Anakiwa and ride up to Te Mahia Saddle and back. That is a 24-km trip, taking about 3 hours, through some of the best forest on the track. However, it is also the busiest section of the track.

The Kenepuru Epic Fit cyclists keen to stretch their legs can ride Queen Charlotte Drive and Kenepuru Road to Kenepuru Saddle and then back along the Queen Charlotte Track. From Anakiwa, the round trip is close to 100 km and can be completed comfortably in two days, or, it can be completed uncomfortably in two days from Picton. This saves the cost of the boat trip and covers some of the most scenic road riding in New Zealand.

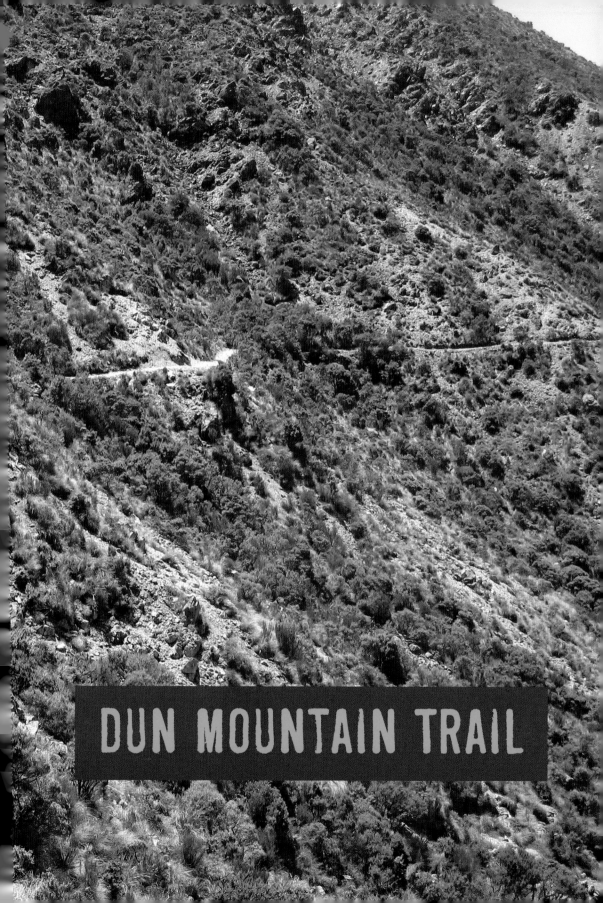

DUN MOUNTAIN TRAIL

The Dun Mountain Trail is a stunning one-day mountain-bike ride crossing a landscape of outstanding natural beauty and fascinating history.

From Nelson city, it follows New Zealand's first railway line, climbing at an easy gradient through beech forest to a large clearing at a shelter called Third House. From there, the railway line continues, but the forest becomes stunted and is suddenly left behind as you enter a dramatic landscape, beaten by the elements and devoid of almost any significant vegetation — a place where building a railway line seems crazy. The tracks were laid down in 1862, by those in search of not gold but chromite. They never found enough to bankroll their misguided endeavour, and the railway line, which ends at Coppermine Saddle, was only used for a few years.

From the saddle, a massive downhill leads to the Maitai Dam, where Nelson city stores its water. Apart from the obvious — gravity is suddenly your best friend — you will also notice that the gradient is steeper and trail surface rougher. Those with full suspension bikes will love it, but others will have to take it easy and be ready to pick their way through a slalom course of rocks. From the dam, the trail follows the water pipeline towards Nelson, before dropping through forest onto a gentle country road that drifts down valley, right back to the city centre.

SUMMARY

Start and end point Nelson
Distance 45 km
Likely time 4–7 hours
Grading Grade 3 (Intermediate) from Nelson city up to Coppermine Saddle; Grade 4 (Advanced) from Coppermine Saddle down to Maitai Valley
Surface 50% historic rail trail, 40% single track, 5% sealed road, 5% gravel road
Bike type Mountain bike
Map A trail map is available from the Nelson i-SITE
Trail website www.nzcycletrail.com
In emergencies Up to 50% of the trail has cellphone coverage (the area close to Nelson)
Bike hire and tours Trail Journeys Nelson, phone 0800 292 538, trailjourneysnelson. co.nz; Biking Nelson, phone 0800 224 532, www.bikingnelson.co.nz; Crank House Nelson (bike hire and repair), 114 Hardy Street, phone 03 548 1666, www.crankhouse.co.nz
Getting there Nelson is 110 km (1 hour 45 minutes) from Picton and 415 km (5 hours) from Christchurch. The trail is signposted for cyclists from the Nelson i-SITE

HIRA FOREST

Maitai Valley Rd

Sunday Hole
(swimming)

NELSON

Maitai R.

Brook St

Maitai Valley
Motor Camp

Maitai R.

Maitai Dam

P

Tantragee
Saddle

Cummins Spur

4-way
intersection

Third House

Wooded Pk

Maitai R. South

Dun
Mountain
1129m

BARNICOAT RANGE

Windy Pt

Coppermine
Saddle 878m

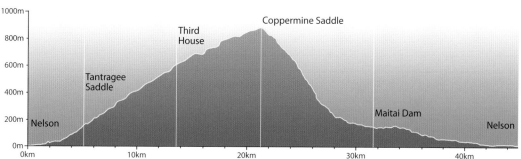

ROUTE DESCRIPTION

Nelson to Coppermine Saddle

21 km, 2.5–4 hours, Grade 3– (Intermediate)

From the Nelson i-SITE, take the signposted cycle route to the start of the trail, 1.5 km away (just past 135 Brook Street). There you will find an interpretation board (but virtually no car parking, so leave your car behind).

The first few kilometres of the trail are known as Codgers Track, because this section was reopened by a group of old codgers working as volunteers about 10 years ago. Follow the easy climb for 20 minutes till you pop out on the gravel Tantragee Road. Ride up this road for 300 metres and then veer right at the Dun Mountain Trail sign. The area around this part of the rail trail was first farmed, then planted in pines, which were logged in 2009–10. It is now being left to naturally revert to native forest.

After about an hour's riding on an easy gradient, you'll come to a well-signposted four-way intersection. Follow the Dun Mountain track straight ahead — through lovely beech forest, all the way to Third House. Sitting at the top of a grassy clearing, this shelter overlooks Tasman Bay and is a rewarding goal in itself.

From Third House, you have three good options: return the way you came (the easiest option), carry on to Coppermine Saddle and then retrace your tyre tracks (a good intermediate option), or carry on over Coppermine Saddle to complete the full loop.

For the second and third options, leave the Third House clearing on the signposted Dun Mountain Trail. Do not take any minor tracks off to the side, as they are all epic. The old rail trail has a few short washouts here and there, but is 99 per cent rideable. You can still see the odd railway sleeper — just a few of the 24,000 that were laid down. Not long before breaking out above the tree line, you'll cross a prominent spur, which was the site of Fourth House. On stormy days this is the last sheltered resting spot. Shortly after, the track becomes rougher and the vegetation suddenly stunted by the poisonous ultramafic soils below. There are signposts clearly marking the site of Windy Point, and stunning views on a clear day.

Windy Point is a good place to reassess the weather — you've got another hour of exposure above the bush line to complete this marathon. If the weather looks good, then carry on for 2 km, across the rocky landscape to Coppermine Saddle (878 metres).

Coppermine Saddle to Nelson
24 km, 2–3 hours, Grade 4 (Advanced)
From the large signboard at Coppermine Saddle, follow the well-formed trail as it swings and dips down towards the sun-bathed Maitai Valley 10 km away. This is one of the longest mountain-bike downhills in the country. There are a few rough stream crossings, lots of switchbacks and countless places to take stunning photos. After several kilometres the trail leaves the mineral belt and re-enters tall native forest.

Eventually you'll reach, and cross, the Maitai River South Branch via an arched wooden bridge. From here, there's even more sweet riding to a T-intersection above the main Maitai River. Turn left to follow 3 km of narrow track beside Nelson's water pipeline, finishing with a particularly flowing section of single track that ends at the gravelled Maitai Valley Road.

Turn left at Maitai Valley Road and coast down past the motor camp, and a few large picnic areas beside the river. Just past the motor camp there is an option to follow signposts up and over Tantragee Saddle and then down the Codgers Track back to Brook Street. Otherwise, it's about another 20–30 minutes' pedalling gently down valley to the centre of the sunshine capital, Nelson.

First stop on the way to Third House, Dun Mountain.

TRAIL TALES

Early Maori frequently travelled up the Brook Valley and on to the mineral belt. There they dug out pakohe (argillite) and shattered it with large boulders from the Nelson Boulder Bank to create sharp adzes and other tools that could be traded throughout the country.

The first European residents of Nelson named Dun Mountain for its colour, taking the word 'dun' from the Old English word meaning brown. Dun Mountain attracted mineral-hunting geologists throughout the 1850s and beyond. In 1859, an Austrian geologist, Ferdinand von Hochstetter, discovered that the mountain was made of a rock particularly dense in two minerals: olivine and chromite. Hochstetter named the new rock 'dunite' after the name of the mountain.

In 1853, 20 London speculators invested £10,000 to form a company to mine copper on Dun Mountain. They knew they would need a railway line to transport minerals to Nelson's port, and so rails were shipped from England and arrived in 1858. By that time it was known that there was virtually no copper, but deposits of chromite had been discovered. Chromite was popular for colouring dyes, as it replaced the poisonous alternative of arsenic.

In 1860, engineers William Doyne and Abraham Fitzgibbon arrived in Nelson to scope out a railway up Dun Mountain. They soon dismissed the option of taking the rail up the Maitai Valley and chose Brook Valley instead. Doyne used an aneroid barometer to

Dun Mountain Railway, Junction Saddle, 1862.

determine the height of the main points between Brook Street and a chromite seam near Windy Point, and he calculated a grade of 1:20.

Construction took place in two parts: the long and difficult section climbing through the bush-covered hills first, followed by the 4.4-km flat section to Nelson city and the port.

Most of the railway workers were ex-gold miners. They worked with pick and shovel and lived in tents beside the railway line during its construction. Around 65 men worked on the 6-km section from the chromite mines near Windy Point down to Third House, while another 100 men built the 11-km section between Third House and Brook Street.

At a cost of £75,000 to construct, the 21.5-km railway used more than 24,000 wooden sleepers provided by local sawmills. The first rails were laid in September 1861 and the last ones were hammered in five months later, in January 1862. In that first year of mining, 3843 tons of chromite were transported by rail and sail to English dye companies. Over the following two years, half that amount was extracted, and then the deposits dwindled to nothing.

While the mine was in full swing, rail wagons were drawn by horse (beating New Zealand's first steam train by nearly two years). The horses pulled empty wagons uphill to

Coppermine Saddle. Once there, the horses were unhitched and taken back down to Brook Street to rest. Meanwhile, the chromite ore was loaded into wagons and gravity-propelled down the mountain, under the control of a brakeman. It took just over two hours to descend to Brook Valley. There were more than 700 corners on the trip and derailments were common. As a result, the brakemen were forbidden on threat of dismissal from completing the trip in any quicker time.

At this time, Third House was the site of a two-storeyed set of stables, and not far from Coppermine Saddle was the mine manager's house and miners' accommodation.

When the Dun Mountain Railway Company applied for permission to take a rail line across Nelson's city streets and through to the port, the provincial council and government acquiesced on the proviso that the company run a regular passenger train. The company agreed, and on 3 May 1862, opened the horse-drawn City Bus Service from Trafalgar Street to the port. And so New Zealand's first public rail transport was created.

The deposits of chromite ran out surprisingly quickly. By January 1866, the mining engineer Joseph Cook had the unpleasant task of informing the directors of the company that 'the present condition and future prospects of your mine are extremely unsatisfactory'.

The company ceased mining operations, but the rail continued to be used for bus excursions to the mineral belt and for transporting firewood, timber, lime, gravel and flagstones, and the City Bus Service was kept alive for another 30 years. But when the City Bus failed in 1901, the line was closed, and in 1907 the rails were dismantled.

The disused railway line became a popular walkway, and in the 1980s, pioneer mountain bikers took to the tracks. Considerable upgrading work between 2008 and 2011 made the Dun Mountain Trail fully rideable, and in November 2011 it became the third New Zealand Cycle Trail to officially open.

FOOD AND ACCOMMODATION

Nelson Plenty of accommodation, shops, bike rentals, food: www.nelsonnz.com. There is a holiday park with cabins on Maitai Valley Road near the end of the trail. Maitai Valley Motor Camp, phone 03 548 7729, www.maitaivmc.co.nz

SHORTCUTS AND DETOURS

Third House and back This popular 2–3-hour, 24-km, easy ride simply goes from the start of the trail beside 135 Brook Street, up to Third House and back the same way. This is the easiest section of the Dun Mountain Trail. Near the bottom you will pass through the Codgers Mountain Bike Park. It is well worth exploring on the return journey if you enjoy narrow, challenging tracks.

GREAT TASTE TRAIL

For a leisurely cycling holiday, in a region famous for wine, food, art and fashion, you can't beat the Great Taste Trail. There are so many things to see and do, you could easily stretch this two- or three-day trip into a week and wonder where the time has gone.

The Great Taste Trail has two excellent multi-day options — the full loop for keen cyclists, and the Coastal Route for those who want to really cruise and spend time taking in the sights. Both rides start from Nelson city, or the airport.

The full 175-km loop is best done in a clockwise direction. From Nelson, it heads south past the airport, through the small town of Brightwater, to Wakefield. From there, it climbs over Dovedale Saddle to Woodstock and flies down to Motueka or Kaiteriteri, before heading back to Nelson via Mapua.

The 77-km Coastal Route also starts from Nelson, then just south of the airport it heads west, skirting around the Waimea Estuary and across farmland and Rabbit Island to Mapua. From Mapua it heads to Motueka via Ruby Bay and Tasman View Road. The final section heads around the coast at Motueka and through Riwaka to Kaiteriteri. From there, a shuttle can take you back to Nelson.

The Great Taste Trail has more cycle-friendly businesses supporting it than any other trail. The region is famous for good weather, great scenery, creative arts, award-winning wineries, orchards and the World of Wearable Art and Classic Cars Museum.

SUMMARY

Start and end point Nelson
Distance 175 km full loop; 77 km Coastal Route; 14 km Spooners Tunnel Route
Likely time 2–4 days
Grading Mostly Grade 2 (Easy) cycle path, with some Grade 3 (Intermediate) country
    roads to complete the full loop
Surface A mix of smooth asphalt path, through to gravel road
Bike type Mountain bike, cycle-touring bike or comfort/hybrid bike
Map Pick up a pamphlet map from the Nelson i-SITE
Trail website www.heartofbiking.org.nz
In emergencies There is cellphone coverage on almost all of the trail
Bike hire and tours Nelson Cycle Hire (at Nelson Airport), phone 03 539 4193,
    www.nelsoncyclehire.co.nz; Biking Nelson, phone 0800 224 532,
    www.bikingnelson.co.nz; The Gentle Cycling Company (bike hire and tours),
    phone 0800 WE BIKE (932 453), www.gentlecycling.co.nz; Trail Journeys Nelson,
    phone 0800 292 538, trailjourneysnelson.co.nz; Wheelie Fantastic
    (bike hire and transport), 0800 2 CYCLE (29253), www.wheeliefantastic.co.nz

Great Taste Trail

Kaiteriteri

Tasman Bay

60

Riwaka

Brooklyn

Motueka

ARTHUR RANGE

West Bank Rd

Motueka R.

Ngatimoti

Tasman

60

Ruby Bay

Woodstock

ferry

Thorpe

Mapua

Rabbit Is.

Dovedale

NELSON

Stanley Brook

Dovedale Rd

6

Trail under
construction

Dovedale Hill
Summit 326m

Waimea
Estuary

Richmond

Pigeon Valley Rd

Tapawera

6

Brightwater

Wai-iti Domain

Wakefield

...va R.

Kohatu

6

Belgrove

6

GORDON RANGE

...ris Gully Reserve

Spooners Tunnel

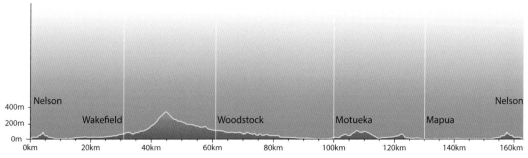

Easy riding just past Richmond.

Getting there Nelson is 110 km (1 hour 45 minutes) from Picton and 415 km (5 hours) from Christchurch. Nelson Airport is right beside the trail, with a bike-hire company on site (see Nelson Cycle Hire) and a new bike assembly area.

Trail transport Mapua to Rabbit Island Ferry, phone 03 540 3095 or 027 473 2888, www.mapuaferry.co.nz to check sailing times before your trip

ROUTE DESCRIPTION

Nelson to Wakefield

31 km, 3–4 hours, Grade 2 (Easy)

From the Nelson i-SITE, ride west on Halifax Street, then south on the St Vincent Street cycle path to Totara Street. Take the Railway Reserve cycle path for a couple of kilometres, then ride down Beatson Road to a roundabout.

At the roundabout, hop onto the footpath on the right side of the road and, around the corner, ride down the right-hand side of Whakatu Drive. This leads you over Langdon Bridge, crossing Annesbrook Drive. Follow the cycle signs carefully. They direct you over another bridge and then through a tunnel under SH6. Head towards Richmond via the signposted Coastal Route.

Nelson Airport is 8 km from Nelson i-SITE, and only a few hundred metres off the Great Taste Trail.

Just before Richmond (and 4 km from the airport), the path splits in two where there is a big trail signboard and a large root ball. The far side of the root ball has been carved into an armchair! To the right are Mapua and Motueka, and straight ahead are Brightwater and Wakefield.

After checking out the sign, ride straight ahead and within 5 minutes you will reach some traffic lights. Cross at the traffic lights, then turn right and cycle for 50 metres to the cycle path on your left. It is signposted to Brightwater (23 km from Nelson) and passes through vineyards, crosses a large suspension bridge and finally weaves through a few suburban streets — keep an eye out for trail markers as you enter Brightwater.

Most riders stop for a while at Headquarters Cafe and Bar, which is right beside the trail.

Through Brightwater, the trail weaves along a mix of streets and paths to a tunnel under

SH6 that takes you to Lord Rutherford Road. Just before the tunnel, on your right, is the Lord Rutherford Memorial, with lots of interpretation panels.

Ride through the tunnel and head south along Higgins Road to Edward Street, Wakefield. This small town has a great cafe, a supermarket and a park with toilets.

Wakefield to Woodstock
31 km, 2–4 hours, Grade 3 (Intermediate)
Cross SH6 at Edward Street and ride up Pigeon Valley Road. Several kilometres of this road is gravel, and it climbs 300 metres to a saddle in a pine forest. This temporary section of the Great Taste Trail is by far the toughest climb and will take 40–60 minutes.

Kiwi Station has been relocated to Tapawera.

From Dovedale Saddle, a long and scenic downhill leads to Woodstock — nothing more than a few houses these days. This is where you will meet the other end of the Great Taste Trail. Turn right at the Motueka Valley Highway, ride north for 300 metres and turn left to cross a bridge to West Bank Road.

Woodstock to Motueka
38 km, 2.5–4 hours, Grade 3 (Intermediate)
Head north down the valley on a quiet, tree-lined road. Here you'll find roadside stalls selling various kinds of produce such as fruit, eggs and jam (pay by cash only).

Exactly 7 km down the West Bank Road is a hall with toilets.

After 12 km, you have the option of riding 1 km off-route to a great swimming spot in the Motueka River, and another 500 metres to a real-fruit ice-cream shop near Ngatimoti. Just turn right down Peninsula Road to a narrow road bridge. The swimming spot is beside the bowling club. Leave the gate as you found it, and follow a narrow

Beside the road to Woodstock.

foot track to the river 50 metres away. For an ice cream or coffee (and chimes!), cross the road bridge and turn left down the Motueka Valley Highway for 650 metres. If it's open it will be signposted on your right.

Back at West Bank Road, continue to Brooklyn (27 km from Woodstock), then turn right onto Old Mill Road. Turn left up Anderson Road and right at Umukuri Road, which leads to a corner on SH60. Follow the main road right to head to Motueka. There is a cycleway on the side of the highway bridge over the Motueka River.

In future, an off-road trail will be built along the stopbank from Old Mill Road to the Motueka River Bridge.

Optional side trip to Kaiteriteri

14 km one way, 2 hours, Grade 3 (Intermediate)

At the Umukuri–SH60 intersection (4 km north of Motueka), turn left and ride 2 km down the main road to the Riwaka Park (with cafe opposite). Alternatively, if riding from Motueka to Riwaka, follow the cycle path and cycle route signs, which will take you around the back of Riwaka to the cafe and park.

From Riwaka, a path leads beside the highway to Goodall Road, then down an orchard driveway to a new bridge across the Riwaka River. It then follows the coast for a couple of kilometres, before passing under the Riwaka–Kaiteriteri Road at the southern entrance to Kaiteriteri Mountain Bike Park. From there, an easy mountain-bike track weaves through pine forest to the southern edge of Kaiteriteri.

Pigeon Valley Road.

Kaiteriteri has one of Nelson's most stunning beaches. During the summer holidays it is absolutely packed with swimmers and sunbathers. It has a huge holiday park, and is only 8 km from Marahau, the entrance to Abel Tasman National Park. Accommodation must be booked in advance, or you'll end up sleeping on the beach.

The Kaiteriteri Mountain Bike Park has a range of excellent tracks. The area also has fabulous sea kayaking and tramping in nearby Abel Tasman National Park. From Kaiteriteri, you can ride back to Nelson or catch a shuttle or boat back.

Motueka to Mapua
30 km, 1.5–2.5 hours, Grade 3 (Intermediate)
The cycle trail avoids the bustling centre of Motueka by following paths beside the scenic coast. There are plenty of side roads leading to the shops if you need anything, but the traffic is very busy in town.

Near the south end of town, the trail crosses the main road and leads to the popular T.O.A.D Hall Store and Cafe. Here you can enjoy healthy food, stock up on fresh produce, and there is a playground for kids.

From T.O.A.D Hall, take the cycle path beside High Street, Wildman Road and the Moutere Highway to the famous Riverside Cafe just 20 metres past Community Road. It's a lovely place to stop.

From there, ride up Community Road (it's a bit steep) and along Tasman View Road to Harley Road. Tasman View Road is an unmaintained road with a few hills to keep you fit.

Coast down Harley Road, and just before the bottom, turn right at the 'To Rush Lane' sign and nip through a tunnel under the main highway to a small park at Tasman.

About 600 metres from the park is a corner store with great pies and a gallery a few houses away.

From Tasman, follow Aporo Road southeast, past the cosy and quirky Jester House Cafe with its supposedly tame eels (don't tempt them with your fingers). An off-road path was built beside Aporo Road in 2014. Three km from Tasman, turn right up Marriages Road, which becomes Pomona Road, and veer left up Pine Hill Road West. At this dead end, there is a 300-metre-long path leading to the other section of Pine Hill Road. This brings you back to the main coastal road to Mapua. The cycle trail heads out to the coast briefly, before arriving at the vibrant village of Mapua.

Mapua to Nelson
33 km, 3–4 hours, Grade 2 (Easy)

From Mapua, catch the Mapua Ferry to Rabbit Island, a pine plantation with areas set aside for recreation. Follow a smooth gravel path through the forest and into a long picnic area beside the beach. It has tables, barbecues, changing sheds and toilets. Cycle signs then lead you across the island and back to the mainland. Turn left to cross Cotterell Road before following an easy gravel path over farmland, through the wildlife reserve at Pearl Creek and on to a large suspension bridge over the Waimea River.

From here, the trail follows Lower Queen Street for a few minutes, then turns left and

Boarding the ferry at Rabbit Island.

heads back to the coast. It weaves around the coastline and across the Waimea Estuary on boardwalks, a highlight of the trip. The trail reconnects with the main cycle path between Richmond and Nelson beside Whakatu Drive (just south of Richmond). Turn left and follow the cycle paths back to the city centre 12 km away.

Optional extra: Spooners Tunnel
14 km, 2 hours, Grade 2 (Easy)

At the time of writing (2017) there was a 5-km gap in the trail between Wakefield and Wai-iti Domain. Only experienced cyclists should attempt to ride State Highway 6 to bridge this trail gap. Hopefully by the time you get there, the trail will be complete.

From Wai-iti Doman (5 km south of Wakefield), follow the trail signs along a smooth path to Belgrove Tavern, 4.9 km away.

From Belgrove, the trail continues south for another 6 km to Spooners Tunnel. At 1.35 km long, this is the longest rail tunnel open to cyclists in the Southern Hemisphere. The tunnel is very cold and pitch black inside — lights are essential. Continue beyond the tunnel to Norris Gully Reserve (14 km from Wai-iti Domain), where the trail ended in 2017. It is likely that the trail will be extended 6 km to Kohatu in the summer of 2017–18. Kohatu has a cafe and accommodation.

The Belgrove Tunnel under construction, 1902.

Taking in the great views from the suspension bridge near Brightwater.

TRAIL TALES

The railway formation used by this trail has a tortuous history. From the 1860s, Nelsonians lobbied for a railway through to the Main Trunk Line and work began in 1871. The first 30 km, crossing the easiest terrain, opened in 1876. Work on extending the rail continued in fits and starts and as it approached the challenging Spooner Range, immigrants from China, Japan and Italy were brought in to maintain progress. The 1352-metre Spooners Tunnel opened in 1893 and the line as far as Kohatu (50 km from Nelson) was completed in 1897.

Construction of the railway continued slowly, was held up by World War I and finally stopped for good in January 1931, when the country entered the Great Depression. The line had made it to the Buller River. The missing link to the Main Trunk Line at Inangahua Junction was less than 70 km — a gap that would never be closed.

After World War II, the government's transport focus shifted to road building, and it was announced that the railway would close when the highways around the Nelson region were completed. This prompted a huge public outcry, culminating in a 12,000-signature petition urging the government to keep the line open. The government responded with an impossible challenge to the locals — guarantee an annual freight of 25,000 tons or the line would close.

The last scheduled train ran on 2 September 1955, and the rails were scheduled for removal later that month, with work to begin from Kiwi Station. Ruth Page led a group of nine women, including activist and future Labour MP Sonja Davies, on a sit-in on the line at Kiwi Station to prevent the rail's removal. When the demolition train arrived a week later, they were all arrested and the slow work of taking up the tracks and sleepers began.

These days, the Great Taste Trail follows parts of the original railway line, through the Railway Reserve in Nelson and on to Brightwater.

West of Nelson, the cycle trail skirts around the Waimea Inlet — the largest enclosed estuary in the South Island. It formed about 6500 years ago after the sea rose to its present level and created Tasman Bay.

The first Maori settled in this area over 600 years ago, around 1400. The land provided fertile ground for crops and the waterways through the inlet remained accessible even at low tide. Maori established extensive gardens in the area, adding charcoal to the soil to provide carbon and help absorb heat from the sun with its dark colour, encouraging crop growth.

Starting from the 1960s, about 179 ha of the Waimea Inlet were lost through sedimentation and land reclamation. The inlet that remains is internationally significant as an environment for 60 bird species, including migratory and rare species such as the bar-tailed godwit, the variable oystercatcher and the kotuku (white heron). Forest and Bird have done considerable habitat restoration, and since 2008, local walker Ian Jonson has been removing rubbish. In one year alone, he pulled 186 dumped tyres from the inlet.

In the middle of Waimea Inlet sits Moturoa, also known as Rabbit Island. It has been a recreation destination since the 1860s, when a horse and wagon regularly transported visitors across mud flats to the island for picnics, horse races along the flat beaches or shooting excursions (rabbits were introduced there in 1865). In 1909, the island was officially set aside for recreation, but this changed in 1920 when the majority was given over for pine plantation.

South of Waimea Estuary, the town of Brightwater was settled in 1855. Its name was chosen by Alfred Saunders, the owner of the local flax mill, from a hit song about the benefits of non-alcoholic drinks. Brightwater also became home to one of New Zealand's most famous scientists, Ernest Rutherford. Rutherford's discoveries about the nature of atoms provided the grounding principles for developments in nuclear science and earned him the 1908 Nobel Prize for Chemistry.

At the western end of the Great Taste Trail lies Kaiteriteri. Explorers from the New Zealand Company's Nelson expedition were the first Europeans to set foot on Kaiteriteri Cove in 1841. The explorers planned to develop a major settlement there, but after further exploration of the bay, they chose the current site of Nelson instead.

Nelson boomed and was proclaimed a city by royal charter in 1858, but Kaiteriteri was not forgotten. In 1916, local farmer Syd Rowling bought 136 acres of the beautiful bay, cleared the gorse and planted apple, pine and gum trees. On the side, he started a low-key camping business, which quickly became popular. Today, Kaiteriteri is one of New Zealand's top summer holiday destinations, and the main gateway for Abel Tasman National Park, established in 1942. Abel Tasman is the smallest of New Zealand's national parks but also its most popular — the options for tramping, kayaking and camping attract over 100,000 visitors every year.

FOOD AND ACCOMMODATION

There are over a hundred cycle-friendly businesses along the Great Taste Trail. Go to the trail website at www.heartofbiking.org.nz and take a look at the official partners under trip planning.

Nelson More cafes, supermarkets, cycle shops and accommodation than you could shake a stick at. Take your pick: www.nelsonnz.com

Richmond (beside the trail) Supermarket, cafe, takeaways, accommodation.

Wakefield Supermarket, cafe, takeaways, accommodation: Wakefield Hotel, 48 Edward Street, phone 03 541 8006; Dunpuffin Railway Cottages, phone 03 541 8265, www.dunpuffin.nz

Riwaka Cafe and accommodation: Eden's Edge Lodge (cycle-friendly accommodation), phone 03 528 4242, www.edensedge.co.nz

Motueka Shops, cafes, restaurants, accommodation: www.nelsonnz.com/i-Site/motueka-isite.html; Motueka Top 10 Holiday Park (also offers bike hire), phone 0800 668 835, www.motuekatop10.co.nz/motueka-cycle-hub.html

Kaiteriteri Cafe/restaurant, general store, accommodation and campground: Kaiteriteri Beach Motor Camp, www.experiencekaiteriteri.co.nz; Kaiteri Lodge, phone 0508 KAITERI or 03 527 8281, www.kaiterilodge.co.nz; Bethany Park Holiday Park, phone 03 527 8014, www.bethanypark.co.nz; Torlesse Motels, Little Kaiteriteri Beach, phone 03 527 8063, www.torlessemotels.co.nz

Mapua Shops, cafes, restaurants, accommodation: www.mapua.gen.nz/stay.html; Cats Pjamas B&B: phone 03 540 3404, www.cats-pjamas.com; Mapua Chalets,

The Headquarters Cafe and Bar in Brightwater.

phone 03 540 3310, www.mapuachalets.co.nz; The Gates Accommodation, phone 03 540 2793, www.thegates.co.nz

Belgrove Tavern and food, phone 03 541 8105

SHORTCUTS AND DETOURS

Most locals ride short sections of the Great Taste Trail. Here are two popular options:

The Coffee Run From anywhere in Nelson or Richmond, ride out to a cafe in Brightwater or Wakefield and back. This is an easy 2–4-hour, off-road ride with no transport issues. If the first cafe in Brightwater is packed (as it often is now), go to the next cafe just around the corner.

Rabbit Island For families with young kids we recommend driving to Rabbit Island, then riding 11 km to the western end of the island and catching the ferry across to Mapua for an ice cream and a swim before heading back. It's flat, easy and fun. Allow 2 hours' riding time and 1–2 hours for catching the ferry and checking out Mapua. Starting from the northwest end of Lower Queen Street is also a great option, extending the ride to Mapua by 20–30 minutes.

Weekend escape Grab a flight to Nelson. Grab a friend to ride with. Grab some bikes from the Nelson Cycle Hire office at the airport and start riding. It is 69 km to Kaiteriteri, via galleries, cafes, beaches and fabulous coastal scenery. You will take in most of the highlights of the Great Taste Trail, including Waimea Inlet, Rabbit Island, Mapua and Kaiteriteri Beach. A weekend allows an easy pace and time to explore at your leisure. Arrange a shuttle back to the airport with Nelson Cycle Hire (they can also book accommodation). Over summer you can also catch a sea shuttle between Kaiteriteri and Nelson (phone 0800 732 748, www.abeltasmanseashuttles.co.nz).

West Bank Road: a cycle tourer's dream.

ST JAMES CYCLE TRAIL

This tough but scenically stunning track provides skilled, fit riders with an opportunity to experience the raw beauty of the retired St James Station. Be warned though, this is not an easy cycle path. It requires river crossings and bike pushing in places and is suitable for experienced bikers only. The St James Cycle Trail is a back-country adventure for those wanting to get away from it all.

Hanmer Springs tourist resort, 130 km north of Christchurch, is the base for this ride. It offers fine restaurants, divine hot pools and an array of accommodation options. It is such a contrast to the world that lies ahead: majestic mountains, untouched rivers and forest-lined high-country lakes. Once you enter the St James, there are no shops, no cellphone coverage, not even a coffee cart! The best accommodation you can hope for may be the insect-proofed tent strapped to your carrier. This track is all about challenge, achievement and the great outdoors. If Barry Crump had been a mountain biker, he would have loved it. The track is often closed in winter because of deep snow.

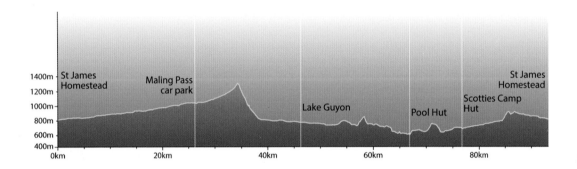

SUMMARY ·····································

Start point Maling Pass or St James Homestead (13 km north of Hanmer Springs)
End point St James Homestead
Distance 66 km point-to-point; or 93-km loop
Likely time 1–2 days
Grading Grade 4 (Advanced)
Surface 25% gravel road, 25% 4WD track, 50% single track
Bike type A mountain bike is essential
Map NZTopo50 BT24 Ada Flat. Also pick up the St James Cycle Trail DOC pamphlet
    from nearby i-SITEs or DOC offices
Trail website www.doc.govt.nz or www.nzcycletrail.com
In emergencies There is no cellphone coverage in the St James Station area. An
    emergency personal locator beacon (PLB) is recommended

L. Tennyson

Maling
Pass
1308m

Maling Pass car park

P

Tophouse Rd

Clarence R.

Lake Guyon Hut

L. Guyon

S T J A M E S   R A N G E

Fowlers
Pass

Fowlers Pass Track

Fowlers Hut

Waiau R.

bridge

Saddle Spur

Clarence R.

Homestead Loop

Edwards R.

Peters Pass 900m

Pool Hut

bridge

Peters Valley

Charlies
Saddle
754m

Scotties Camp Hut

P

St James Homestead

Tophouse Rd

Waiau R.

Jacks Pass

H A N M E R   R A N G E

St James Cycle Trail

i

HANMER SPRINGS

Bike hire Hanmer Springs Adventure Centre, phone 0800 FOUR FUN (0800 368 7386),
www.hanmeradventure.co.nz

Getting there Hanmer Springs is 133 km (1 hour 45 minutes) from Christchurch via
SH1, SH7 and SH7A. From Hanmer Springs, head out of town on Jacks Pass Road
and turn right onto Clarence Valley Road to climb over Jacks Pass to the Clarence
Valley. After descending into the Clarence Valley, turn left at Tophouse Road. The old
St James Homestead is on your left, 13 km from Hanmer Springs

Extra equipment If you are doing this as a 2-day trip you will need camping gear.
A tent is optional, but recommended, as the huts could be full

Trail transport For a lift from Hanmer Springs to the trail, contact St James Journeys,
phone 03 315 5086 or 027 315 6106, www.stjamesjourneys.co.nz

The semi-wild St James horses.

ROUTE DESCRIPTION

Optional Start: St James Homestead to Maling Pass car park

26 km, 1.5 hours, Grade 3 (Intermediate)

By starting from St James Homestead, which is the official end to the trail, and riding
26 km up a scenic gravel road, your car will be waiting for you at the end of the trip.
The historic homestead has a car-parking area, toilets and an information board. It is
also the start of the easy 3-hour Homestead Loop (see Shortcuts and Detours).

From the St James Homestead, head north along Tophouse Road for 26 km to the
Maling Pass car park on your left, 2 km before Lake Tennyson.

Maling Pass car park to Lake Guyon

20 km, 2–4 hours, Grade 3– (Intermediate)

Maling Pass car park is the official start of the St James Cycle Trail. An old farm track leads from the car park, through open tussock land, up to Maling Pass, an hour away. At 1308 metres, this pass marks the highest point on the trail. On the other side awaits a 30-minute downhill into the Waiau Valley.

Down in the valley, a purpose-built cycle trail branches off the 4WD track, and leads across grasslands and matagouri scrub to a signposted intersection. Approximately 15 minutes (2 km) away, on your left, lies the picturesque Lake Guyon, where a basic four-bunk hut awaits those who wish to stay overnight. It's also a welcome swimming spot on a hot summer's day.

From the car park to Lake Guyon is mostly downhill, so you may wish to continue to Pool Hut, another 2–4 hours away. However, this next part of the track is challenging in places and involves some 5- to 10-minute 'foot cycling' sections.

Remember to follow BLUE marker poles. Other tracks are marked with other colours.

Lake Guyon to Pool Hut

21 km, 2–4 hours, Grade 4 (Advanced)

From Lake Guyon, head back to the main track and continue following the blue marker poles down this broad valley. The track becomes a lot rougher, and after crossing the Waiau River on an impressive swing bridge, you will have to walk most of the way to the top of Saddle Spur. Some people get lost here as the marker poles are scarce. Keep your eyes peeled and follow your progress on the map.

There are great views from where you cross Saddle Spur, and it is mostly downhill or flat to Pool Hut, 5 km away.

The bridge near Pool Hut, with a great swimming spot below.

Riding into the massive Waiau Valley.

Pool Hut has four mattresses, but no cookers. It is not insect proof, and the small creek just behind the hut is a perfect breeding ground for sandflies. You may prefer to camp if you have an insect-proof tent. There are good spots closer to the river.

Pool Hut to Scotties Camp Hut
9 km, 1–2 hours, Grade 3+ (Intermediate)
About 5 minutes south of Pool Hut, there is another large swing bridge. The trail is often loose and rocky from here to Scotties Camp Hut with a few walks required over steep bluff sections. The exception is the final downhill from Charlies Saddle to the hut, which is smooth and fast.

There is a new bridge across the Edwards River just before the hut. Allow at least 1 hour to ride from Pool Hut to Scotties Camp.

Scotties Camp Hut to St James Homestead
17 km, 1.5–3 hours, Grade 3 (Intermediate)
From Scotties Camp Hut up to Peters Pass junction involves lots of easy 4WD track, several rough stream crossings and a long steep hill that some people will have to walk up. Give yourself at least 1 hour for this 10-km section.

There are two routes back to St James Homestead from Peters Pass junction. One follows a relatively boring 4WD track and the other is a fantastic new cycle trail. To take the fantastic route — why wouldn't you? — turn right at the junction and continue following blue marker poles down Peters Valley. The next 7 km was upgraded in early 2013 and is now the best section on the whole trail.

The trail officially ends at St James Homestead.

From the homestead car park it is 13 km (10 km of which is downhill) to Hanmer Springs, where cafes and hot pools await. On a fine day, the outstanding scenery is best appreciated from the saddle of your trusty steed.

TRAIL TALES

On Saturday 20 November 2010, the St James Cycle Trail became the first of the New Zealand Cycle Trail Great Rides to be opened. In 2008, the 78,196-ha St James Station had been purchased by the government for the princely sum of $40 million from the Stevenson family, who had owned it since 1927. The government's main aim was to protect the area from intensive farming and development and guarantee public access to a unique high-country wilderness, which includes the St James Walkway.

The property spans three mountain ranges and comprises a range of exceptional natural features, including glaciated valleys and moraine deposits, streams, wetlands, lakes and alpine tarns. The area also hosts over 400 indigenous plants and 30 native birds.

William Newcombe at Lake Guyon homestead, circa 1870.

As was the case with many large Canterbury stations, St James Station was an amalgamation of several smaller runs, starting with the Edwards Block, which was bought by G Edwards in 1862.

Little is known of these early runholders. Edwards would have operated his block as a cattle and sheep station, and it is thought that he built a cob homestead somewhere in the Edwards River Valley. Today, however, only remnants of cob fencing can be found scattered at various places throughout the valley.

The Lake Guyon homestead site still includes the remains of the cob homestead, the poplar trees planted as a shelter belt, the garden and orchard area with its rock walls, and the sheep dip and yards.

The St James Station of the Clarence River Valley was developed by J McArthur sometime in the 1880s. The homestead itself burnt down in 1947, but the original woolshed, the cookhouse and the stables remain intact.

The 'Count de la Pasture', whose family had fled the French Revolution, ran the original 8000-odd acres of the nearby St Helens lease and, at various stages, this run included much of the Molesworth Station, and the St James Station, as well as other runs. It is difficult to give precise dates to these acquisitions because the runholders changed so often and the lease sizes seemed to expand and contract with each block sale.

Finally, after decades of title changes, the Stevenson family bought the St James property in 1927 and remained the owners for 81 years. They began breeding the St James horse herd, which became known as a powerful semi-wild hunting type of horse with exceptional endurance — attributes highly prized by the farmers working the rugged high country of the South Island stations. Remnants of the herd can still be seen today, sometimes right beside the St James Cycle Trail.

Farmers in the early days endured isolation, loss of stock through extreme winter snowstorms, and pests in the form of rabbits. From Maling Pass to the north, you can still find the remains of a 125-km rabbit-proof fence that was completed in 1889 and extended from the Main Divide to the Pacific Coast.

The pioneering farmers were aware of and sought out the Hanmer hot springs as they drove stock on the route through to Canterbury. Maori also used the springs regularly on their trips back and forth from the West Coast, but the springs were only 'officially' discovered in 1859 by William Jones, a farm manager from Culverden. News of the luxurious pools spread quickly, and by 1871, the manager of the Jollies Pass Hotel had constructed a dressing shed close to the most popular pool. In 1897, the government built the first 'sanatorium' accommodation unit at the pools, and in 1918 confirmed Hanmer Springs as a tourist resort and hospital. Today it is a major tourist destination with 20 different pools including a swimming pool.

Riders heading off on the easy Homestead Loop.

FOOD AND ACCOMMODATION

Hanmer Springs Food, accommodation, bike hire: www.visithanmersprings.co.nz

St James Homestead Camping area, toilets and a day shelter: www.doc.govt.nz

Lake Guyon Hut costs $5/night (i.e. one hut ticket), www.doc.govt.nz

Pool Hut and Scotties Camp Huts are free, but they are very basic: www.doc.govt.nz

Camping This is the only New Zealand Cycle Trail that I took a tent on and was glad of it.
Waking in the hills is a special experience.

SHORTCUTS AND DETOURS

Homestead Loop An easy, 15-km, half-day ride starts and finishes at St James Homestead.
I recommend doing it in an anticlockwise direction to finish with the best 7 km of the
cycle trail. From the homestead, ride up Tophouse Road for 2.6 km, before turning left
onto a cycle trail, which cuts across to the 4WD track heading up to Peters Pass. From
Peters Pass, turn left again and follow the brilliant new track back down to
St James Homestead. Hot tip: There is one off-camber corner on the way down, which,
if you overcook, will have you eating dirt quicker than you can say 'green eggs and ham'.

Fowlers Pass Epic The Grade 5 (Expert) Fowlers Pass Track runs from Lake Guyon up over
a high alpine pass and down to Fowlers Hut beside Tophouse Road. Ride the top or
bottom half of the St James Cycle Trail to Lake Guyon and then over Fowlers Pass.
The downhill is arguably the best historic stock route to ride in the country. Beware
though, there are many challenges, and dozens of walking sections on the Fowlers
Pass Track. Fowlers Hut was built around 1890 to house the men brought in to control
the rabbit numbers in this area.

THE OLD GHOST ROAD

The Old Ghost Road is the most spectacular and wild of all the cycle trails. From the ghost town of Lyell, deep in the Buller Gorge, it climbs steadily through native forest on a mining trail built in the 1870s. You will sweat your way past massive slips and archaeological sites, up to the stunted forest of the tree line, before breaking out on to what feels like the top of the world. The endless views stop you in your tracks, demanding to be admired — on a fine day. On a bad day, you'll cower from the elements, reaching for every layer of clothing you have brought, because a storm on the Lyell tops is a powerful experience.

Beyond Ghost Lake, the trail narrows and descends through alpine scrub to Dragon's Creek before crossing a saddle and climbing over the Skyline Ridge, with its granite armadillos. From there a flight of wooden steps leads to a long, flowing descent, through native forest and across several rivers and streams to 'earthquake country', where huge rocks dominate the landscape.

The last leg of this journey follows the mighty Mokihinui River as the trail clings to the side, passing the remains of mining settlements, almost completely reclaimed by the forest, before ending just a few kilometres from the welcoming Seddonville Village.

SUMMARY

Start point Lyell, Buller Gorge

End point Seddonville

Distance 88 km

Likely time 2–3 days

Grading Grade 3 (Intermediate) to Grade 5 (Expert)

Surface Gravel and dirt

Bike type A mountain bike is essential, full suspension recommended

Map New Topo map The Old Ghost Road

Trail website www.oldghostroad.org.nz to make bookings

In emergencies There is virtually no cellphone coverage on the trail. An emergency personal locator beacon (PLB) is recommended

Bike hire Habitat Sports, Westport, phone 03 788 8002, www.habitatsports.co.nz; Buller Adventures, Westport, phone 0508 486 877, www.bulleradventures.com

Getting there The trail starts at the ghost town of Lyell, beside SH6 in the Buller Gorge. It is 34 km west of Murchison and 50 km inland from Westport. Driving time is 4 hours from Christchurch and 2 hours from Nelson

Trail transport A shuttle from Westport to and from the two ends of the trail is offered by Bazil's Hostel, phone 03 789 6410, www.bazils.com; Hike n Bike Shuttle, phone 027 446 7876, www.hikenbikeshuttle.co.nz; and Habitat Sports and Buller Adventures (see above for contact details)

Extra equipment Sleeping bag, good outdoor clothes, first-aid kit and food

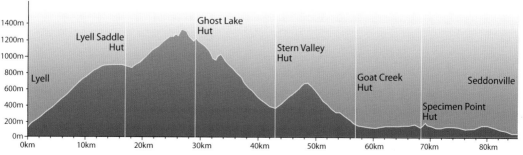

High-altitude riding on the Lyell Range.

ROUTE DESCRIPTION

Lyell car park to Lyell Saddle Hut

17.5 km, 2.5–3.5 hours, Grade 3 (Intermediate)

From the Lyell car park, ride to The Old Ghost Road sign and then walk down some steps to a high suspension bridge. On the far side, a mining track built in the 1880s climbs through beech forest at a gradient of four degrees. The Eight-Mile historic site is a lovely spot for your first rest. There are information boards and historic relics to look at.

The second good spot to stop is at a particularly massive slip. From the edge, you can look right up the Lyell Valley to the Lyell tops where you are heading. Walk carefully across the slip because a fall off the side would mean certain death. The hut near Lyell Saddle is about 1 hour away, and the gradient becomes easier and easier.

The hut is 5 minutes before the saddle. Look out for a side track on your left that climbs to the hut 100 metres away. Next to the main hut, there are a couple of 'sleepout' huts that can also be booked through the trail website.

Lyell Saddle Hut to Ghost Lake Hut

11.5 km, 2–3 hours, Grade 4 (Advanced) to Grade 5 (Expert)

From Lyell Saddle Hut, the track climbs for 5 km to the bush edge. It then sidles south of Mount Montgomery, and north of Rocky Tor. There is an 800-metre section called the

Alpine Goat Track which is Grade 5 — there is no room for error.

From there, the track leads past the Tombstone and Heavens Door, mostly downhill to Ghost Lake Hut. Ghost Lake is in a natural alpine amphitheatre. This section of trail faces the full brunt of wind, rain and snow, so go well prepared.

Ghost Lake Hut to Stern Valley Hut

13 km, 2–2.5 hours downhill, Grade 4 (Advanced) to Grade 5 (Expert)

From Ghost Lake to the Skyline Steps the track is narrow, loose and steep in places. Be prepared to walk.

The 290 Skyline Steps lead down to a fantastic section of track, flowing downhill most of the way to Stern Valley.

Stern Valley Hut to Goat Creek Hut

14 km, 2–3 hours, Grade 3 (Intermediate)

From Stern Valley Hut, the trail climbs a gentle valley to twin lakes at point 471 and then weaves through a massive boulder field called The Boneyard before cresting Solemn Saddle. It then follows Goat Creek down to Goat Creek Hut (DOC, three bunks, no charge), 5 minutes off the main track.

Goat Creek Hut to Specimen Point Hut

A curious South Island Robin.

11.5 km, 1–2 hours, Grade 3 (Intermediate)

From Goat Creek Hut, the trail heads through forest for another 10 minutes before crossing the stunning Mokihinui River South Branch.

From the crossing, the trail weaves down river flats and through majestic podocarp forest to Mokihinui Forks Hut. DOC did a great job of upgrading this old New Zealand Forest Service hut, which is a popular destination for hunters and fishers.

The Old Ghost Road then heads west for a few kilometres to Specimen Point Hut (built specifically for the cycle trail and offering excellent views of the river). Specimen Point also has a couple of private 'sleepout' huts that can be booked through the trail website.

Specimen Point Hut to Seddonville

20 km, 3–4 hours, Grade 3 (Intermediate)

From Specimen Point Hut, the trail is back onto the historic mining track built over a century ago. Much of this track was destroyed by landslides in the 1929 Murchison earthquake. Two men died on the track when the quake struck, and are assumed to have been buried in one of the landslides triggered by the quake. The once dangerous 'Suicide Slips' are now crossed on long land bridges, but there are still two walking sections along precipitous bluffs. Mostly though, it is easy pedalling along a fast trail.

When you reach the car park, it is a cruisy 3 km down a gravel road to Seddonville, where you can hang out at the pub or the holiday park.

TRAIL TALES

Gold was discovered in the Lyell area long before gold-feverish Europeans arrived. Maori often saw it during their search for pounamu. In 1862, a Maori prospector named Eparara, along with four others, found a 'dumbbell' shaped nugget of gold weighing in at 19.5 oz when they were fossicking up Lyell Creek.

Once the rumour was out, thousands of men abandoned older gold mines to flock to the Lyell. Despite being inhospitable terrain, a town sprang up and boomed to a population of 2000. By 1863, miners had found many huge nuggets, with one group of five Irishmen claiming to have uncovered 1.4 kg of gold in five days — equivalent to $100,000 for a week's work!

Miners converged from around the world — Greece, Italy, Switzerland, England, India and America — and 12 men quickly organised themselves into a 'Vigilance Committee' to control theft and the size of claims. On two occasions at least, they threatened some Australian miners with lynching for attempting to take Maori prospectors' finds.

Lyell was no easy place to live, and for a long time it could only be accessed from the epic Buller River. Partly in response to so many drownings in the river, a road was built up the gorge to Lyell. By 1874, Lyell had six hotels, a school, a blacksmith, and several stores including a bakery. The bakery was owned by Frederick Ulmer, whose son Ron, grandson Gary and great-granddaughter Sarah all became champion cyclists.

As business boomed, mining companies turned their attention to the quartz reefs located behind the township. They developed a water-powered piston battery to bash the quartz and extract the gold hidden within it. This new method of mining provided stable work for many of the gold diggers and quickly became the main form of mining in the area. The largest mine was the United Alpine with a 20-head battery. It was situated 6.5 km up Lyell Creek and opened in 1874. The mine ran for over 30 years.

However, the town's water supply was under constant pressure, and when a fire struck in 1874, there was not enough water to contain it. Eighteen buildings burnt to the ground in that fire, and only a few were rebuilt as by this time most of the easy gold had been claimed, and everyone saw the writing on the wall.

Most mining had ceased in the area by 1913 and a large proportion of the population had dispersed, but the Post Office Hotel and a small number of loyal residents remained. In June 1929, a magnitude 7.8 earthquake struck the area. No buildings in Lyell suffered serious damage but the town was completely cut off by slips. Most people were now convinced that Lyell was too difficult a place to live in. The final blow fell in 1963 when the hotel burnt to the ground and the die-hard residents soon moved away.

At the other end of the trail, the Mokihinui boasts an equally colourful history. The valley was originally used by Maori as an inland route to Karamea via Rough and Tumble Creek.

On one occasion, a raiding party making its way down the coast was chased by Ngai Tahu Maori. The raiders reached a large unnamed river. Their leader, concerned about splitting his group and leaving a small number vulnerable to attack from the chasing party, commanded his warriors to construct a raft large enough to take the whole group in one go. Thus the river was named Mokihinui, meaning 'big reed raft'.

The settlement of Lyell, circa 1890.

They left the raft on the banks of the river, and it was reported to have been used to help with river crossings — when Charles Heaphy first travelled through the area in the early 1840s with his guide Kehu, they fully expected to use the raft themselves.

But there was a more novel form of transport across the river. Between 1865 and 1880, during the early gold-prospecting era, a flying fox/chair was built. On 23 January 1884, the *West Coast Times* reported on the 'dangerous state of the Rough and Tumble chair',

One of the bridges over the Suicide Slips, Mokihinui Gorge.

but it wasn't until the early 1900s that it was replaced by a large iron bridge, the remains of which can still be seen lying in the river today.

Gold was discovered in the area in 1866, at the mouth of the Mokihinui River. Mining operations soon spread up valley, the mines having colourful names such as Red Queen, Old Derby, Guiding Star, Invincible, and Southern Lights. The Red Queen continued to be mined until the 1940s, with the main focus around the Maori Creek and Jones Creek area. Historic plans show that a settlement named Seatonville once existed in this area, and if you keep your eyes peeled while riding down the gorge you will see two pelton wheels, rock walls and other reminders of the lively past of this area.

FOOD AND ACCOMMODATION

On the trail There are several huts along the trail. Two of them (Mokihinui Forks Hut and Goat Creek Hut) are basic DOC huts. The other four huts (Specimen Point, Lyell Saddle, Ghost Lake and Stern Valley) have communal huts as well as 'sleepouts'. These huts should be booked well in advance at www.oldghostroad.org.nz and the DOC huts through www.doc.govt.nz/parks-and-recreation/places-to-stay/

Seddonville Seddonville Hotel, phone 03 782 1828, seddonvillehotel.co.nz; Seddonville Holiday Park, phone 03 782 1314, www.seddonvillepark.co.nz; Rough and Tumble Lodge, phone 03 782 1337, www.roughandtumble.co.nz

Granity Ghost Lodge, phone 021 267 5102, www.ghostlodge.nz; Absolute Beach House, phone 03 782 8993; Drifters Cafe (food and internet), phone 03 782 8087 (Wed to Sun 9 a.m. to 4 p.m.); Miners on Sea and Tommy Knockers (food and accommodation), phone 0508 646 377 or 03 782 8664, www.minersonsea.co.nz

Westport Lots of food and accommodation, and a bike shop: www.westport.nz.com; one budget bike-friendly business is Bazil's Hostel, phone 03 789 6410, www.bazils.com

Murchison Plenty of accommodation and places to eat: www.visitmurchison.nz

The old Lyell dray road.

SHORTCUTS AND DETOURS

In and Out The two most obvious shortcut options are to ride from either end for as long as you like and then turn around and head back out. If you are fit and love the alpine zone, then start from Lyell. If you prefer flattish tracks, or really like rivers, then start from the Seddonville end. Both are fantastic day rides during fine weather, or you may want to do overnighters. Lyell to Ghost Lake Hut is 60 km return. Seddonville to Goat Creek Hut is also 60 km return, but has much less climbing.

The Roundabout The Ghost Road Roundabout doubles the length of The Old Ghost Road. Start from Lyell and ride to Seddonville on The Old Ghost Road. That will take 2–3 days. Then ride the Charming Creek Walkway to Granity, down the highway to Waimangaroa and over the Denniston Plateau to Lyell. All up, you will need 4–5 days. Full details are in *Classic New Zealand Cycle Trails*.

WEST COAST
WILDERNESS TRAIL

ombine beautiful forests, lakes and rivers with fascinating pioneering history and genuine West Coast hospitality, and you have the Wilderness Trail. It is one of the most interesting trails in the country, with something different to see and experience around almost every corner.

From Greymouth Station, the trail follows the Grey River to the coast before tracing the restless Tasman Sea south to the Taramakau River and the Bridge Bar and Cafe. After a well-earned drink, you'll head inland to Kumara, a historic mining town that is being rejuvenated by the cycle trail. It's an ideal stop for the first night.

From Kumara, the trail really lives up to its name as it heads towards the Alps, weaving through forest, past lakes and over wild rivers. It is a full day of discovery en route to Cowboy Paradise, a replica western town, complete with saloon, boardwalks and a shooting range.

The third day is mostly downhill, travelling beside the mighty Arahura River, over a small hill to Lake Kaniere and then beside a historic water race to the relaxing cafe and accommodation at Hurunui Jacks, a destination renowned for good art and food. From there, the final leg takes you to Hokitika, the tourist capital of the coast.

The final day has more highlights, as the trail takes to the Mananui Tramline on its way to an impressive treetop walkway beside Lake Mahinapua. Tucked inside one of New Zealand's oldest scenic reserves, the walkway gives rare views over ancient forest to the coast and the Southern Alps. South from here, the trail mostly follows the old railway line to Ross, a classic West Coast mining town that refuses to give up the ghost.

SUMMARY

Start point Greymouth or Ross
End point Ross or Greymouth
Distance 139 km
Likely time 3–4 days
Grading Mostly Grade 2 (Easy) with some sections of Grade 3 (Intermediate)
Surface Mostly smooth gravel, with some sealed road
Bike type Comfort/hybrid bike or mountain bike
Map and trail website www.westcoastwildernesstrail.co.nz
In emergencies Cellphone coverage is patchy along this trail, especially between Kumara
    and Kaniere
Bike hire Colls Sportsworld in Greymouth, phone 03 768 4060,
    www.coastsportsandcycles.co.nz; Mann Cycles Greymouth, phone 03 768 0255,
    www.manncycles.co.nz; or Hokitika Cycles and Sports World, phone 03 755 8662,
    www.hokitikasportsworld.co.nz

West Coast Wilderness Trail

Tasman Sea

GREYMOUTH

Grey R.

6

Paroa

Bridge Bar and Cafe

NEMONA FOREST

Kumara Junction

Taramakau R.

Kumara

6

WAIMEA FOREST

Kapitea Reservoir

Kumara Reservoir

Arahura R.

Loopline Rd

KAWHAKA FOREST

HOKITIKA

Kaniere

Hurunui Jacks

Lake Kaniere Rd

Kawhaka Ck

Milltown

Kawhaka Pass 317m

L. Mahinapua

Mananui Tramline

treetop walkway

L. Kaniere

Cowboy Paradise

Ruatapu

6

Totara R.

Ross

Hokitika R.

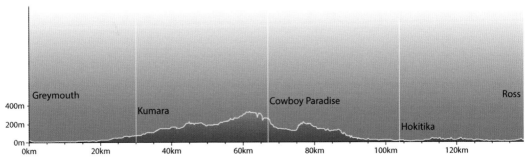

Getting there Greymouth is 290 km (4 hours) from Nelson via SH6, SH69 and SH7. Greymouth is also 520 km (7 hours) from Queenstown via SH6, and 3 hours from Christchurch via SH73. The most enjoyable way to get there is the scenic TranzAlpine train from Christchurch to Greymouth (the train carries up to four bikes at one time)

Trail transport Wilderness Trail Shuttle, phone 03 755 5042 or 021 263 3299, www.wildernesstrailshuttle.co.nz; Trail Transport, phone 03 768 6618 or 027 661 8024, www.trailtransport.co.nz

Looking west through a World War II lookout box towards the Greymouth Bar.

ROUTE DESCRIPTION

Greymouth to Kumara

30 km, 3–5 hours, Grade 1 (Very easy)

From Greymouth Station, on Mackay Street, head to the Grey River stopbank just across the road. On top is a smooth cycle trail heading out to the coast via a lagoon and the famous Greymouth Bar — a 400-metre stretch of reclaimed land from where you can watch fishing boats come and go. Check out the gun emplacement near the start of the bar.

Back-track to the start of the bar and head south along the coast. After 7 km, you will pass the Seaside Holiday Park, which sells a range of snacks. Carry on south, enjoying the stunning coastal vistas, and when you are almost 13 km from town, turn left to the Paroa Hotel (a stone pub).

From behind the Paroa Hotel, the trail crosses Saltwater Creek and follows the highway, sometimes branching away to weave through forest, before breaking off and heading inland, across the historic Taramakau River road and rail bridge. In 2015, a clip-on path was built for walkers and cyclists, so the crossing is now safe.

At the far end of the bridge, cross the road and follow a new path to Tram Road.

The trail follows bits of the old tram line through bush and across farmland to the small town of Kumara. This is a great place to explore for a few hours, with historic story boards, an art gallery, short walks and the restored Theatre Royal Hotel.

Kumara to Cowboy Paradise

37 km, 4–6 hours, Grade 2+ (Easy)

From the Theatre Royal Hotel in Kumara, ride south on Second Street, left onto Tui Street and turn right down Fifth Street, then veer left onto Larrikins Road and then left again up Larrikins Track. You will pass near the historic Londonderry Rock and later climb gently up a cool single track to the stunning Kapitea Reservoir, with a mountain backdrop.

Hokitika's iconic clock tower, built in 1903.

Ride down to the far end of the reservoir, between Kapitea and Kumara reservoirs, and head along a sweeping boardwalk. From the other side, the trail follows Loopline Road and Old Christchurch Road before taking a minor road left to Kawhaka Reservoir, crossing the weir and heading into the real wilderness. You will follow a historic pack track up the Kawhaka Valley to Kawhaka Pass at 317 metres. From there, the trail runs beside a water race for a couple of kilometres and descends into virgin forest and across the Wainihinihi Gorge. The day finishes at the replica western town of Cowboy Paradise.

Cowboy Paradise to Hokitika

36 km, 3–5 hours, Grade 3– (Intermediate)

From the end of the western town, a fun trail sweeps gently down to the Arahura River. This 4-km downhill is so sweet you might feel like riding back up to repeat the experience!

Follow Milltown Road down the Arahura Valley. This area has special significance to Maori as a source of quality pounamu. There is a toughish 1-km climb out of the valley, through native forest, followed by a descent to Lake Kaniere. It's a beautiful lake with good swimming for hardy souls. As soon as the road leaves the lake, turn right onto the old Kaniere water-race track. After 3 km, turn left down Ward Road and, immediately after a bridge at the bottom of the hill, turn right onto a new trail that weaves through

The Theatre Royal, lovingly and luxuriously restored.

regenerating forest on the way towards Kaniere (a suburb of Hokitika).

Shortly after crossing a small weir, the trail passes Hurunui Jacks — a brilliant spot to enjoy West Coast hospitality. If you like art and the outdoors, you'll want to stop here and relax for a while.

From Hurunui Jacks, the trail runs beside Lake Kaniere Road to the outskirts of Hokitika — a vibrant town famous for greenstone art, its annual Wildfoods Festival and drunken attempts to climb its clock tower.

The final few kilometres into town are along the Old Kaniere Tram, right beside the river with awesome views. Straight after passing under the highway bridge, turn left to take Gibson Quay for one block before turning right to go to the centre of town, 100 metres away.

Hokitika to Ross
36 km, 3–5 hours, Grade 3 (Intermediate)
This section is due to be upgraded from its current Grade 4 state to Grade 3 in mid-2017. It includes a 1-km diversion to the treetop walk beside Lake Mahinapua.

From the clock tower in Hokitika, ride south down Sewell Street and turn left past the large signs advocating the therapeutic value of whitebaiting. Ride onto the obvious cycle path and across the Hokitika River bridge clip-on.

Head south beside the highway and turn right on Golf Links Road. Where the end of this road meets the highway, a short cycle path leads to an information shelter.

From the shelter, cross the road and follow the orange trail signs to the Mananui Tramline (Mahinapua Walkway). This is 7 km from town and takes you inland, across a bridge, past some stunning wetlands and through native forest.

About 5 km down the walkway, you can take a side walk to a lakeside picnic area — this section is not rideable. The tram line is 6.5 km long. At the far end, you'll pop out onto Woodstock-Rimu Road. Turn right and cruise for 2 km to the turn-off to the treetop walk.

The Westcoast Treetop Walk and Cafe lies 800 metres to your right. It was built in 2012, is 47 metres high, and gives stunning views of Lake Mahinapua and the Southern Alps. The walk takes 40 minutes.

From the treetop walk, head south down Woodstock-Rimu Road to SH6, turn right and cruise along the highway for 2 km before turning left down Paiere Road. This soon ends, and you'll ride onto the old railway formation. You'll cross 12 bridges along this stretch, with good views from the larger ones, especially the last bridge, which is 200 metres long and crosses the Totara River.

From the Totara River Bridge, a gravel path leads to Beach Road, where you turn left and roll into Ross. This is one of the most interesting small towns on the West Coast and deserves a couple of hours' exploration, or even a night's stay — it is loaded with history. Check out the information centre and the historic Empire Hotel just across the road.

TRAIL TALES

In pre-European times, pounamu (greenstone) was the West Coast's most significant resource, and Maori searched the length of the land for it. Pounamu was valued for its beauty and strength, which made it perfect for tools (chisels and adzes), weapons (clubs) and jewellery.

When the first European explorers, Thomas Brunner and Charles Heaphy, walked to the coast from Golden Bay with their Maori guide Kehu in 1846, they were welcomed as guests to the Mawhera pa (where Greymouth is today). The Grey River was then known as Mawheranui River (mawhera meaning 'wide-spreading mouth').

Europeans discovered gold in the Taramakau and Greenstone areas in 1863, and the following year 70 diggers arrived from Nelson. The town's first buildings were little more than tents, but they were developed into more substantial structures as businesses became better established.

As the gold rush slowed, coal and timber provided a more reliable foundation for the local economy. The first coal was transported by canoe down the river to Greymouth in 1864. Demand only really took off in the 1870s, however, when major work was done to improve the harbour. Steamers, such as the SS *Nelson*, were soon travelling regularly between Nelson and the West Coast.

Cyclists exploring the West Coast in the 1880s.

By 1881, Greymouth was booming, although activity at the port declined through the twentieth century, especially after the opening of the Otira rail tunnel in 1923, which linked east with west. The port is now mainly used by fishermen.

Vessels attempting to enter the West Coast river ports faced the hazards of formidable weather and submerged sandbars that shifted with every storm. The ships were often forced to wait up to a week or more for favourable conditions to enter the harbours, and the waiting proved almost as dangerous as the attempts to enter. Hokitika port alone experienced 108 strandings between 1865 and 1867, an average of one every 10 days.

In 1877, a tram line south of Greymouth was extended to Kumara in response to the discovery of gold. The Kumara area had been overlooked in the first rush of the 1860s, but when coarse gold was found there in glacial gravels in 1876, miners rushed to stake a claim. Surveyor Arthur Dobson named the town after bush lawyer flowers — kohimara.

One of the first people to gravitate to Kumara was shopkeeper Richard Seddon. He opened a hotel there in 1876 and the next year was made mayor. He soon moved to national politics, becoming the country's longest-serving premier, in office from 1893 until his death in 1906. Seddon never forgot his ties to the West Coast and was one of the strongest supporters for extending the railway line down to Haast and over the pass to connect with the Otago Central Railway.

By 1909, the railway extended from Greymouth to Hokitika and Ross. Seddon's vision of it continuing south through to Otago was clearly impossible, but passenger services continued until 1972 and the line finally closed to all traffic at the end of 1980.

Ross was the centre of one of New Zealand's richest alluvial gold fields in the late 1800s. In a familiar story, the town sprang up after gold was discovered in 1864, by a Welshman named Jones at Jones Creek. The area had never been settled and was only rarely visited by Maori, who had never named it. Two prospectors discovered New Zealand's largest gold nugget, weighing 2.8 kg, at Ross in 1909. The nugget was nicknamed the Honourable Roddy after the then Minister of Mines, Roderick McKenzie. The government purchased the nugget and gave it to King George as a coronation present.

There was enough gold in the Ross area to sustain miners for several decades, after which the town continued to survive as a timber-milling and lime-processing centre.

Passing through Mawhera Reserve is one of the trail highlights.

However, recent developments in mining combined with rising gold prices mean that there is the possibility of extracting more of the precious metal from the area, but not without considerable environmental impact.

The first person to cycle the West Coast wilderness was AP Harper, who, in 1900, rode down the West Coast in search of gold. After finishing prospecting on the coast, Harper decided to take his bicycle over Haast Pass to Lake Wanaka as that was much shorter than the way he had come. However, carrying his bike over Haast Pass 65 years before the road was built proved so difficult that Harper wrote to the *Press*, strenuously advising others not to attempt the same. Today it is considered one of the best cycle-touring routes in the world.

Crossing the historic Totara River rail bridge.

FOOD AND ACCOMMODATION

Greymouth Restaurants, great cafes and accommodation: www.greydistrict.co.nz

Kumara Tearooms, pub, accommodation (www.kumarawestcoast.org): The Theatre Royal Hotel, phone 03 736 9277, www.theatreroyalhotel.co.nz; Maggies Cottage, phone 03 736 9802.

Milltown Cowboy Paradise offers food and accommodation near Milltown, phone 03 280 9559, www.cowboyparadise.co.nz. The trail goes through Cowboy Paradise.

Lake Kaniere Accommodation: www.holidayhouses.co.nz/Lake-Kaniere.asp; or phone the Hokitika i-SITE on 03 755 6166.

Hurunui Jacks Accommodation at Lake Kaniere Road (12 km from Hokitika), phone 03 755 8683, www.hurunuijacks.co.nz

Kaniere Cottage accommodation at Westside Rides, phone 03 755 6508, or 021 260 9233, www.westsiderides.co.nz

Hokitika Shops, supermarkets, cafes, accommodation: www.hokitika.org

Ross Shops and accommodation: Ross Motels, phone 03 755 4153, www.rossmotels.co.nz; The Empire Hotel (camping facilities), phone 03 755 4005.

Day trippers exploring the Kumara to Cowboy Paradise section.

SHORTCUTS AND DETOURS

Off Yer Bike There are three 20–30 minute walks from the centre of Kumara, and plenty of history you can learn about just by walking the main street and reading all the interpretation panels.

Lake Kaniere Loop Those hankering for some difficult Grade 5 mountain biking might like to try riding around Lake Kaniere on their way to Hokitika. It is a tough trip, with at least half an hour of walking. Allow 2–3 hours for this 21-km loop. From Lake Kaniere Village, ride 10 km of gravel road before turning right onto the signposted Lake Kaniere Walkway.

Westcoast Treetop Walk Halfway between Hokitika and Ross is the walkway and cafe (phone 0508 TREETOPS, www.treetopsnz.com). The walk weaves around the top of massive rimu and kahikatea trees, and there is a lookout tower giving amazing 360-degree views. The walk costs $38 per adult and is signposted from the cycle trail. Book online to save 10 per cent

ALPS 2 OCEAN
CYCLE TRAIL

New Zealand's highest mountain, Aoraki/Mount Cook, forms the cornerstone of the country's longest cycle trail. Starting from the Southern Alps, this 300-km trail descends 540 metres through the Mackenzie Basin and down the Waitaki Valley to Oamaru and the Pacific Ocean.

The Alps 2 Ocean (A2O) trail has eight distinct sections, which can be ridden individually, or combined to create one of the most memorable cycling holidays of your life. The first half from Aoraki/Mount Cook or Lake Tekapo to Omarama has spectacular mountain scenery, and three sections of fantastic off-road trail. The trail sections around the base of Lake Pukaki, the base of Lake Ohau and across the Quailburn are absolutely world class. The cycling can be complemented with a trip onto Tasman Glacier, a swim in Loch Cameron, or a glider flight at Omarama.

The second half of the trail also has some great bits of cycle path, mixed in with quite a lot of road riding past lakes Benmore, Aviemore and Waitaki. It then enters the fascinating Vanished World Heritage Trail, with Elephant Rocks and fossilised creatures from another epoch such as giant penguins and vicious-looking dolphins. The strange landscapes have been used for a few movie sets, including *The Chronicles of Narnia* movies.

Finally, the trail enters Oamaru on a disused railway line and passes through the Victorian Precinct before suddenly emerging at a long pier on the edge of the Pacific Ocean.

If you don't have time to do the whole trail, cherry-pick the sections from Lake Pukaki to Lake Ohau and over the Quailburn to Omarama. They have the best scenery and the least traffic.

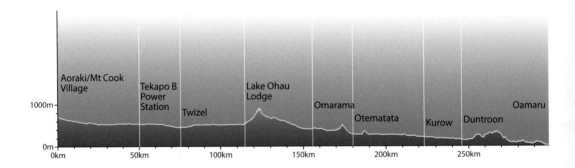

SUMMARY ··

Start point Lake Tekapo or Aoraki/Mount Cook Village
End point Oamaru
Distance 300 km, with an optional extra 55 km
Likely time 4–6 days
Grading A mix of Grade 2 (Easy) off-road trail and Grade 3 (Intermediate) on-road sections

Alps 2 Ocean Cycle Trail

Aoraki/Mount Cook

Aoraki/Mount Cook Village

helicopter shuttle

P

Jollie River

Tasman R.

80

L. Pukaki

Braemar Station

BEN OHAU RANGE

TWO THUMB RANGE

L. Tekapo

Tekapo

MACKENZIE BASIN

Tekapo B Power Station

8

Pukaki

Twizel

L. Ohau

Quailburn

8

BENMORE RANGE

L. Benmore

KIRKLISTON RANGE

Omarama

8

refer to Pukaki to Omarama map

Ahuriri Pass

83

Otematata

L. Aviemore

Sailors Cutting

L. Waitaki

83

Kurow

ST MARYS RANGE

Duntroon

Elephant Rocks

Waitaki R.

Maerewhenua R.

OAMARU

Weston

Surface 60% smooth off-road trail and 40% on-road trail

Bike type Mountain bike, hybrid/comfort bike or touring bike with fat tyres

Maps Available on the trail website and from local businesses

Trail website www.alps2ocean.com

In emergencies 95% of this trail has cellphone coverage

Bike hire Refer to the trail website for a range of operators offering bike hire, transport and
guided tours

Getting there The most popular starting point is Lake Tekapo Village, which is 230 km
from Christchurch via SH1, SH79 and SH8. If driving your own vehicle, you can park
at Oamaru and get a shuttle to the start of the track

Optional start The official start to the trail involves a helicopter flight from Aoraki/Mount
Cook airport across to the east side of the Tasman. This 2-minute trip costs around
$800 for one to six people. It will not fly in bad weather. Few riders are choosing this
option. Alternatively, if you want to start from Lake Tekapo, you can cycle down the
canal roads (see Route Description)

Following an old farm track en route to Quailburn Station.

ROUTE DESCRIPTION

Tekapo Village or Aoraki/Mount Cook Village to Lake Pukaki

30 or 50 km, 5–8 hours, Grade 2 (Easy) to Grade 3 (Intermediate)

The most popular start for this ride is Lake Tekapo Village. From the shops, follow A20 signs to the Tekapo Canal Road, which is only open to walkers and cyclists. It is very easy cycling and there are great views of the Southern Alps ahead. At the canal outflow, a cycle lane leads down to a T-intersection where you should turn left, riding parallel to Lake Pukaki.

The original start to this trail is at Aoraki/Mount Cook Village, but it requires a helicopter flight that is now almost $800 per load (six riders maximum). All the same, Aoraki/Mount Cook Village is a great place to visit, with interesting short walks, a museum in the Hermitage Hotel, and good cafes to enjoy before your cycling adventure.

From the White Horse Hill Campground, ride 7 km on a new cycle path to the Aoraki/Mount Cook Airport. Then take a helicopter flight across the Tasman River and ride down the east side of Lake Pukaki to Braemar Station. Flights are cancelled in bad weather. Perhaps in future a jetboat or hovercraft will be available.

Braemar Station (at the 37-km mark) has good accommodation available. Most of this section is riding down Hayman Road beside Lake Pukaki. About 5 km before the purpose-built trail begins, you will pass Tekapo B power station. Only 1 km before SH8, there is a signpost pointing right to the cycle path. There is a picnic table there and a magnificent view.

Lake Pukaki to Twizel

26 km, 2–3 hours, Grade 2 (Easy)

From Tekapo B power station, ride down Hayman Road for 5 km before turning right onto the signposted A20 Trail. Tekapo B is the only power station in New Zealand surrounded by water.

This purpose-built trail skirts around the bottom of the lake and across the dam to a rest area with toilets and a small cafe that specialises in salmon.

From the rest area, cross the highway and follow signs to another section of trail that crosses Pukaki Flats to Twizel. It is 21 km from the start of the single track around Lake Pukaki to Twizel — all off-road.

As you enter Twizel there is a mouth-watering cafe on your left called the Musterers Hut. A couple of hundred metres further on you will see the town centre, also on your left. It has cafes, two supermarkets and a bike/hardware store. Twizel was built in 1968 to house the hydro scheme workers, and has since successfully morphed into a holiday town.

Twizel to Lake Ohau Lodge
39 km, 3–5 hours, Grade 2 (Easy)

From Twizel, ride to the right of the shopping centre and take Nuns Veil Road out to Glen Lyon Road. Turn left and cruise down to the Pukaki Canal. On the way you pass right by the best swimming spot in the region, Loch Cameron. It's signposted on the right and is much warmer than any of the lakes or rivers around here as the water trickles into it slowly.

Just after Loch Cameron, you will cross the canal and turn left to follow the road beside it to Lake Ohau, 20 flat kilometres from Twizel. The canal has a salmon farm in it, and sometimes a number of people fishing nearby for escaped salmon.

Skirting around the bottom of Lake Ohau with Ben Ohau ahead.

At the lake, turn left across the dam and then right onto a 4WD track that leads around the lake to a weir. About 20 metres past the weir, turn hard right (just by a toilet) and follow a new single track around the lake edge to Lake Ohau Road. This is another brilliant section of trail.

At Lake Ohau Road, turn right and ride 9 km to Lake Ohau Lodge. You will pass a beautiful council campground about halfway down this road at Lake Middleton, where

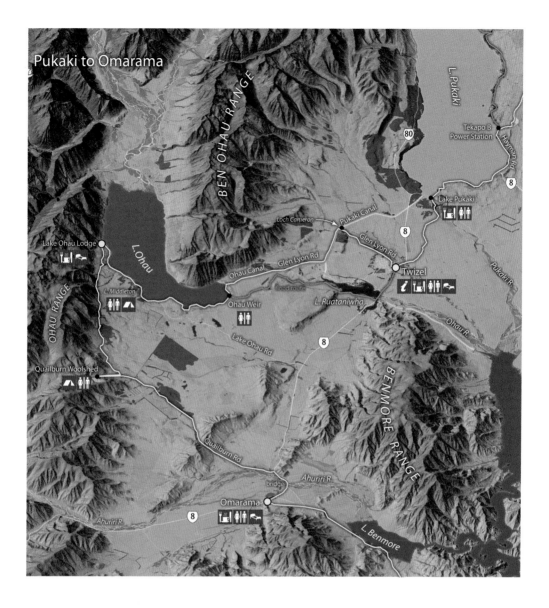

Pukaki to Omarama

there are toilets. But if you like to end a day's cycling with a soak in a spa pool, a delicious meal and a comfortable bed, then carry on to the lodge. It is one of the trail highlights.

Alternative flood route: Every so often, maybe a few weeks a year, the hydro lakes fill up so much that water has to be spilled over the Ohau River weir. When this happens the cycle trail is diverted around the southern side of Lake Ruataniwha. From Twizel, head out to SH8 and head south on a path beside the highway. Straight after crossing the bridge at the outlet of Lake Ruataniwha, turn right and follow a gravel road around the south side of the lake and then beside Ohau River all the way to the cycle path around the edge of Lake Ohau.

Climbing through beech forest after leaving Ohau Lodge.

Lake Ohau Lodge to Omarama
41–45 km, 4–6 hours, Grade 3 (Intermediate)

From the lodge's driveway, the trail heads around the base of the Ohau Range, offering excellent views and fun cycling. If you are from a flat city, the first half might be a bit tough; it climbs 300 metres. Beyond the climb, a sweeping downhill awaits.

After 18 km, you will meet Quailburn Road. A few minutes up to the right is a historic woolshed, a toilet and an idyllic campsite beside a small stream. Otherwise, turn left and change into a big gear! The road is slightly downhill, and there is usually a tail wind. It's gravel for several kilometres and leads most of the way to Omarama.

When you reach the highway, look to your right, and you'll see the cycle trail heading off-road, through some willows. This fun section leads to a picnic area with toilets just before the Omarama Bridge. Stop and make sure there is no traffic on the highway before nipping across the bridge and, after 100–200 metres' riding, onto another cycle path that leads right into Omarama.

Omarama has some amazing hot pools. You'd be mad not to check them out. It also has a great curio and second-hand bookshop, as well as a good clothes shop. And it has thermals that make it a glider's paradise.

Omarama to Otematata

24 km, 1.5–2 hours, Grade 3 (Intermediate)

From the small settlement of Omarama, the trail runs beside SH83 to what is locally known as Sailors Cutting. Start on the right-hand side as you leave town. From the top of the first climb you will see the trail weaving down to Lake Benmore and onto Sailors Cutting. There is a campground beside the lake here. After Sailors Cutting, the ride is on the highway up to Ahuriri Pass and then you'll be flying downhill to Otematata, a busy holiday town in summer. An off-road alternative may be built in 2017–18.

If you feel like a break from your bike, the Otematata Wetlands Walk is well worth it. Give yourself 1 hour, starting from the centre of town. There is some great swimming along the way — at the right time of year.

Otematata to Kurow

43 km, 3–5 hours, Grade 3 (Intermediate)

From the west end of Otematata, turn off the highway on Loch Laird Road and ride to Benmore Dam — one of the largest in New Zealand. There is an information building near its base. The climb to the top of the dam is 100 metres high. Cross the dam and follow the road around Lake Aviemore to Aviemore Dam. A few large camping areas (with toilets) lie sprawled out along the edge of the lake, many of them permanently occupied by caravan owners. In summer, an estimated 5000 people camp beside Lake Aviemore.

About 2 km before Aviemore Dam, you will cross Deep Stream and see a walking track on your left. A 10-minute walk takes you up to a picnic table beside a good swimming spot.

At the time of writing, you had to take the highway from Aviemore Dam to Kurow, but there were plans to replace this with an off-road path in 2017 or 2018.

Kurow to Duntroon

28 km, 2–3 hours, Grade 2 (Easy)

Kurow is an interesting town with several shops, including cafes and antique stores.

From Kurow, an off-road trail leads all the way to Duntroon. You are likely to have a tail wind pushing you along.

Soon after leaving town you will see Western House B&B on your right and then the large Pasquale winery with a cafe on your left (open 10 a.m. to 4 p.m.). A few kilometres before Duntroon there are the Maori drawings, with a car park and picnic area on your right.

After checking out the rock drawings it is only another few kilometres into Duntroon. Make sure you check out the tiny jail and Vanished World Centre. Duntroon has two holiday cottages.

Duntroon to Oamaru

53 km, 4–6 hours, Grade 3 (Intermediate)

From Duntroon to Oamaru, the trail follows an interesting mix of roads, cycle paths and rail trail. Keep your eyes peeled for the A2O signs to stay on the right track.

Check out the Elephant Rocks (popular for rock climbing) and Anatini Valley, which has the oldest kowhai tree in New Zealand, and was used as a film set for the *The Chronicles of Narnia* movies. With huge granite rocks and fossils aplenty, you may want to take your time exploring this fascinating area.

The last 5 km are along a railway line and through the Oamaru Gardens, before riding down a few streets to the long pier at the end of Wansbeck Street.

Oamaru is famous for its historic precinct: a fascinating selection of shops celebrating the best elements of the Victorian era with cafes, bakeries, tearooms, bookshops, antique stores, breweries and art galleries.

TRAIL TALES

New Zealand's highest mountain, Aoraki/Mount Cook, has a dual history to reflect its dual name. Maori legend describes four brothers sailing around the world in the oldest brother's waka *Te Waka o Aoraki*. As they paddled through the rough seas, the waka was thrown onto a reef and became stranded. The four travellers climbed up the high side of the waka to escape the freezing-cold water and wait for the storm to ease. They waited and waited until they were frozen in place by the bitter south wind. And there they remained as the four highest peaks of the Southern Alps — Aoraki (Mount Cook) the oldest and tallest brother, Rakiroa (Mount Dampier), Rakirua (Mount Teichelmann) and Rarakiroa (Mount Tasman), with their waka becoming the South Island.

European history centres on tourism and mountaineering. The first accommodation at Aoraki/Mount Cook Village was a small cob building, constructed in 1884

A cycle tourer near Aoraki/Mount Cook Village, circa 1900.

and called the Hermitage. It has undergone numerous reincarnations since then and is now an impressive multi-storeyed hotel, even with its own museum.

The first attempt to climb Aoraki/Mount Cook was made in 1892 by an Irish climber and his Swiss guide. It is possible they made it to within 100 metres of the summit. However, the honours for a successful ascent and descent went to three local climbers: Jack Clarke, Tom Fyfe and George Graham, who reached the top on Christmas Day 1894.

Aoraki/Mount Cook is 3754 metres tall, but it has been taller. In 1991, the top 10 metres of the mountain fell away as a massive landslide sent millions of cubic metres of snow and rock crashing down the side to the Tasman Glacier.

Away from the Alps, the most obvious landmarks along the trail have all been constructed by man. In 1904, the Hay Report outlined the potential for hydro-electric power from many of the South Island rivers, including the Waitaki.

Work began in 1928, and the first dam on the Waitaki was also the last to be built completely by hand. Most of the construction formed part of a 'Make Work' scheme during the Great Depression. At the peak of construction, the dam employed 1250 workers, plugging away under extremely arduous conditions. The practising doctor from the local town of Kurow, Dr McMillan, the town's Presbyterian minister, Rev. Nordmeyer, and the district's school teacher, Mr Davidson, responded to the hardships they witnessed by developing a world-leading welfare system. It was so effective that the New Zealand government used it as a template for the nation's first social security scheme, introduced in 1938.

A historic rail tunnel between Duntroon and Oamaru.

Through to 1985, another seven hydro dams and many kilometres of canals were built between Lake Tekapo and Kurow on the Waitaki River. Canals were developed to control the water flow and stop glacial gravels from travelling with the water into the mechanical workings of the power stations. Towns such as Twizel and Otematata were built to a Scandinavian design, especially to house the construction workers and their families.

The memorable Quailburn section of the cycle trail passes through a retired sheep station. A Scotsman by the name of McMurdo claimed the land for farming and called it Benmore after his birthplace. He built up the sheep numbers to 80,000. After shearing, the wool was packed into bales and bullock teams took it slowly but surely down to the port

The Otematata Wetlands Walk.

at Oamaru. Part of Benmore was sold off and became Quailburn Station, named after the native quail that inhabited the area at one stage. But the quail quickly disappeared.

The sheep competed with the birds for food and then, in 1888, a population of ferrets was established at Quailburn to control the rabbit infestation that plagued the region. Settlers and ferrets alike enjoyed quail for their dinner and ate them to extinction.

The Quailburn woolshed, just off the trail, was constructed in the early 1920s from beech trees taken from Quailburn Bush. It is now a lovely place for a picnic.

Further down the trail at Duntroon, a fascinating and ancient history is being uncovered. For more than 30 years now, scientists have been discovering the remains of animals that died near Kaikoura 25 million years ago. Movements in the earth's tectonic plates have shifted the long-settled remains of some now-extinct species over 400 km, from sites offshore from Kaikoura to the valleys inland from Oamaru.

Today, the Vanished World Heritage Trail and Centre in Duntroon is a fascinating home to many interesting extinct species such as a squalodon-like dolphin and the world's largest penguin.

Equally fascinating is the ancient Maori rock art found just out of Duntroon. Carved into or painted and drawn on the stone, the art depicts animals and sailing ships. Maori created the paint from a mixture of animal or bird fat, vegetable gum and soot or red ochre. There are good interpretation panels at the site explaining the drawings.

The trail ends at the most interesting part of Oamaru — the Victorian Precinct. Oamaru was first settled in the 1850s and grew swiftly as an important port. However, the original jetty was poorly built, with little regard for the vicious storms that could sweep up the coast. Between 1862 and 1875, over 22 ships were wrecked trying to make berth at the port. Finally, a 600-metre breakwater was constructed, which enabled larger steamers to find a safe haven at the port.

Oamaru was also the site of New Zealand's first recorded bicycle race. In 1889, two years after the world's first bicycle race in Paris, the *Otago Witness* reported on two velocipedes racing a mile along North Road. The winner was Thomas Woonton, racing on a locally made machine at an average speed of 14 kph.

The history of Oamaru, and bicycles, is celebrated in the Victorian Precinct, through which the last 500 metres of the A2O travels.

Anatini Valley, one of the *Narnia* film locations.

Eating what you like is just one reward of cycling.

FOOD AND ACCOMMODATION

The trail website www.alps2ocean.com has up-to-date lists of accommodation options along the trail.

Tekapo Cafes, supermarkets, restaurants, accommodation: www.tekapotourism.co.nz

Aoraki/Mount Cook Village Cafes, restaurants, accommodation: www.mackenzienz.com

Braemar Station Back-country lodges, phone 03 680 6844 or 027 254 4206,
    www.braemarstation.co.nz

Lake Pukaki Information Centre and Mt Cook Alpine Salmon Shop, phone 03 435 0427,
    www.alpinesalmon.co.nz

Twizel Supermarket, cafes, restaurants and a range of accommodation: www.twizel.info; Jake's
    Hardware (limited bike parts and basic repairs), 24 Market Place, phone 03 435 0881.

Lake Middleton Camping ground (late September–early May only): Waitaki District Council
    Camp Administrator, phone 0800 108 081, www.waitaki.govt.nz

Lake Ohau Accommodation and meals (bookings recommended): Lake Ohau Lodge,
    phone 03 438 9885, www.ohau.co.nz

Omarama General store, restaurants, cafes and a range of accommodation options:
    www.discoveromarama.co.nz

Otematata General store, cafe and accommodation: Otematata Holiday Park and Lodge,

The wonderfully bizarre Steampunk HQ, Oamaru.

phone 03 438 7826, www.otematata.kiwi.nz; Otematata Country Inn, phone 03 438
7797; Otematata Eatery, Bar and Lodging, phone 03 438 7899, www.bestdampub.co.nz

Kurow Food, petrol, a range of accommodation and a museum: www.kurow.org.nz

Duntroon Accommodation options can be found on the trail website. There is also a
domain for camping, and a garage that sells Italian-made chainsaws. For more details,
go to www.duntroon.co.nz. Also be sure to check out the Vanished World Heritage Trail
and Centre, www.vanishedworld.co.nz

Oamaru Supermarkets, cafes, restaurants, accommodation and bike shops:
www.waitakinz.com

SHORTCUTS AND DETOURS

Weekend escape The very best bits of off-road trail are around the bottom of lakes Pukaki
and Ohau, and across the Quailburn. If you are reasonably fit and start early you will
be able to ride from Hayman Road to Lake Ohau Lodge on the first day (65 km). Then
from the lodge to Omarama via the Quailburn will be easy on the second day (45 km).

OTAGO CENTRAL
RAIL TRAIL

At an official opening in 2000, the Otago Central Rail Trail became New Zealand's first multi-day rail trail. It is considered a flagship of the cycle trails and in 2012 was voted number 5 in the AA's 101 Must-do activities. The small towns along the trail had long been in decline, but are now revitalised by the increase in visitors. They offer warm southern hospitality and understand what cyclists need, especially those who haven't been on a bike for a while.

The trail runs from Clyde to Middlemarch, or Middlemarch to Clyde. Exactly which direction is best depends on which way the wind blows. Although parts of it are exposed to wind, there are no steep hills on the trail. It can be ridden by anyone of almost any age or cycling ability. The trail looks like a narrow gravel road, and some sections are a bit rough.

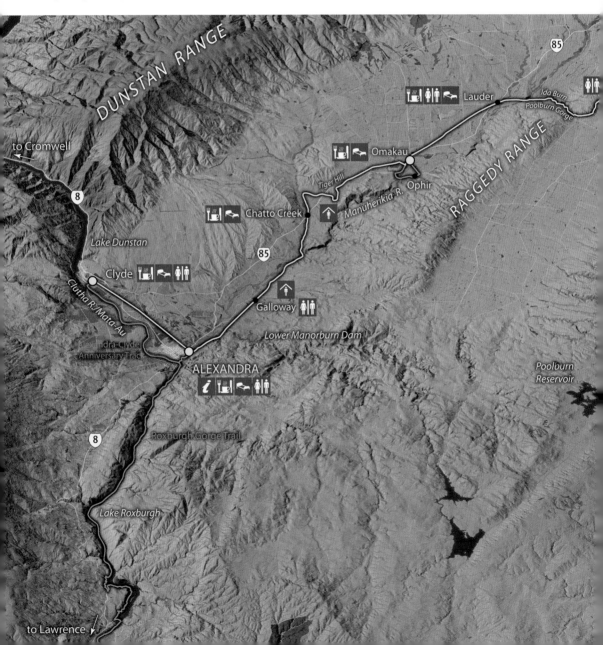

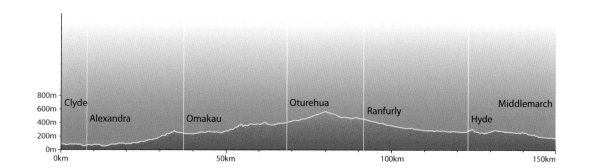

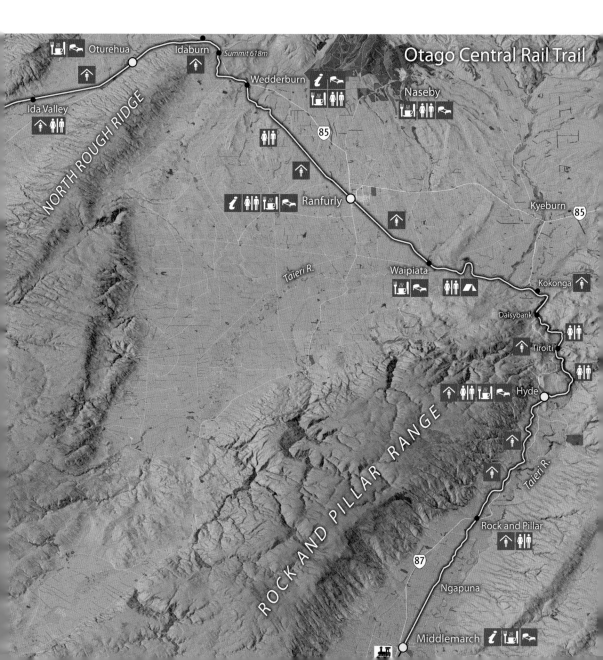

Wide tyres and a big comfy seat will help if you are not used to cycling.

Central Otago is famous for its wide open spaces, layered with rock and tussock beneath a rich blue sky. It's a relaxing landscape, enhanced by the trail's historic tunnels and bridges. The trail has no motorised traffic on it, although there are several road crossings. There are towns at regular intervals, and several operators will carry your bags from one town to the next.

April is a popular riding time, because the colours of the deciduous trees are stunning and the temperature is not too hot or cold. Over Easter, accommodation on the trail can be booked out.

A new feature of the trail is the Otago Central Interplanetary Cycle Trail between Clyde and Ranfurly. Along the trail there are built-to-scale models of our solar system and the planets.

A passenger service still runs on the old railway line from Middlemarch to Dunedin and is highly recommended for its scenic and historic value.

SUMMARY ···

Start point Clyde or Middlemarch
End point Middlemarch or Clyde
Distance 151 km
Likely time 3–5 days
Grade 1+ (Very easy)
Surface Wide gravel, a bit rough in places
Bike type Hybrid/comfort bike, touring bike or mountain bike
Map A good pamphlet map is available at Otago i-SITEs, or see the trail website
Trail website www.otagocentralrailtrail.co.nz
In emergencies There is generally good cellphone coverage, although there are a few
    black spots
Bike hire and tours Trail Journeys in Clyde, phone 0800 030 381, www.trailjourneys.co.nz;
    Altitude Bikes in Alexandra, phone 03 448 8917, www.altitudebikes.co.nz; Bike it
    Now in Clyde, phone 0800 245 3669, www.bikeitnow.co.nz; Off the Rails in Ranfurly,
    phone 0800 633 7245, www.offtherails.co.nz; Cycle Surgery in Middlemarch, phone
    0800 292 534, www.cyclesurgery.co.nz
Getting there Start from either Clyde or Middlemarch. From Dunedin, you can start in style
    by catching a historic train to Middlemarch or Pukerangi. Middlemarch is 80 km (1 hour
    10 minutes) from Dunedin, and Clyde is 83 km (1 hour 10 minutes) from Queenstown
Taieri Gorge Railway For details about the train from Dunedin to Middlemarch or Pukerangi,
    phone Taieri Gorge Railway on 03 477 4449, or check out www.dunedinrailways.co.nz

Typical Central Otago weather on the trail.

Special considerations Autumn is the best season for this cycling trail — the climate is moderate and the autumnal colours are stunning. Winter can be extremely cold, and summer blisteringly hot. Carry extra water during summer and a torch for the tunnels

ROUTE DESCRIPTION

Clyde to Alexandra

8 km, 1 hour, Grade 1 (Very easy)

Before you start your trip, you might want to buy a Rail Trail Passport. It costs $10 and you have it stamped at towns along the ride to prove you did the whole trail.

The trail officially starts/ends at Clyde and runs in a straight line for 8 km to Alexandra. There is an alternative route on the other side of the Clutha River/Mata-Au — the Alexandra–Clyde Anniversary Track. Here are details on both options.

The Otago Central Rail Trail starts from the Clyde Station platform, on the opposite side of SH8 to Clyde township. It is on the corner of SH8 and Springvale Road, and you will see the large Trail Journeys building there. It is 8 km to Tarbert Street in Alexandra. Turn right to head for the main shops, or cross the road and continue along the rail trail.

Alternatively, from the cute row of shops in Clyde township, ride down Matau Street and cross the Clutha River/Mata-Au on the old iron bridge. The Alexandra–Clyde

Anniversary Track was built to celebrate the region's 150th anniversary. This gravel track follows the southern bank of the river for 12 km to a second bridge over the Clutha, which leads to the shops in Alexandra. It is more scenic and fun than the rail trail, but also 4 km longer and a little bit harder.

Alexandra to Omakau

29 km, 2–4 hours, Grade 2– (Easy)

From Alexandra, the trail starts 800 metres north of the shopping centre, at the corner of Tarbert Street and Little Valley Road. It crosses a narrow bridge over the Manuherikia River and passes Tucker Hill, a poor gold-mining area that yielded just enough to pay for food and supplies. After 17 km, you will reach Chatto Creek and see lots of bike racks out the back of a popular hotel.

The trail then climbs up Tiger Hill, with great views of the Dunstan Range. The next town, Omakau, was built for the railway line and has food and accommodation. It is only 2 km away from a much older town, Ophir. Gold was discovered there in 1863, and the town quickly boomed to have a population of 1000. It has many old buildings including New Zealand's oldest post office.

Omakau to Oturehua

29 km, 2–4 hours, Grade 2– (Easy)

The trail crosses reasonably flat terrain to Lauder, where there is a hotel and cafe, and then crosses the highway. Before long you'll reach an impressive 110-metre-long curved bridge. You will then enter the Poolburn Gorge where there are two tunnels with beautiful rock work at either end, followed by another impressive bridge. Give yourself plenty of time for this stunning section.

The trail then crosses the Ida Valley and passes Hayes Engineering (book ahead for a fascinating tour) en route to Oturehua. The highlight here is Gilchrist's Store, New Zealand's longest-running store, trading since 1898. Don't miss it.

Oturehua to Ranfurly

25.5 km, 2–3 hours, Grade 2– (Easy)

After 12 km of gentle climbing you will reach the summit of the rail trail at 618 metres, which coincidentally is at 45 degrees south latitude. From there it is downhill for a few kilometres to Wedderburn, a small village with a rustic tavern and accommodation. Check out the Red Barn information centre and cafe in Wedderburn.

It's downhill from here to Ranfurly; the service centre of the region. Ranfurly has many accommodation options, some interesting small shops, and a few art deco buildings.

A very busy day at Ranfurly Station.

Ranfurly to Hyde

32 km, 2–3 hours, Grade 1 (Very easy)

The section from Ranfurly to Daisybank includes a 96-metre-long steel truss bridge at Waipiata across the Taieri River, where there is a picnic and camping area. From Daisybank, at the 109-km mark, there are three bridges, a tunnel and good views of the river and trees en route to Hyde. There is also a 152-metre-long tunnel, so you may want to carry a torch. From the tunnel it is not far to Hyde, home of the iconic Otago Central Hotel. It has accommodation and a cafe.

Hyde to Middlemarch

27.5 km, 1.5–2.5 hours, Grade 1 (Very easy)

The rail trail has a slight downhill gradient most of the way from Hyde to Middlemarch. It hugs the Rock and Pillar Range for the first half, to a rest area also called Rock and Pillar. From there, the line is straight and relatively boring to Middlemarch.

Middlemarch is a small town that has been transformed by the rail trail. There is now plenty of accommodation and places to eat.

If travelling on to Dunedin, the ideal way to end your trip is to catch the Taieri Gorge Railway to Dunedin. It leaves Middlemarch at 1 p.m. on most Fridays and Sundays over summer. During the rest of the week it leaves from Pukerangi (25 km south of Middlemarch). Dunedin is 75 km away via SH87.

TRAIL TALES

It is hard to believe that much of the landscape you will cycle across on this trail was once underwater. The fossilised remains of turtles, crocodiles and fish, dating from 16 to 18 million years ago, show that Central Otago was once awash with the vast Lake Manuherikia. This shallow body of water stretched from beyond the southwestern end of the rail trail at Clyde to its northern reach.

Then, about five million years ago, the movement of the earth's tectonic plates pushed up a series of parallel mountains, including the Raggedy Range and Rough Ridge, which the trail skirts around. The lake drained and transformed into rivers and creeks, the largest river being the Manuherikia, which flows into the Clutha River/Mata-Au at Alexandra.

Only a thousand years ago, much of the land in Central Otago was cloaked in forest. Maori arrived in the region, drawn up the river valleys to hunt moa. To facilitate hunting, they burnt off much of the forest of inland Otago. The forest was replaced naturally by tussock and with cabbage trees that Maori planted as a food source for their trips across to the West Coast in search of pounamu.

Europeans began to explore the lower South Island from the 1790s. The sealers came

William Williams (with rifle) on a railway jigger during a rabbit-hunting expedition on the Otago Central Railway, circa 1900.

first, then the whalers. In March 1848, the first two immigrant ships arrived from Greenock, Scotland. They sailed into Otago Harbour and established the city of Dunedin (the Scottish Gaelic name for Edinburgh).

Maori had a close relationship with the early European settlers as they commonly worked together in the whaling and sealing industries. When Europeans began to explore further inland, they relied heavily on Maori knowledge of routes and food sources to help them through.

In the 1850s, settlers from Dunedin turned their sights inland, taking out leases on vast tracts of land for sheep runs. These pioneering farmers had their work cut out, mustering sheep in extreme weather and protecting their herds from packs of wild kuri (Maori dogs).

When gold was discovered in Central Otago in the 1860s, thousands from around the world flocked to the interior,

There are numerous history boards along the trail.

and many towns sprang up, such as Naseby, St Bathans and Alexandra. In time, many gold seekers moved on, but many settled to either farm the land or supply services to farmers. Soon these settlers were demanding a railway line to link their towns with Dunedin. A government report in 1877 offered a variety of possible rail routes, and eventually the decision settled on the Otago Central railway line as it had the least tricky terrain.

In the winter of 1879, work began near Dunedin, but with 12 viaducts and 10 tunnels to be built through the Taieri Gorge, the line progressed at an excruciatingly slow pace, finally reaching Middlemarch 12 years later. This section of the line is still open today and is an ideal add-on to the rail trail ride.

Only seven years later, in 1898, the next 59-km section was completed through to Ranfurly, a town purpose-built for the railway. Ranfurly holds the record as the coldest town in the country. It recorded minus 25.6 degrees Celsius in 1903. In 1930, a series of devastating arson attacks resulted in much of the town being rebuilt in the art deco style favoured at that time.

The Otago Central line finally reached Clyde in April 1907, 28 years after construction began. In 1921, it was pushed through to its final destination of Cromwell (284 km from Dunedin), although this section was later flooded with the construction of the Clyde Dam.

Two of the most historic sites on the rail trail lie at Oturehua. The first is Gilchrist's Store, built in 1898 and still open today as New Zealand's oldest continuously operating general store. Then just out of town is Hayes Engineering, where the ubiquitous wire fence strainer was invented in 1927. They are still used in their millions on farm fences around the country.

For the first half of the twentieth century, trains were one of the most popular modes of transport in New Zealand and around the world. But the Otago Central line didn't run without problems. Infestations of rabbits stripped the vegetation from the banks and cuttings, resulting in continuous slips across the lines; sparks from the steam engines set off trackside grass fires, and on 4 June 1943 the train derailed while travelling at twice the permitted speed through a cutting just south of Hyde. Twenty-one passengers were killed and 47 were injured.

The popularity of the train dwindled as people began to use private cars more after World War II. Then, in 1979, during a period of global oil shortages, the Otago Excursion 'weekender' train ran from Dunedin to Cromwell, and the rail's popularity was revived for a time.

Eleven years later, the Cromwell to Clyde section of the rail was closed when construction work began on the Clyde Dam, and shortly after, the line from Clyde to Middlemarch followed suit. It took one year to lift the line that had taken a multitude of engineers, stonemasons, blacksmiths and labourers 16 years to lay.

Abandoned rail corridors have proved extremely popular for recreation overseas, and in 1993 DOC bought the 150-km rail corridor between Clyde and Middlemarch with the aim of creating a similar recreation destination here. Some landowners were sceptical, but many locals got behind the project. A charitable trust formed in 1994 to help DOC realise the vision, and the first section of rail trail opened within the year — 11 km from Hyde to Daisybank.

Seven years and $850,000 later, the full 150-km Otago Central Rail Trail was officially opened. It now attracts around 30,000 riders a year, who contribute an estimated $12 million to the local economy. The rail trail is widely credited for revitalising Central Otago.

FOOD AND ACCOMMODATION

Food and accommodation services along the trail are comprehensively listed on the trail
website: www.otagocentralrailtrail.co.nz

Because the trail is now so popular, you should book your accommodation in advance
during public holidays and on weekends.

If you want someone to organise your whole trip along the rail trail, contact Trail Journeys
in Clyde. They have over 500 hire bikes and also organise accommodation, meals and
transport. Altitude Bikes in Alexandra offers a similar service, as do Bike it Now, Off the
Rails and Cycle Surgery (see Bike hire for details).

SHORTCUTS AND DETOURS

The Highlights For those short on time, the most interesting parts of the rail trail (those
with tunnels and viaducts) are from Oturehua to Omakau (29 km) and Ranfurly to
Hyde (32 km).

Ophir Detour It is worth branching off the rail trail at Omakau to visit Ophir and take
a look at the Ophir Bridge. Ophir is 2 km from Omakau, and the bridge is a further
kilometre.

Naseby A living museum 14 km north of Ranfurly, the scenic and historic small town of
Naseby is a common overnight destination. Most people arrange a shuttle to take them
there, although it is only 10 km from the rail trail via the Gimmerburn–Ranfurly Road.
In April the autumnal colours around the small lakes are stunning, and in winter it is
famous for curling. See www.nasebyinfo.org.nz

ROXBURGH GORGE TRAIL

There is no other landscape like it in New Zealand. The Roxburgh region is a desert without sand. A desert with the country's largest river flowing through it, but for most of the year hardly a drop of rain falls upon the rocky ground. Massive schist boulders lay stacked precariously upon each other, and under many of them are the hovels dug out by nineteenth-century men hungry in their search for gold, willing to suffer in search of the mother lode.

The Roxburgh Gorge Trail is totally unique. The first third leaves the bustle of Alexandra behind as it enters the gorge and passes through the spectacular Narrows on its way to a jetty near Doctors Point. Riders then hop on a boat for a completely different view of the gorge, one that gives a better appreciation of the scale of the landscape, and of the diabolical mining that was mostly done by hand. The final third leaves Lake Roxburgh and sidles up into a crooked side stream before finishing beside Roxburgh Dam. By 2020, it is likely that the trail will have been constructed all the way down the gorge. There is currently a 12-km gap in the middle that is being closed by boat operators.

This trail starts near one end of the venerable Otago Central Rail Trail, and finishes a stone's throw from its sister trail, the wonderful Clutha Gold Trail. All three trails combined make for one of the best week-long cycling holidays in the world.

SUMMARY •••

Start point Alexandra
End point Roxburgh Dam
Distance 34 km
Likely time 4–6 hours
Grading Grade 2+ (Easy, but some sections are precipitous)
Surface Smooth gravel
Bike type Mountain bike or comfort/hybrid bike
Map The one in this book is currently the best available
Trail website www.cluthagold.co.nz
In emergencies There is no cellphone coverage in the gorge, but the trail is not long

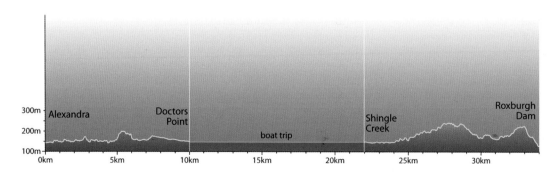

Roxburgh Gorge Trail

Bike hire Altitude Bikes in Alexandra, phone 03 448 8917, www.altitudebikes.co.nz

Getting there Alexandra is 92 km from Queenstown via SH6 and SH8, and 192 km
    from Dunedin. Otherwise, ride the Otago Central Rail Trail to Alexandra

Trail transport You can arrange transport from the end of the trail at Roxburgh Dam to
    Alexandra with Altitude Bikes (see Bike Hire above)

Doctors Point jetty to Shingle Creek The middle section of the trail is by boat. Contact
    Clutha River Cruises in Alexandra to arrange transport, phone 0800 CLUTHA (258 842)
    or 022 068 3302, www.clutharivercruises.co.nz, or Beaumont Jet, phone 027 784
    5649 or 03 485 9455, www.beaumontjet.co.nz

Trail donation A donation of $25 per adult or $50 per family covers the cost of trail
    maintenance for both the Roxburgh Gorge and Clutha Gold trails

ROUTE DESCRIPTION

Alexandra to jetty opposite Doctors Point
10 km one way, 1–2 hours, Grade 2+ (Easy)

Starting from the Alexandra shopping centre, cross the road bridge heading south on
SH8. The bridge is narrow, but it has a pedestrian path on the western side. At the far
end, turn right down a gravel path that leads to the Clutha River/Mata-Au, then turn right
again to head downriver on the Roxburgh Gorge Trail.

If you are driving to the trail, head through the centre of town on Tarbert Street and,
at the southern end, turn right into a large parking area below the bridge. Ride from

A lookout near The Narrows, Roxburgh Gorge.

the trail information board across the bridge to the trail.

The trail passes through an exotic woodland, before entering a rocky desert with good views of the gorge. Many of the larger boulders were home to gold miners in the 1860s and 1870s. The trail goes right past a couple of rock dwellings, complete with stone fireplaces, and built rock walls. They must have been miserable hovels in winter.

After crossing a bridge over Butchers Creek the trail climbs a moderate hill and descends to the stunning Narrows, where there are two tight switchbacks serving as brilliant lookout points. The last few kilometres of this trail descends to a jetty built in 2013.

From the end of the trail, either head back the same way, or hop on a boat to be taken downriver to Shingle Creek. Make sure you have arranged a boat beforehand. There is no cellphone coverage in the gorge.

Doctors Point jetty to Shingle Creek

12 km, 1 hour

A trail has not been built along this section because of land access issues. These may be resolved in five or 10 years' time as part of the land tenure review process, as this is actually public land that was leased 99 years ago and the lease is now up. Until then you must take a boat down the river for 12 km to the next section of track. You must book ahead.

The middle section of the trail is by boat.

The perspective of Roxburgh Gorge from the water is completely different. Once you pull away from the land, you can appreciate the scale of the water races that were built, rock by rock, across massive hills. The water was being diverted for many kilometres, to gold-mining areas. You can see abandoned sluicing equipment in several places. Your boat captain can show you interesting relics and explain their history along the way to Shingle Creek.

Shingle Creek to Roxburgh Dam
12 km one way, 1–2 hours, Grade 2+ (Easy)

Beside the small bay at Shingle Creek stands an old tin shack that you can shelter in if it is raining. Navigation is easy from here as there is only one track to follow. It climbs gently down valley, affording good views as it gains height.

To avoid a steep ravine at Elbow Creek, the track heads away from Lake Roxburgh for a few kilometres, turning in and out of side gullies before heading back to the lake. A final and impressive set of switchbacks heralds the end of the Roxburgh Gorge Trail. At the top corner, take a look back at the view of Roxburgh Gorge for the last time.

From the top of the hill it is only a few minutes to a small car park. From the car park, a steep gravel 4WD track leads down to a large lookout area above Roxburgh Dam.

Those continuing on to the Clutha Gold Trail should ride a few hundred metres down the sealed road to a T-intersection — turn left and ride across the dam. The Clutha Gold Trail starts 600 metres from the far end of the dam.

The impressive Lake Roxburgh switchbacks.

Cyclists in front of the Alexandra road bridge, circa 1901.

TRAIL TALES

The town of Alexandra, at the start of this ride, dates back to the first gold discoveries in the Otago region in the 1860s. It was originally named Lower Dunstan, then Manuherikia, then The Junction. Finally, in 1863, the name Alexandra was settled on, in honour of Princess Alexandra of Denmark, future Queen of the United Kingdom and wife to King Edward VII.

Alexandra is based at the confluence of the mighty Clutha and Manuherikia rivers. Residents originally used punt ferries to cross the rivers. The first ferry was just a packing case that men stood on as it was hauled across by a cable. The punts expanded in size until the last ferry was able to carry loads of up to 30 tons.

Locals lobbied hard for a bridge across the Clutha and in the winter of 1879 builder Jeremiah Drummery started constructing a suspension bridge with two magnificent 30-metre-tall towers, which still stand today. The bridge took three years to build and was opened on 2 June 1882 at a final cost of £32,000. It served for over 70 years, and the schist block towers can be seen from the start of the trail. By the time a second bridge was built in 1958, the old bridge was in poor condition. Bus passengers were sometimes advised, for their own safety, to hop off the bus and walk across!

In the 1860s, the Roxburgh Gorge was quite a different place, both geographically and socially. Frenchmans Point, nicknamed the 'Jewellers Shop', at the confluence of the Manuherikia and Clutha rivers was originally a crescent-shaped terrace, about 400 metres long with a sandy beach at its front.

Gold hunters probed the beach, but found nothing of merit . . . initially. Then, in the winter of 1864, the river flowed lower than usual and a party of miners struck the lode they'd been looking for. Immediately, 15 claims were pegged out, but the workings were precarious — every time the river rose to any extent, the claims would be flooded. The

Please do not disturb the rabbits.

miners persevered and, by 1872, more than 35,000 ounces of gold had been discovered along the banks of the Roxburgh Gorge. The miners lived in tiny stone cottages, and rudimentary shelters under schist slabs. The hardships were borne with the knowledge that they were temporary — the miners would find gold, or not, and then move on. By mid-1873, all the best gold in the area was gone and so was the terrace formation, dispersed to the waters of the Clutha through the miners' sluicing efforts.

Huge gold dredges worked the river throughout the late 1880s, with the most successful being the *Dunedin*, which extracted around 528 kg of gold over the time that it ran the river.

In 1947, the Roxburgh Dam site was selected as the ideal location for a hydro-electric power scheme. Demand was high for electricity and at one stage 1400 people were working on the construction in an effort to finish the job as quickly as possible. In the first year, most of the efforts focused on diverting the river along a 14-metre-deep, 30-metre-wide and 550-metre-long temporary diversion channel. The final cost of the Roxburgh Dam was

Dr Barrie Wills in one of the small rock shelters beside the trail.

£17,000,000. It was completed ahead of schedule and the first electricity was generated in July 1956. In the process, 30 km of the gorge was flooded and Lake Roxburgh was formed.

Riding the trail today, it is hard to imagine how impressive the gorge once was. Over millennia, New Zealand's most powerful river had carved a ravine up to 400 metres deep, where massive rapids accelerated through steep-sided constrictions. The gorge proper started 700 metres down from Alexandra, at a place once called the 'Gates of the Gorge' where schist bluffs squeezed the river to less than 40 metres in width. The most spectacular feature of the gorge was further down, at a place now called The Narrows. Centuries ago, the left wall of the gorge collapsed, blocking the river. The Clutha poured over the top, creating huge falls known as the Golden Falls. They were so powerful they scoured out a large basin below them and pushed up shingle into an island in the centre, which was named Island Basin. Miners working in the vicinity had to shout to be heard over the noise of the Golden Falls.

The Roxburgh Dam was originally designed with a 'life' of 50 years. In 2007, this 'life' was extended another 35 years. The dam's owner, Contact Energy, has stated that the most significant issue associated with the dam has been the regular flooding of Alexandra, which has been exacerbated by the build-up of sediment in the lake. Eventually this, along with the dam's ageing structure, will lead to it being decommissioned, at which time the now flooded gorge may be restored.

Butchers Creek bridge, 6 km from Alexandra.

FOOD AND ACCOMMODATION

Alexandra A lovely town with lots of cafes, restaurants, shops and accommodation:
www.alexandra.co.nz

Roxburgh Dam Lake Roxburgh Lodge, restaurant, bike and kayak hire (highly
recommended), phone 03 446 8220, www.lakeroxburghlodge.co.nz

Roxburgh A small town 10 km from the end of the trail with a few cafes, shops and several
accommodation options: iSite, phone 03 262 7999; Riders Rest, phone 03 446 8988,
www.ridersrestroxburgh.com

SHORTCUTS AND DETOURS

The Narrows Short on time? Ride from Alexandra to The Narrows lookout and back. It
is 6 km each way, with just a few small hills. The Narrows was formed by a massive
landslide that completely dammed the river.

The Alexandra–Clyde Anniversary Track This is a fun and easy 12-km extension to the
Roxburgh Gorge Trail. This trail is shown on Google Maps as 'Clyde–Alexandra Riverside
Trail'. From Clyde, it starts from the end of the old bridge across the Clutha at the end of
Matau Street and then follows the south side of the Clutha River/Mata-Au to Alexandra,
where it meets the Roxburgh Gorge Trail.

The Narrows lookout.

CLUTHA GOLD TRAIL

The magic of the Clutha Gold Trail is hard to pin down. The trail is easy to ride, but also fun because of the way it weaves through forest and around the hills, providing a constant sense of discovery. There are also the extraordinary tales of Maori, European and Chinese exploration, in search of pounamu and gold. And there are the remains of once-large towns, ready to welcome us modern-day, two-wheeled travellers with their southern hospitality. Whatever the reason, there is no doubt that the Clutha Gold activates the simple joy of riding a bicycle, and provides one of the best Great Rides.

The Clutha Gold Trail starts just below the Roxburgh Dam, although I recommend you combine it with the Roxburgh Gorge Trail, which starts 34 km up the valley at Alexandra. From the dam it follows the Clutha River/Mata-Au to three towns — Roxburgh, Millers Flat and Beaumont. There is hardly a hill in sight. Much of the trail is purpose-built for cycling, while other sections use old road and rail formations. It's absolutely brilliant.

From Beaumont the mighty river is left behind as the trail climbs east and passes through a long-disused railway tunnel, descends to Evans Flat and rolls into the lovely small town of Lawrence. The built trail is 73 km long but the ride itself is 80 km if you branch off to cafes and accommodation beside the trail.

SUMMARY

Start point Roxburgh Dam (near the end of the Roxburgh Gorge Trail)
End point Lawrence
Distance 80 km
Likely time 2 days
Grading Grade 2 (Easy)
Surface Wide, smooth gravel paths
Bike type Comfort/hybrid bike or mountain bike
Map An official trail map is available at i-SITEs in Alexandra, Roxburgh and Lawrence, and most businesses around the trail
Trail website www.cluthagold.co.nz
In emergencies There is 70% Spark coverage and 30% Vodafone coverage on this trail.
Bike hire Altitude Bikes in Alexandra, phone 03 448 8917, www.altitudebikes.co.nz; iBike Hire in Lawrence and Dunedin, phone 0800 480 680, www.ibikehire.co.nz; Trail Journeys in Clyde, phone 0800 030 381 or 03 449 2150, www.trailjourneys.co.nz
Getting there A good option is to drive to Lawrence, get a shuttle up to Roxburgh Dam (or even Alexandra) and ride back to your car. Lawrence is 92 km (1 hour 10 minutes) from Dunedin. It is a further 70 km (1 hour) from Lawrence to Roxburgh Dam. From Roxburgh Dam, it is a 125-km (1.5 hours) drive to Queenstown
Trail transport Altitude Adventures in Alexandra, iBike Hire in Dunedin and Lawrence and Trail Journeys in Clyde (see Bike Hire)

Clutha Gold Trail

to alexandra

Roxburgh Gorge Trail

Roxburgh Dam

Clutha R. / Mata-Au

Roxburgh

Hercules Flat

Pinders Pond

Dumbarton Rock

Teviot

Ettrick

Teviot Rd

Teviot R.

L. Onslow

LAMMERLAW RANGE

arched bridge

Millers Flat

Clutha R. / Mata-Au

Lonely Graves

Horseshoe Bend

Millennium Track

Raes Junction

Beaumont

Clutha R. / Mata-Au

BLUE MOUNTAINS

tunnel

Bowlers Creek

Evans Flat

Gabriels Gully

Lawrence

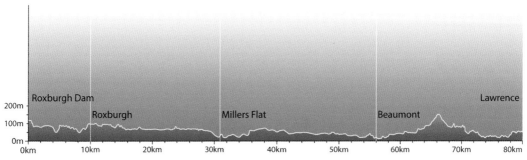

Roxburgh Dam	Roxburgh		Millers Flat		Beaumont		Lawrence
200m							
100m							
0m							
0km	10km	20km	30km	40km	50km	60km	70km	80km

ROUTE DESCRIPTION

Roxburgh Dam to Roxburgh township

10 km, 1 hour, Grade 2– (Easy)

The trail head is signposted 500 metres below the Roxburgh Dam, beside Roxburgh East Road. There are marker posts every kilometre, showing the distance from the start and the end. It follows the eastern edge of the Clutha River/Mata-Au, sometimes weaving through trees, and other times crossing open space beside the river. There are a couple of 50-metre stretches you may want to walk, but most of this section is as easy as any rail trail, except a lot more engaging. If you feel like a swim, jump in at Bunny Cove (signposted).

A sheltered bay beside the Clutha River.

The trail pops onto the road at the first bridge across the Clutha. Roxburgh township is on the far side. It has shops, galleries, accommodation, an i-SITE and a small museum. Allow a couple of hours to explore this interesting and welcoming small town.

Roxburgh township to Millers Flat

21 km, 2 hours, Grade 1+ (Very easy)

From the main street in Roxburgh head back down Jedburgh Street and across the road bridge over the Clutha River/Mata-Au. Turn right and continue following the trail as it weaves through willows beside the river. Easy cycle trails don't get any better than this. After 6 km, you'll reach Pinders Pond on your left. This is a popular picnic and swimming spot and has toilets next to a car park.

From Pinders Pond the trail passes the massive Dumbarton Rock, which once stretched all the way across the river. The valley then spreads out, offering long views over farmland on both sides of the Clutha. About 10 km from Roxburgh you'll meet a fork in the trail, where a side track leads to the historic Teviot Goods Shed. Give it a miss and go straight ahead for more lovely riverside riding. After crossing Teviot Road a few times, the trail rolls into Millers Flat on the main street. This is a small settlement with a few places to stay, a general store, a swimming pool and, over the arched bridge across the Clutha River/Mata-Au, a cafe and gallery. The general store has limited hours during the weekend. It is right next to the old bakehouse.

The old Millers Flat bakehouse, before it was restored.

Millers Flat to Beaumont
25 km, 2–3 hours, Grade 2 (Easy)
From the old bakehouse, cross the road and ride through the park on your right to continue following the trail down valley. After riding between two large concrete bridge piles, switch back up onto the old road, which runs parallel to the new road. Here, the new road is actually on the old railway formation.

A few short sections of the trail share the gravel road, called the Millennium Track. This part of the Clutha River/Mata-Au is a popular spot for kayaking, and there are several short tracks leading down to the river's edge.

The trail meets SH8 at the Beaumont Bridge. The trail carries straight on ahead to

Lawrence, but most people cross the bridge on the right to drop into the local tavern. It also has accommodation and a campground.

Much of the trail follows the mighty Clutha.

Beaumont to Lawrence

22 km, 2 hours, Grade 2 (Easy)

From the Beaumont Bridge, ride down Weardale Street, then left on Eastferry Street to head past the old school and on to the next part of off-road trail.

The section branches away from the Clutha River/Mata-Au and mostly follows the old railway line to Lawrence. You will be climbing almost imperceptibly away from Beaumont before a last-minute steep section to an old railway tunnel. Either take a torch for the tunnel, or walk through.

From the far end, the trail descends gently to Lawrence, except for one more short hill. There are several points of interest, including two brick buildings on your right, which are the remains of New Zealand's largest Chinese settlement, about 2 km before Lawrence. Straight after the brick buildings you will ride past a forest restoration project to a car park, 900 metres from Lawrence. Ride beside the highway and turn left at Back Road to cruise into town.

Lawrence was New Zealand's first gold-rush town. The Lawrence information centre and museum, and nearby Gabriels Gully mining area, are well worth investigating. Lawrence also has some great cafes and places to stay.

Chinese gold miner Wing Chung with a cradle on the banks of the Clutha River.

TRAIL TALES

The Clutha River/Mata-Au is New Zealand's largest by volume and, along with the surrounding district, was called Molyneux (Mill of the Water) by early Otago settlers. The Maori name, Mata-Au, meaning 'surface current', is an apt warning of the many swirling eddies along the river's length. This river has a massive catchment and discharges almost twice the volume of water of New Zealand's longest river — the Waikato. To swim down the Clutha River/Mata-au, a person would have to be crazy, or desperate.

In the early 1850s, explorer Nathanael Chalmers met chief Reko from Tuturau and convinced Reko and another Maori guide to take him north through Central Otago in return for a three-legged pot. Chalmers became the first European to reach lakes Wakatipu, Wanaka and Hawea and explore the valleys of the upper Clutha. But it was not without cost. His clothes were torn to shreds, his boots disintegrated and had to be replaced with flax sandals, and he became critically ill with dysentery. Fearing for Chalmers' life, Reko and his companion built a flax raft and the team made a swift and frightening trip down the Clutha and out to settlements on the coast.

Towns along this trail were settled from the coast inland. Lawrence was home to New Zealand's first major gold strike — one of the biggest in the world. Gabriel Read discovered gold in what became known as Gabriels Gully in 1861. At the height of the gold rush, Lawrence had a population of over 11,000 men, making it one of the largest settlements in the country. After a few years, the European miners had found the easy gold and many moved on to more lucrative strikes.

Fearing that the departure of the gold miners would bring the local economies to a standstill, the Dunedin Chamber of Commerce invited Chinese miners to come and pick over the old workings. In the 1800s, many Chinese left their homes in central Asia to

Chinese miners in front of a stone cottage, Otago.

seek wealth in the gold fields of America, Australia and New Zealand. A steady flow of Chinese began to arrive in Otago from Australia in the spring of 1865.

However, welcome as these hard workers were, they were prohibited from settling in existing townships. Instead, they were forced to set up virtual ghettos on the outskirts. In 1883, more than 500 Chinese lived in 60–70 buildings on less than half a hectare of land about 1 km west of Lawrence, between the road and the railway line.

The railway line reached Lawrence in 1877, and there it stalled for 30 years before being slowly extended to Beaumont. In 1928, the railway, so crucial to the economic viability of the commercial fruit industry, finally made it to Roxburgh — the end of the line. Any thought of it connecting with the Otago Central line ended with the construction of the 70-metre-high Roxburgh Dam. The railway proved useful for transporting goods during the construction of the dam, but closed soon after construction was complete. The last trip was in May 1968.

Like so many of the towns in Otago, Roxburgh has its origins in gold. When a party of four men travelling up the Clutha reached Teviot Creek one of them offered to carry two of the other three across. The two dry men then continued on their way, leaving the other two to hang their clothes out to dry. While waiting, they tried their luck at gold panning and decided then and there to stake out a claim. Others followed, and a gold-mining settlement, known as Teviot Village, soon grew on the eastern side of the river. Over some years, it gravitated to the western side. In April 1877, it was renamed Roxburgh. By this time, the area had already developed a reputation for its stone fruit. As early as the 1860s, the Tamblyn brothers had begun growing commercial fruit in the region and sent the first consignment of 40 cases of peaches to Dunedin in 1877.

Millers Flat, 17 km downriver from Roxburgh, is another important fruit-growing area and played a significant role in the gold-dredging prospects of the river. In 1892, around a dozen dredges plugged the river for gold between Coal Creek (near Roxburgh Dam) and Beaumont.

The arched bridge at Millers Flat is famous for being opened not once but twice. The completion of the long-awaited bridge in 1898 was cause for much celebration. When the time came for the grand opening, it was discovered that Premier Richard John Seddon was not scheduled to open the bridge for some months. It was left to a honeymooning couple to officiate an impromptu opening, after which a heavy chain was strung across the bridge closing it to 'vehicular traffic' until the official opening on 23 February 1899.

The dramatic Clutha River/Mata-Au has touched many lives in many different ways. Early in 1865, the body of a young man was discovered on the banks of the river, near Horseshoe Bend. At an inquest it was decided that the body must be that of Charles Alms, who had been thrown from his horse while swimming cattle across the river. The body was buried in an unmarked grave and more or less forgotten. Later that year, though, a gold miner named William Rigney came across it and made a simple headstone from a piece of black pine. Upon it he inscribed the words 'Somebody's Darling Lies Buried Here', and the Lonely Graves site was formed.

Further downstream, a builder working on the construction of the Beaumont Bridge in 1884 had luck on his side. The clumsy John Polglaise fell off the scaffolding while working on the bridge . . . twice! He was swept downstream, and rescued both times.

One of New Zealand's most famous authors, Janet Frame, changed her last name to Clutha by deed poll, partly in a bid to protect her privacy but also to acknowledge how important this dramatic river was to her.

The river, and in particular Beaumont, was also on the long journey undertaken by Maori travelling from Southland to the West Coast for pounamu. They would stay at Beaumont for a few months, tending crops and building up their supplies before moving on.

The idea for the Clutha Gold Trail developed in 2006, after locals had seen the success of the Otago Central Rail Trail. In 2010, it gained funding from the cycle trails project, and in late 2013 the full trail was officially opened.

For over a century Roxburgh has been famous for its apricots.

FOOD AND ACCOMMODATION

Roxburgh iSite, phone 03 262 7999, and Lawrence Information Centre, phone 03 485 9222, can help with booking accommodation.

Alexandra Cafes, restaurants, shops, accommodation: www.alexandra.co.nz

Roxburgh Dam Lake Roxburgh Lodge and Restaurant, www.lakeroxburghlodge.co.nz

Roxburgh Cafes, shops, accommodation: iSite, phone 03 262 7999; Clutha Gold Cottages, phone 03 446 8364, www.cluthagoldcottages.co.nz; Roxburgh Motels, phone 03 446 8093; Villa Rose Backpackers, phone 0800 132 612 or 021 294 1977, www.villarose.co.nz; The Commercial Hotel/Backpackers, phone 03 446 8160, www.centralotagonz.com; Riders Rest accommodation, phone 03 446 8988, www.ridersrestroxburgh.com; and more at www.centralotagonz.com

Millers Flat Food and accommodation: see www.centralotagonz.com for accommodation; The Millers Flat Tavern: phone 03 446 6025; Millers Flat Four Square is only open on Saturday mornings.

Beaumont Food and accommodation: Beaumont Hotel and Caravan Park, phone 03 485 9431; Beaumont Jet, phone 027 784 5649 or 03 485 9455, www.beaumontjet.co.nz for transport up and down the river, and for accommodation.

Lawrence Supermarket, cafes, shops, accommodation: www.lawrence.nz

SHORTCUTS AND DETOURS

Roxburgh–Millers shortcut If you only have a couple of hours to spare, then start at
Roxburgh township and ride down to Millers Flat. This 21-km section rides beautifully.

Teviot Goods Shed If the Clutha River/Mata-Au is in flood then you will need to take a
signposted 'flood detour'. It starts 10 km down valley from Roxburgh and goes to
Millers Flat via Loop Road. On the way you will pass the remains of a large stone
building, which was once the Teviot Goods Shed.

Birch Island This 1.5-hour jetboat and walking tour starts from Beaumont and heads 12 km
down the Clutha River/Mata-Au to explore the natural and cultural history of Birch Island.
Contact Beaumont Jet (phone 027 784 5649 or 03 485 9455) to arrange a tour.

Easy riding from Millers Flat to Beaumont.

Gabriels Gully Four km north of Lawrence on Gabriels Gully Road is a lovely picnic area at
a historic gold-mining area. Well worth a look if you have time at the end of your ride.

The Grand Tour Riders can complete an 8-day circuit of Otago as follows: Leave Dunedin
via the Taieri Gorge Railway, then bike 140 km of the Otago Central Rail Trail to
Alexandra. Next, ride and boat through the Roxburgh Gorge to the start of the Clutha
Gold Trail. This leads to Lawrence, 1 hour's shuttle ride from Dunedin. Alternatively, the
fit and fearless may prefer to ride via the Lawrence to Dunedin Connector (see *Classic
New Zealand Cycle Trails* for details).

QUEENSTOWN TRAIL

A 100-km network of smooth gravel cycle paths now connects the highlights of the Queenstown area. From downtown Queenstown the trail skirts around Lake Wakatipu, with the Remarkables towering above. It's flat and easy. From Frankton (by the airport) the options begin; will you head for the quaint heritage of Arrowtown, or the buzz of bungy jumping at the historic Kawarau Bridge? Perhaps the famous Gibbston wineries are more appealing, or a 1-hour ride around the picturesque Lake Hayes.

The Queenstown Trail network has been built to cater for everyone and provides an ideal way to explore an area of outstanding scenic beauty. It includes seven bridges, with five crossing the spectacular Arrow River. Almost 100,000 people rode the trails in the first six months, and although most are doing short rides of less than a few hours in length,

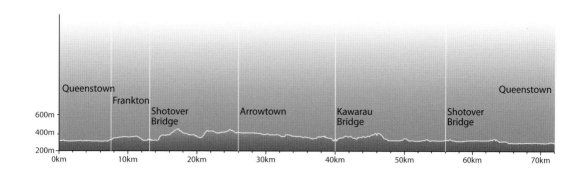

Queenstown
Frankton
Shotover
Bridge
Arrowtown
Kawarau
Bridge
Shotover
Bridge
Queenstown

600m
400m
200m

0km   10km   20km   30km   40km   50km   60km   70km

ARROWTOWN

CROWN RANGE

Arrow R.

Kawarau Bridge

Gibbston
River Trail

Kawarau R.

Chard Farm

Gibbston
Valley Winery

Gibbston
Tavern

Gibbston
Back Road

6

there is an option to do an 80-km, two-day ride, which is described below. This loop trip goes from Queenstown to Arrowtown then down the Arrow River to the wineries region and back via the Kawarau River. There are plenty of alternatives, so trips can cater for any group of friends and family.

Good times on the Queenstown Trail.

SUMMARY ··

Start and end point Queenstown

Distance 72–81 km

Likely time Up to 2 days

Grading Grade 2 (Easy) to Grade 3 (Intermediate), with a few unexpected short steep hills

Surface Mostly smooth, wide, gravel paths

Bike type Comfort/hybrid bike or a mountain bike

Map Download a map from the trail website

Trail website www.queenstowntrail.co.nz

In emergencies There is good cellphone coverage on this trail

Bike hire Go to the Plan and Book section of www.queenstowntrail.co.nz to choose from several bike-hire companies. The Gibbston Valley Winery also offers bike hire and shuttles to and from Queenstown

Getting there Queenstown is 280 km (3.5 hours) from Dunedin and 480 km (6 hours) from Christchurch. There are dozens of flights a day to Queenstown Airport, at

Frankton. The trail can be accessed from several entry points, including Queenstown, Frankton and Arrowtown. Queenstown is 10 minutes' drive from the airport. There are regular airport shuttles and a bus, as well as rental cars available. Many accommodation providers also offer free shuttles to and from the town centre

Stunning autumnal colours around Lake Hayes.

ROUTE DESCRIPTION

Queenstown to Arrowtown

26–35 km, 3–5 hours, Grade 3 (Intermediate)

Coast down to the waterfront at Queenstown and turn left, following an easy cycle path around the edge of the lake to Frankton. At the head of Frankton Arm, you have two choices. The shorter option climbs up to the golf course, past 'Hendo's Hole' (an infamous developer's folly), down Grant Road and through an industrial area to the Shotover River. To take this option, turn left to follow the trail under the new Shotover River Bridge and up to the old Shotover Bridge.

Alternatively, take the scenic route to the same bridge by following the signs alongside the lake and crossing SH6 at the pedestrian crossing by the traffic lights. After a short ride through residential streets, turn right at the kindergarten onto a trail that leads for 7 km around the top of the Kawarau River then up the Shotover River Valley to the old Shotover Bridge.

Cross the bridge and loop around underneath it to continue up river. Now carefully follow the signs along a mix of trail and road to Arrowtown. Be prepared to tackle a couple of steep hills on the way (making this option a Grade 3) plus some tricky navigation through Millbrook Resort.

The trail leads through the west end of Arrowtown to the Chinese huts. Then just nip up to the main street 50 metres away. It is one of those movie-set type towns that radiates character — only it's the real thing!

Riding beside Lake Wakatipu.

Arrowtown to the historic Kawarau Bridge

14 km, 1.5–2 hours, Grade 2 (Easy)

Once again, you have a couple of options, but the choice is quite simple really — if you don't want to be bored, don't follow the path beside Centennial Ave heading south.

The best option is to drop back down to the Chinese settlement beside the Arrow River and follow the path downriver, crossing five bridges on the way to the historic Kawarau Bridge. After crossing a cyclist's bridge tucked under the highway bridge, turn left then follow Arrow Junction Road for a while before the trail begins again on your left and leads to an impressive suspension bridge and then an underpass. No expense has been spared. The trail then leaves the river and follows the original highway to the Kawarau Bridge. If people are bungy jumping, hop off your bike and walk past the action.

There is a cafe at the bridge, and several renowned vineyards dotted along the Gibbston River Trail.

Kawarau Bridge to Queenstown

32 km, 2–4 hours, Grade 3 (Intermediate)

The final leg of this ride involves a few hills. Don't say we didn't warn you! Ride back towards Arrowtown on the track you rode in on for just over 4 km. When you reach Morven Ferry Road again, look for a turn-off 30 metres away to your right. From there, a new trail crosses farmland and drops down beside the Kawarau River. This is a really enjoyable section with stunning views. Eventually it leaves the Kawarau River and takes you 2 km up the Shotover Valley, right back to the old bridge across the Shotover River.

Cross the bridge and take the track downriver, under the new highway bridge, left past the quarry and down to the river again, following the Queenstown Trail signs. This track will bring you out to Robertson Road, where you can nip out to Kawarau Road. Go down to the traffic lights and use the pedestrian crossing on this busy road, then follow cycle paths down to the lake edge. Turn right at the lake, and you'll be back in Queenstown in about half an hour.

TRAIL TALES

Thousands of years ago, the Arrow Basin and Lake Hayes were scoured out by the Wakatipu Glacier. Lake Hayes had originally been an arm of Lake Wakatipu, until the connection was severed by alluvial material washed down over millennia from the powerful Shotover River.

The Maori of Waitaha first discovered the area, followed by Ngati Mamoe and later Ngai Tahu. They made seasonal homes on the sides of Lake Hayes and sought pounamu from the West Coast.

Lake Hayes was originally named Hays Lake after D Hay, an Australian who explored the area in 1859 in search of suitable sheep country. Over time, the name changed as locals began to believe its name was a misspelling of rogue sea captain and early local hotelier Captain 'Bully' Hayes.

Late in 1859, William Rees and Nicholas von Tunzelmann forged a route from Lake Wanaka through to Lake Wakatipu via the Cardrona Valley and over the Crown Range to current-day Arrowtown. Rees became the first European to farm the Queenstown area, building his homestead in what is now the city centre. He burnt off much of the native beech forest and scrublands to make way for grazing and then planted trees such as Douglas fir, larch, willow and poplar to soften the harsh landscape he had created. One of Rees's farm workers, Alfred Duncan, is credited with providing the first written description of the Arrow River as 'flowing like silver threads through the blackened scrub-clothed plains'.

In May 1861, another of Rees's employees, shearer Jack Tewa, made the first gold discovery in the area. In 1862, either William Fox or the team of Thomas Low and John

MacGregor made the next discovery, and despite all attempts to keep their finds secret, by the end of the year over 1500 miners were camped on the Arrow River. In January 1863, the first load of gold was escorted out of the Arrow Gorge, all 340 kg of it, and gold fever was in full swing.

Eventually, William Rees's pastoral lease was cancelled, and the area was declared a gold field. Rees converted his woolshed into a hotel named the Queen's Arms (now Eichardt's), right in the centre of Queenstown, and business boomed.

At the climax of the gold rush, Arrowtown had a population of over 7000. As it became more established, avenues of trees were planted to make it look more like the miners' home towns in Europe.

But the tide turned quickly, and by 1865 most of the European miners had their sights set on the West Coast and abandoned the Otago fields in droves.

Concerned that the economy of the area would dwindle, the Otago Provincial Government invited Chinese miners to replace the European miners in the gold fields. The Chinese miners created their own settlement in west Arrowtown and remained there until 1928.

During the gold-mining period many bridges and roads were built, some of which are incorporated into the Queenstown Trail today. The most famous, the Kawarau Bridge, was completed on 30 December 1880, after hard campaigning by locals to have a road bridge

Three North Island cyclists tour the Southern Lakes District in 1941.

The historic Shotover Bridge — in use for over a century.

replace an unreliable punt service. The bridge continued as a major link to Queenstown for 80 years, but by the 1960s it could no longer cope with the size and volume of modern traffic and was replaced by a new highway bridge.

In 1988, the Kawarau Bridge leapt into the limelight again when AJ Hackett and Henry van Asch chose it for the world's first commercial bungy jump. The following year, DOC, with funding from the bungy-jump operation, started to restore the bridge.

The impressive 172-metre-long Lower Shotover Bridge was built between 1910 and 1915. By 2000, it had seriously deteriorated and was no longer being used by traffic. In 2003, a restoration project was taken up by the Rotary Shotover Bridge Restoration Trust. This was completed in 2005.

From farming and gold-mining origins, Queenstown has transformed into the adventure capital of New Zealand. In 1981, its population was less than 3500 but, a mere three decades later, it now boasts almost 2 million visitors per year. Various attractions can lay claim to this dramatic increase, including the Kawarau Bridge bungy jump, jetboating and skiing, the Remarkables mountain range, the Routeburn Track and the Queenstown Trail.

High riding over the Arrow River.

FOOD AND ACCOMMODATION

Queenstown The main tourist town in New Zealand. The place is buzzing and there are
    more support services than you could ever dream of: www.queenstownnz.co.nz
Arrowtown A much smaller and more historic town, with a good range of shops and
    accommodation: www.arrowtown.com

Gibbston The Gibbston Valley is famous for wines and has a bike-hire shop and
mountain-bike trail network: www.gibbstonvalleynz.com

Kawarau Bridge The bridge has a cafe next to it and, of course, you can join the crowds
lining up to cheat death by doing a bungy jump: www.bungy.co.nz

SHORTCUTS AND DETOURS

Lake Hayes Loop Lake Hayes offers an easy, single-track spin around a beautiful lake.
There are only two short but steep climbs. From Queenstown, head northeast on SH6.
A couple of kilometres past the new Shotover River Bridge, turn into the signposted car
park on the left. Ride down to the lake and complete this 1-hour lap in either direction.

Gibbston River Trail This 7-km, 1-hour, Grade 2 (Easy) path offers stunning scenery and
was fully upgraded in 2014. From Kawarau Bridge car park, you will find a Gibbston
River Trail sign. From there, it leads to several wineries, including: Chard Farm
Vineyard (2 km), Gibbston Valley Winery (1-km side trip) and Peregrine Winery (right
beside the trail), or, if you feel like a hilly loop, take the Gibbston Back Road into
the foothills for 3.5 km before flying down to the Gibbston Tavern, just across the
highway from the trail. At the far end, turn around and ride back the same way.

Jacks Point Track This 14-km, 2–3-hour ride comprises some brilliant Grade 3/4 single
track, with awesome lakeside vistas. From the southern end of the Kawarau Bridge
just out of Frankton, you'll see a sign for Kelvin Peninsula Track. Turn sharp right and
drop down to the water's edge to follow a single track between holiday mansions and
the lake's edge. Carry on around the golf course to the very end of the peninsula.

From the peninsula golf course, continue southeast around the lake. There are some
steep sections to test expert riders.

About 1 km before the impressive rock outcrops of Jacks Point, the track turns away
from the lake and zig-zags up to a road that leads through a new subdivision to SH6.

Off Yer Bike As the adventure capital of New Zealand, Queenstown has a smorgasbord
of exciting activities ready and waiting. The ultimate buzz is bungy jumping off the
Kawarau Bridge. For a longer-lasting adrenalin fix, try rafting the Shotover or Kawarau
rivers, or skiing in winter, or to simply mellow out, head for the 500-metre-high walk
up Queenstown Hill. The views are fantastic.

Queenstown Bike Park The best set of gravity-assisted trails in New Zealand start from
the top of the Queenstown Skyline Gondola. It is open most days from the middle
of September through to the middle of May. These action-packed mountain-bike
tracks range from Grade 3 (Intermediate) to Grade 6 (Extreme). Most people ride full
suspension bikes here. For more information go to www.skyline.co.nz/queenstown

AROUND THE MOUNTAINS

This fantastic trail around the Eyre Mountains south of Queenstown is being rolled out in three stages. One stage is already complete: it follows an existing back-country road with great scenery and virtually no traffic. It goes from the shores of Lake Wakatipu to Mavora Lakes or vice versa.

The second stage, completed in October 2015, is a rail trail from Kingston, at the southern tip of Lake Wakatipu, south to Lumsden and Mossburn.

The final stage is a mix of cycle trail and gravel road between Mossburn and Mavora Lakes, making this one of the best multi-day rides in New Zealand.

SUMMARY ··

Start point Queenstown

End point Kingston

Distance 196 km

Likely time 3–5 days

Grading Grade 1 (Very easy) to Grade 3 (Intermediate)

Surface Smooth rail trail and back-country gravel roads

Bike type Mountain bike or comfort/hybrid bike

Map and trail website www.aroundthemountains.co.nz for a trail map

In emergencies There is little cellphone coverage on much of this trail. An emergency personal locator beacon (PLB) is optional

Bike hire www.aroundthemountains.co.nz or numerous operators in Queenstown

Getting there There are regular flights every day into Queenstown. You'll need to book water transport in advance. Lake Wakatipu's historic steamer, the TSS *Earnslaw*, leaves daily over summer, every 2 hours from 10 a.m. to 8 p.m., www.realjourneys.co.nz; Queenstown Water Taxis offer more flexible times, phone 03 441 1124

Trail transport To get back to Queenstown from Kingston you'll need to book a shuttle. Try www.aroundthemountains.co.nz or Queenstown Bike Taxis, phone 021 296 7643, www.queenstownbiketaxis.co.nz

Special considerations As the most southern ride in New Zealand, this trail is best ridden during November to May. It is best not to ride the trail over winter or spring

Around the Mountains

QUEENSTOWN

Mt Nicholas

Lake Wakatipu

Walter Peak

Von R.

Mt Nicholas Rd

Mavora
Lakes

Mararoa R.

Mavora Lakes Rd

Oreti R.

Centre Hill Rd

E Y R E   M O U N T A I N S

Kingston

Mataura R.

6

Fairlight Station

Garston

Eyre Creek

Athol

94
o Te Anau

97

Oreti R.

6

Mataura R.

Five Rivers

Mossburn

94

Lumsden

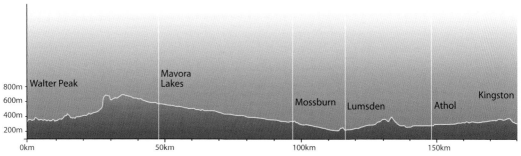

800m
600m
400m
200m

Walter Peak

Mavora
Lakes

Mossburn

Lumsden

Athol

Kingston

0km   50km   100km   150km

ROUTE DESCRIPTION

Queenstown to Mavora Lakes

58 km, 4–6 hours, Grade 3 (Intermediate)

From Queenstown, catch a water taxi or the historic steamboat TSS *Earnslaw* across Lake Wakatipu to Walter Peak Station (phone 0800 65 65 01 to book in advance — $36 per person and $5 per bike). Over summer, the *Earnslaw* is scheduled to leave Queenstown daily every two hours from 10 a.m. to 8 p.m. and it is a lovely trip. You can see right into the engine room of this beautiful boat.

From Walter Peak jetty, cycle 12 km around to Mount Nicholas Station, then head south on the quiet Von Road, which becomes Mount Nicholas Road. There is one serious climb — the Von Hill — that sees you gain 300 metres' elevation. It might take half an hour to walk if it's too steep to ride.

Quality time on Around the Mountains Cycle Trail.

Turn right at Mavora Lakes Road if you wish to visit the lakes. There is a camping area 7 km up this road at the southern end of North Mavora Lake. It is a beautiful area, but the sandflies will keep you moving (unless it's raining).

Mavora Lakes to Mossburn

50 km, 2–4 hours, Grade 2 (Easy) to Grade 3 (Intermediate)

There are plans to build a trail off-road from Mavora Lakes, but they are unlikely to start construction before 2019. Until then, just head back to the intersection and continue

Historic farm building beside the trail.

south on Mavora Lakes Road for 18.5 km before turning left onto Centre Hills Road.

Ride down Centre Hills Road for just over 9 km before turning left and riding down a 4WD track towards the Oreti River for 900 metres. Then turn right onto the purpose-built Around the Mountains Cycle Trail, which leads all the way to Mossburn. It runs roughly parallel to the Oreti River for approximately 20 km to Cumberland Street at the back of Mossburn.

Turn left down the main street of Mossburn to find two cafes and a garage. The Mossburn Hotel is just a few hundred metres down York Street.

Mossburn to Lumsden
21.5 km, 1.5–3 hours, Grade 2 (Easy)

Ride east out of Mossburn on the main road and you'll find the cycle trail, just on the edge of town. It runs parallel to the highway most of the way, but ducks off down a couple of country roads. It's well signposted.

You'll pass the driveway to Brookhaven Country Garden at the halfway mark.

If you are heading all the way to Lumsden, then straight after crossing the Oreti Highway Bridge, turn left twice, to ride under the bridge and then south to Lumsden 3 km away. If you don't want to take the side trip to Lumsden, head north after the bridge.

A cycle tourer at Mavora Lakes.

Lumsden to Athol

35 km, 2–4 hours, Grade 1 (Very easy)

It is 15 km from Lumsden to Five Rivers where there is a nice cafe and art gallery, just a few hundred metres off the main trail. It's all well signposted.

After refuelling, ride back to the main trail and continue north for another 20 km to Athol, a cute little town with cafes.

Athol to Kingston

32 km, 2–4 hours, Grade 2 (Easy)

From Athol, ride north and follow the trail to a pair of magnificent suspension bridges. From there the trail takes you right to the centre of Garston, a small village with a hotel, playground, some interesting historical boards and a honey shop.

Leaving Garston, the trail is on a country road most of the way to another suspension bridge, which crosses the Mataura River at the boundary between Southland and Central Otago. On the far side is Fairlight, a small railway station building, which has seen better days.

Continue north and you'll soon be enjoying a gentle downhill to Kingston, a scenic lakeside village with food and accommodation.

TRAIL TALES

The *Kingston Flyer* is possibly New Zealand's most famous vintage train. The *Flyer* actually refers to a number of engines that first operated in the 1890s from Kingston to Gore, Invercargill and sometimes Dunedin. At that time there was also a boat service from Kingston to Queenstown. The regular passenger service to Kingston ended in 1937, although special holiday trips continued through to Easter 1957.

'Ua' 177 steam locomotive (1900–1937) hauling a goods train at Kingston.

The *Kingston Flyer* was resurrected in 1971 by New Zealand Railways as a heritage service that proved hugely popular, carrying over 30,000 passengers before the line closed again, in 1979, due to flooding damage between Lumsden and Garston. The trains were taken to Kingston and resumed short 14-km trips from Kingston to Fairlight in 1982. At the time of writing, the future of the train is uncertain as it is up for sale.

New Zealand Railways also ran boat transport on Lake Wakatipu. At the beginning of last century, they commissioned a boat-building company in Dunedin to build a 50-metre-long steamship, which they called the *Earnslaw*, after the prominent peak, Mount Earnslaw (2889 metres), which can be seen from Lake Wakatipu. The ship was duly built for the grand cost of £21,000 and then carefully dismantled for transportation. Every part was numbered and packed onto a train bound for Kingston. In February 1912, after months of rebuilding, the TSS *Earnslaw* was finally launched. Along with three other New Zealand Railways ships, the 'Lady of the Lake', as the steamer was known, was a vital transporter of people, livestock and goods to farming stations around Lake Wakatipu. The TSS *Earnslaw* was bought by tourism company Real Journeys and still operates a regular daily service.

GINNY WOOD

Heading towards Hidden Burn.

Mount Nicholas Station is one of the largest farms in New Zealand with 30,000 merino sheep and 2200 Hereford cattle. It was first settled in the 1860s, and many of the farming techniques used on the station remain unchanged. Every year 9000 sheep are mustered down from the high mountains before the winter sets in and the peaks become cut off by snow. One of the main destinations of the fine merino wool is outdoor clothing. Mount Nicholas Station was the first station to supply Icebreaker with wool for their now famous merino garments.

FOOD AND ACCOMMODATION

Accommodation can be booked through www.aroundthemountains.co.nz. When you book through the website a percentage of the profits goes into the marketing and maintenance of the trail.

Queenstown Accommodation, food, shops: www.queenstownnz.co.nz

Walter Peak High-country farm with food and luxury accommodation available:
The Lodge at Walter Peak, phone 0800 766 854, www.thelodge.net.nz

Mount Nicholas Lodge and meals available if you book ahead, phone 03 409 0712, www.mtnicholas.co.nz

Mavora Lakes Campsite with toilets, www.doc.govt.nz

Mossburn A small town with a general store, dairy, two cafes and the Mossburn Railway Hotel, phone 03 248 6399, www.mossburnhotel.co.nz

Lumsden A large town with a wide range of accommodation and places to eat including cafes and restaurants. There is an information centre in the old railway station, phone 03 248 7178.

Five Rivers Has a great cafe and gallery, phone 03 248 7755, www.fiverivers.co.nz

Athol Small town with two stores: Lazybones Cafe with takeaways, internet and crafts, phone 03 248 8847, and the Highway Cafe and Dairy. Athol Lodge and Holiday Park, phone 021 184 5444, www.thelodgeathol.co.nz

Garston Small town with a cafe, the Garston Hotel and Cafe, phone 03 248 8989, and a B&B down the road, Naylor House, phone 03 248 8809, www.naylorhouse.co.nz

Kingston Holiday town with food and accommodation, check out www.kingston.kiwi.nz. Try the Kingston Corner Cafe and Bar for food and Kingston Holiday Park for a range of accommodation, phone 03 248 8501, 0800 807 836, www.kingstonholidaypark.co.nz

SHORTCUTS AND DETOURS

High in the hills above Garston is a network of trails following historic water races through conservation land and a former sheep farm. The trails are narrow in places and provide interesting riding in an exhilarating landscape. Access is organised through Welcome Rock Trails, which also provides maps: phone 027 239 2628, www.welcomerock.co.nz. Bookings are essential.

TOUR AOTEAROA: CAPE REINGA TO BLUFF

Combine nine Great Rides with a dozen Heartland Rides, a few mountain-bike tracks, one stretch of beach riding, and five connecting boat trips, and you have the 3000-km Tour Aotearoa — one of the world's great bikepacking journeys. From the northern tip of New Zealand to the southern toe, this inspirational cycle route reveals diverse landscapes, iconic heritage sites and welcoming rural communities. It is widely regarded by those who complete it as the trip of a lifetime. Brendan Pheasant, from Napier, says:

'I'm not sure I can convey the wonderfulness of it all — what a great route, what a diverse and beautiful little country, what fantastic people I met along the way, and what a lot of tasty food I ate!'

The shape and terrain of Aotearoa naturally ignites an interest in travelling its full length, and as the New Zealand Cycle Trails have been built, the route has become more and more inspiring. It was only a matter of time before a Cape Reinga to Bluff journey became a reality. In February 2016, after four years of careful route design, I was joined by 250 other riders to launch the Tour Aotearoa cycle route. The Tour was a huge success and the route has become the backbone of the New Zealand Cycle Trail network, ridden by hundreds of bikepackers annually.

Tour Aotearoa has 30 photo control points where riders are expected to stop and take a photo to prove they have been there (similar to the stamped passports on European biking journeys). On average, there is one photo control point every 100 km. Your control point photos will make a great album at the end of your trip!

The best time of year to start Tour Aotearoa is mid-February to late March. The weather is generally settled during this period, and although the days are shorter, the peak tourist season has passed and there is more space (on the roads, and in accommodation and cafes).

It is possible to do the whole tour without camping — and travelling light, with no camping or cooking gear, is very enjoyable. However, taking camping gear does give you a lot more flexibility in where to stop and stay along the ride.

You can do the Tour in one hit, or divide it up into North and South islands. Here, the journey is divided into six sections, which start/end at towns with transport options.

As new cycle trails and paths are constantly being built in New Zealand, so the route improves every year. Updates are published for the Tour Aotearoa route at www.touraotearoa.nz and in the *Tour Aotearoa Official Guides,* which are revised annually.

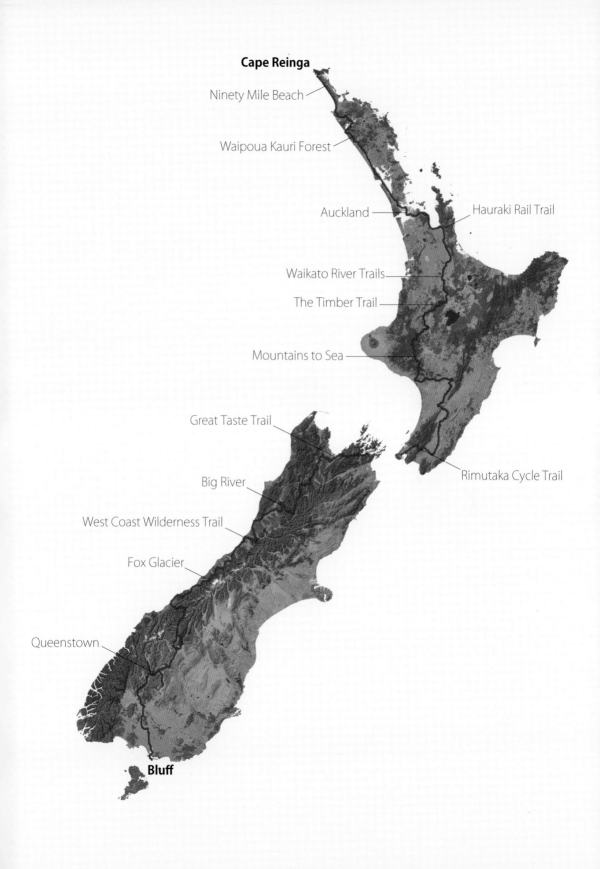

Cape Reinga

Ninety Mile Beach

Waipoua Kauri Forest

Auckland

Hauraki Rail Trail

Waikato River Trails

The Timber Trail

Mountains to Sea

Great Taste Trail

Rimutaka Cycle Trail

Big River

West Coast Wilderness Trail

Fox Glacier

Queenstown

Bluff

Boarding the boat to cross Kaipara Harbour

SUMMARY ··

Start point Cape Reinga

End point Stirling Point, Bluff

Distance 3000 km

Likely time 250–350 hours riding time: 30–50 days

Grading Grade 4 (Advanced)

Surface Just about everything: sealed roads, cycle lanes and cycle paths, gravel roads
and trails, dirt tracks and hard beach sand

Bike type Hard-tail, 29er mountain bike with bikepacking bags. Front suspension
optional. A minimum tyre width of 50 mm (2 inches) is recommended as over half
your riding time will be on gravel roads and cycle trails

Maps See maps in the *Tour Aotearoa Official Guides*

Trail website www.touraotearoa.nz

In emergencies Consider taking a Spot™ tracker, which acts as a personal locator
beacon (PLB) in emergencies and shows your position on the MAProgress
website (see www.maprogress.com) so that your friends and family can follow
your progress down the country

Bike hire It is always best to ride a bike that you are familiar and comfortable with, but if you have to hire one, go to Natural High as you can pick up a bike in Auckland and drop it off in Invercargill

Getting there From Auckland, catch the InterCity bus to Kaitaia and arrange a shuttle from there to the Cape at the i-SITE. Alternatively, you can ride from Kaitaia to Cape Reinga (111 km)

ROUTE DESCRIPTION

Cape Reinga to Auckland

446 km, 4–8 days, Grade 4 (Advanced)

From the iconic Cape Reinga lighthouse (the first photo control point), an hour of road riding leads to Ninety Mile Beach, a desert beside an ocean. It's a stark and exposed landscape, ending at a holiday village called Ahipara.

From Ahipara, a selection of quiet, back-country roads leads to the Rawene Ferry Terminal, from where a ferry runs regularly across the placid Hokianga Harbour.

Beyond the harbour, mangroves and golden beaches are left behind and the Tour climbs into Waipoua Forest, weaving past giant kauri, including the 2000-year-old Tane Mahuta (another photo control point).

Emerging from the forest, scenic farmland leads to Dargaville, a welcome staging post for those still finding their riding legs. To avoid traffic, the route then continues south on a dead-end road to Pouto Point Village, where a boat takes you across the Kaipara Harbour to Parakai Springs, another lovely holiday settlement.

Back roads lead from Parakai to the edge of Auckland, where the Northwestern Cycleway provides safe passage into the heart of the metropolis.

This section ends with a 10-minute ride to the top of an extinct volcano Maungawhau/ Mount Eden — from where Auckland is spread out like a 3D map. The journey has only just begun.

Auckland to Taumarunui

471 km, 5–10 days, Grade 1 (Easy) to Grade 5 (Expert)

From the volcano, the route heads through Cornwall Park, down Onehunga Mall, across the old Mangere Bridge and through the 'burbs to Totara Park, where you leave Auckland on an old coach road. Tour Aotearoa then follows country roads to Clevedon and around the Seabird Coast to Miranda Hot Springs.

After a soak in the springs, the route is suitably relaxed as it follows the Hauraki Rail Trail (the first Great Ride) to Kopu, Paeroa and Te Aroha. Te Aroha has fabulous street art, and hot pools, and there are plans to extend the trail to Matamata and beyond.

Follow a mix of roads from Matamata to the Waikato River Trails, the second Great Ride of the Tour. This is where your mountain-bike tyres will really start paying off. There are lots of hills and switchbacks on the Waikato River Trails.

Just beyond the riverside town of Mangakino, the route leaves the trail and follows a cunning combination of roads and tracks to the Centre of the North Island Track. Beyond there, a forestry road leads to the Timber Trail, one of the best Great Rides in the country. It passes through virgin forest, which is habitat to kiwi, kokako, rare frogs and other native species.

At the end of the trail, you may want to stop for a night at Ongarue, or continue on to the end of this section, at Taumarunui, 'on the Main Trunk Line'.

The 141 metre-long Maramataha Gorge Bridge is the longest on any New Zealand Cycle Trail.

Taumarunui to Wellington
680 km, 6–12 days, Grades 2 (Easy) to Grade 4 (Advanced)
From Taumarunui, beautiful but hilly country roads lead through scenic reserves and farmland to Blue Duck Station at Whakahoro. A Great Ride then climbs up the Kaiwhakauka Track, and down the Mangapurua Track, through Whanganui National Park, to the iconic Bridge to Nowhere. From there a short track leads to Mangapurua Landing where you must choose between a jetboat or canoe trip down the Whanganui River.

Beyond the village of Pipiriki, the riding becomes much faster as you fly along River Road towards Whanganui. This is still part of the Mountains to Sea Cycle Trail. At Whanganui, a short trip up the historic Durie Hill Elevator helps you head east on the Three Rivers Trail to Hunterville — home of the Huntaway sheep dog.

Nearing the end of the Maungatapu Track.

An unavoidable 5 km on State Highway 1 is endured before rolling through some of the most beautiful sheep country in New Zealand on the Gorges to Sea Cycle Trail and then heading down the Pohangina Valley on the Manawatu Cycle Trail to Palmerston North.

From Palmerston North a climb over the Pahiatua Track takes you to the sunny Wairarapa, where back roads lead through Pahiatua, Eketahuna and Masterton to the wine country of Martinborough, which has a mouth-watering number of vineyards and cafes.

Next comes the Rimutaka Cycle Trail, following a historic railway line through to the Hutt Valley and then a riverside trail to Wellington Harbour.

The route around the harbour to the capital is a work in progress, and the works will be ongoing from 2017 through to 2022.

In Wellington you can enjoy a well-deserved rest while waiting to catch a ferry across the Cook Strait to the South Island, 92 kilometres away.

Crossing from the North to South Island is a milestone worth celebrating. Not only is it 100 km over the halfway point, but you've been gaining fitness which will enable you to easily ride further and faster each day on the journey ahead. Riding the length of the South Island takes most people around 40 per cent of their total riding time. But the toughest hills (Maungatapu and Crown Range) lie ahead.

Picton to Hokitika

600 km, 6–12 days, Grade 2 (Easy) to Grade 5 (Expert)

From the ferry the route skirts the Marlborough Sounds on Queen Charlotte Drive, one of the best road rides in New Zealand. The miles fly by, until you reach the dreaded Maungatapu Saddle — the toughest climb of the whole 3000-km journey — which towers above the Pelorus Valley in the east and the Maitai Valley in the west. Both rivers provide fantastic swimming holes. A mellow downhill follows the Maitai Valley to the centre of Nelson.

The Great Taste Trail starts in Nelson and provides excellent riding to Richmond, Brightwater, Wakefield and even through Spooners Tunnel — the longest rideable tunnel in the Southern Hemisphere. It cuts out a major climb and leads to a series of roads, through Tapawera and Tadmor Valley to Kawatiri Junction, which was as far as the railway line ever made it.

The next stop is one of the most beautiful lakes in the country, Lake Rotoroa, with a backdrop of Nelson Lakes National Park. You are now on the Pioneer Heritage Trail, which passes through beech forests, farmland and small towns on the way to the West Coast. One of the most memorable sections is the Big River to Waiuta Track in Victoria Forest Park. A narrow single track weaves through lush native forest to the ghost town of Waiuta.

Greymouth is where the Tour's favourite Great Ride begins — the West Coast Wilderness Trail. It is a smooth gravel path packed with beautiful heritage scenery en route to Hokitika via a replica western town called Cowboy Paradise.

Hokitika to Queenstown

535 km, 5–10 days, Grade 2 (Easy) to Grade 4 (Advanced)

Pushing off from Hokitika, there is another 35 km of the West Coast Wilderness Trail leading to Ross, before a long section of mostly highway riding leads down the coast, through glacier country, to Haast. The best time to ride this section is March or April, when the weather is generally good and the tourist peak is over. A highlight is a 6-km side trip to the Fox Glacier.

Haast Pass is the lowest route through the Southern Alps, surrounded by Mount Aspiring National Park and providing a long descent to lakes Wanaka and Hawea. An off-road path leads from Hawea to Wanaka township, where you'll find the first bike shop since Hokitika!

After restocking at Wanaka, a long gentle climb leads past the historic Cardrona Hotel and over the Crown Range to Queenstown. The vistas from the summit extend across the Wakatipu Basin to the Remarkables mountain range and beyond. Off-road trails lead to Arrowtown and then, via three stunning rivers, to New Zealand's tourist capital — Queenstown.

The Braeburn Track, en route to Murchison.

Queenstown to Bluff

244 km, 2–4 days, Grade 2 (Easy) to Grade 3 (Intermediate)

The final leg of the journey begins with your fifth water section — a 13-km ferry trip across Lake Wakatipu to Walter Peak Station on the historic steamship TSS *Earnslaw*. After disembarking, a lonely gravel road disappears up the Von Valley, flanked by the Eyre and Thomson mountains. This is part of the Around the Mountains Cycle Trail, the last Great Ride of the Tour.

Emerging from the mountains, the route crosses the Southland Plains and skirts around Invercargill on a gravel path that is being built to Bluff (it wasn't complete at the time of writing in 2017). When you can smell the sea air and see the port of Bluff, you know it's not far. And when the bright yellow signs at Stirling Point finally come into view, with 3000 km having passed beneath your tyres, you can feel a sense of accomplishment, knowing you have cycled the length of this beautiful little country called Aotearoa.

Journey's end.

TRAIL TALES

The Length of New Zealand (LONZ) journey has attracted many types of adventurers. One of the oldest was 85-year-old writer AH Reed, who walked from top to bottom in 1961. Dog-lover Grant 'Curly' Jacobs from Taranaki ran the length of New Zealand with his best friend Buddy, unassisted, in two and a half months. In 2012, David 'The Judge' Wilson from Oamaru became the first person to ride a penny-farthing from Bluff to Cape Reinga. And the LONZ has even been skateboarded, by five overseas tourists in 2008 — they took 53 days and wore out several half-pairs of shoes.

No one is sure when the first person cycled the length of the country but history suggests it may have been around 1899 when the New Zealand Cyclist Road Map was published showing routes from Ahipara to Invercargill. From then, up until quite recently, cycle tourists followed the main roads, but as traffic volumes grew, this became less attractive and the advent of the mountain bike saw more and more people looking for the path less travelled.

The first person to cycle the Tour Aotearoa cycle route was Mike 'The Scout' Brien, a school teacher from Nelson, who tested the route in December 2015, completing the ride in just under a month.

FOOD AND ACCOMMODATION

For those who can ride around 100 km per day, it is possible to ride the length of the country without having to camp or cook. This does require careful planning, and booking ahead. For most of the ride, there are food and accommodation providers 20–40 km apart. They are all listed in the *Tour Aotearoa Official Guides*.

It is the occasional long gap between towns that needs planning. These are as follows:
Cape Reinga to Hukatere via Ninety Mile Beach: 70 km
Mangakino to Timber Trail Lodge via the Centre of North Island Track: 90 km
Murchison to Springs Junction via Maruia Saddle: 78 km
Reefton to Ikamatua via Victoria Forest Park: 56 tough km
Haast to Makarora via Haast Pass: 78 km
Queenstown to Mossburn via Mavora Lakes: 103 km

That's only six long-hauls. Have a substantial breakfast, and head out well stocked up with food and water! It's all part of the great adventure.

Celebrations well deserved at the end of a 3000-km journey.

EXTRA INFORMATION ON GRADES

	FITNESS (are there steep/ long climbs)	SKILL (is the track narrow or rough)	TRAFFIC (how much traffic and is the road narrow)	OVERALL TRAIL GRADE (1 Very easy to 5 Expert)
Twin Coast Cycle Trail Pou Herenga Tai	Low	Easy	Low	2 — Easy
Hauraki Rail Trail	None	None	Low	1 — Very easy
Waikato River Trails *Karapiro* *Arapuni* *Waipapa* *Maraetai* *Whakamaru*	Low Average Average Low Low	Easy Average Average Average Average	Low Low Moderate None None	2 — Easy 3 — Intermediate 3 — Intermediate 3 — Intermediate 3 — Intermediate
Te Ara Ahi-Thermal by Bike	Low (except for Rainbow Mountain which is Average)	Easy (except for Rainbow Mountain which is Average)	Low for the first half. Moderate for the second half	3 — Intermediate
Motu Trails *Dunes Trail* *Motu Road* *Pakihi Track*	None High Low	Easy Easy High	None Moderate Low	2 — Easy 3 — Intermediate 4 — Advanced
The Timber Trail	Average	Average	None	3 — Intermediate
Great Lake Trail	Average	Average	None	3 — Intermediate
Mountains to Sea	Average	High in places	High in places	4 — Advanced
Hawke's Bay Trails *Coastal Ride* *Water Ride* *Puketapu Loop* *Wineries Ride* *Tukituki Loop*	None None None None Low	None None None None None	None None Low Low High	1 — Very easy 1 — Very easy 1 — Very easy 2 — Easy 4 — Advanced
Rimutaka Cycle Trail *Hutt River Trail* *Rail Trail* *Cross Creek to Orongorongo*	None Low Average	Easy Easy Average	None None Moderate	2 — Easy 2 — Easy 3 — Intermediate
Queen Charlotte Track	High	Average	None	4 — Advanced

	FITNESS (are there steep/long climbs)	SKILL (is the track narrow or rough)	TRAFFIC (how much traffic and is the road narrow)	OVERALL TRAIL GRADE (1 Very easy to 5 Expert)
Dun Mountain Trail	Average	High (just for the downhill)	Low	3–4 — Intermediate to Advanced
Great Taste Trail	Low	Easy	Mostly low	2–3 — Easy to Intermediate
St James Cycle Trail	High	Average	None	4 — Advanced
The Old Ghost Road	High	High	None	4 — Advanced
West Coast Wilderness Trail	Low	Easy	Moderate in a few places	2–3 — Easy to Intermediate
Alps 2 Ocean Cycle Trail	Average	Easy	High (for 28 km between Sailors Cutting and Kurow)	3 — Intermediate
Otago Central Rail Trail	Low	None	None	1 — Very easy
Roxburgh Gorge Trail	Easy	Average in a few places, otherwise Low	None	2 — Easy
Clutha Gold Trail	Low	Easy	Low	2 — Easy
Queenstown Trail (not counting Jacks Point or Gibbston tracks)	Average (there are a few short steep hills)	Easy	Low	2–3 — Easy to Intermediate
Around the Mountains	Low (apart from 2.4 km of Grade 3 on the way to Mavora Lakes)	Easy	Low	1–3 — Very easy to Intermediate
Tour Aotearoa	High	High in places	High in places	4–5 — Advanced to expert

Traffic grades

Grade 1 means that, apart from road crossings, there is no traffic on the trail.

Grade 2 means there may be some traffic, but it will be low in volume and speed.

Grade 3 means that part of the trail (possibly only a few kilometres) is on an open speed limit road. Even if the road is only used by a dozen cars or trucks a day it is Grade 3 or above.

Grade 4 means there are up to 1000 vehicles a day on average using a 100 kph road. There will only be more traffic if there is ample space for cyclists on the shoulder of the road.

Grade 5 means there are over 1000 vehicles a day on the road, and there may be little or no shoulder.

To put that into context, anyone who cycles regularly in a big city will have no problems riding anything in this book, even Grade 5. However, when cycling on a busy open road, I recommend you make yourself stand out by wearing hi-vis clothing, and/or turning your lights on. Also, listen out for traffic and, if appropriate, move well left.

The situation to really look out for is when two vehicles, coming from either direction, are likely to pass each other, and you, at the same time. It happens very rarely, but if it does on a narrow road, you should be prepared to get off the road and give them space.

GEAR LISTS

Minimum to take
on every ride:

Helmet
Sunglasses
Sunblock
Wallet
Cellphone
Map
Windbreaker coat/
    rain coat
Spare inner tube
Tyre levers
Pump
Multi-tool/Allen keys
Food and water

Optional extras:
Camera
First-aid kit
Insect repellent
Survival blanket

GPS device
PLB (emergency personal
    locator beacon)
Pocket knife/Leatherman
    multi-tool
Chain breaker for
    repairing broken
    chains
Bike oil
Front and rear lights
Bike lock

Extra gear for
overnight trips:

More clothes
More food and water
Toothbrush and
    toothpaste
Cellphone charger
Rear pannier bags and a
    small handlebar bag

Dry bag/plastic bags to
    keep gear dry
Camping gear if camping

Extra tools per group on
long remote trips:

Spoke tool
Crank tool
Freewheel tool
Spare brake blocks/pads
Spare cables
Another spare tube and
    puncture
    repair kit
Spare tyre (lightweight)

ACKNOWLEDGEMENTS

Riding buddies

Bronnie Wall for riding half the Great Rides with me, then researching the history of the trails and checking numerous drafts. Your support has been invaluable.

Paul McArdle for teaming up on a week-long research trip in the North Island — Twin Coast, Hauraki, Te Ara Ahi, Taupo trails and, your favourite, the Hawke's Bay Trails.

Murray Drake and Ginny Wood for the rides on West Coast Wilderness, The Old Ghost Road, St James and Dun Mountain.

Kevin Hague, who seemed to be at just about every trail opening!

Kath Kelly, human dynamo, for rides on Clutha Gold, A2O and Queenstown Trail.

Mary Molphy from Ireland for riding with us on the A2O.

Gerry Dance for joining me on a ride on the Twin Coast Cycle Trail.

And the many other lovely people I rode with for just an hour or two along one of the trails.

Cycling enthusiasts

For emailing me their experiences of riding the trails: Barbara Cuthbert, Patrick Morgan, Lyn Manning, Martin Langley, Jude Ellis, Kathy Ombler and Thijs Haustraete.

Trails people

Thanks to everyone who has worked so hard on the New Zealand Cycle Trail project. Especially to John Dunn, programme manager of the project, for his tireless enthusiasm.

Richard Balm for his generosity and trail advice.

Rod Peirce and Peter Cummings for meeting on the Clutha Gold Trail and imparting their knowledge and enthusiasm.

Jason Menard on A2O for driving us to the trail head and creating a great website for the trail.

Hamish Seaton for excellent route details when the A2O hadn't yet put signs up.

Barrie Wills for riding with us on Roxburgh Gorge Trail and sharing his extensive knowledge.

Dave Crawford from Beaumont Jet for taking us down the Roxburgh Gorge before the trail was officially open.

Jeff Dalley for sharing his knowledge of the St James Cycle Trail.

Glyn Wooler for answering endless questions about the Waikato River Trails.

Andrew Young from Far North District Council and Ray Clarke for their time and knowledge on the Twin Coast Cycle Trail.

John Stock for showing us around the first leg of the Timber Trail and checking I had my facts straight.

Roy Grose and Mark Nelson for sharing their knowledge of the Queen Charlotte Track.

Evan Freshwater for riding the Around the Mountains with me on a rainy day.

Phil Oliver, local fount of knowledge, for driving us around the Otago trails.

Jim Robinson, a champion of the Motu Trails.

Mark 'The Steam' Bradshaw for his knowledge of Northland's railways.

People who worked on this book

Everyone at Penguin Random House New Zealand, especially Margaret Sinclair and Sarah Yankelowitz.

My awesome brothers: Simon for such a great job double-checking the route directions, and Paul for taking my raw GPS data and massaging it into meaningful data for Geographx to turn into wonderful maps.

Suzanne Blackwell — for researching the non-cycling attractions along the trail.

Milica Legetich — our intern from Whitireia Publishing for reviewing a draft manuscript.

Andrew McLellan for reviewing text and providing feedback on the trails.

Dean Johansson for researching the 2015 and 2017 updates.

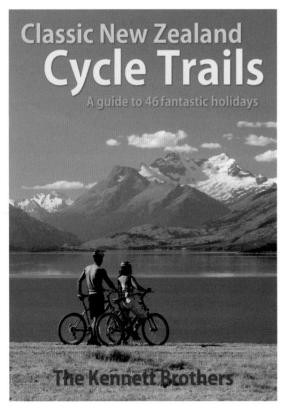

For more information on the New Zealand Cycle Trail network, check out this handy guide at www.kennett.co.nz

INDEX